THE WORLD OF
MARIAN APPARITIONS

THE WORLD OF

Marian APPARITIONS

WINCENTY ŁASZEWSKI

SOPHIA
INSTITUTE PRESS

Sophia Institute Press
Box 5284, Manchester, NH 03108
1-800-888-9344

www.SophiaInstitute.com

Sophia Institute Press® is a registered trademark of Sophia Institute.

Hardcover ISBN: 978-1-64413-202-9

ebook ISBN: 978-1-64413-203-6

Library of Congress Control Number: 2021930983

Fifth printing

Contents

Introduction

The first apparition of Mary happened in the year 40, when Mary was still alive. She was living in Jerusalem and appeared to the Apostle James the Greater in Spain. The apparition was controversial in Spain but was later approved by the Congregation of Rites in 1723 under Pope Innocent XIII. This first apparition was really a bilocation since Mary was physically present in Jerusalem when she appeared in Spain. The supernatural aspects of the account were described in the book *The Mystical City of God* by the Venerable Mary of Agreda in 1665.

The Marian apparitions at Fatima, Portugal, are probably the most famous of the Marian apparitions. This is because they include arguably the most dramatic miracle since biblical times, a secret message, and prophecies about the coming Second World War. They addressed secular politics directly and have become a rallying point for ideological movements in the Church. Subsequent apparitions have confirmed and spread the Fatima message to this day.

Marian apparitions generally include four components: the visionary, the experience, the message, and the miracles. But within this framework, there has been a wide variety. The visionaries are sometimes children, sometimes professed religious, and sometimes lay adults. The experiences all include Our Lady, but sometimes she appears in her fullness, other times merely as a voice, and still other times as a statue or image that moves or speaks. The messages are almost always centered on prayer and repentance, but sometimes they include dire warnings for the world. The accompanying miracles vary widely, from enduring images to one-time spectacles, but they are almost always testable by outside experts, so the Church and the world have some proof that something extraordinary happened.

Once a report of such an event is made—or an ongoing event is noticed—the local bishop makes two important determinations. First, he discerns whether the messages connected with the apparition are

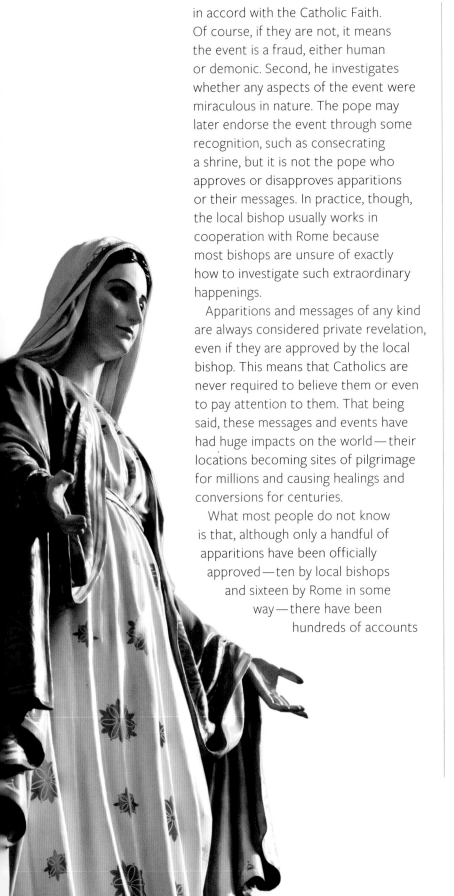

in accord with the Catholic Faith. Of course, if they are not, it means the event is a fraud, either human or demonic. Second, he investigates whether any aspects of the event were miraculous in nature. The pope may later endorse the event through some recognition, such as consecrating a shrine, but it is not the pope who approves or disapproves apparitions or their messages. In practice, though, the local bishop usually works in cooperation with Rome because most bishops are unsure of exactly how to investigate such extraordinary happenings.

Apparitions and messages of any kind are always considered private revelation, even if they are approved by the local bishop. This means that Catholics are never required to believe them or even to pay attention to them. That being said, these messages and events have had huge impacts on the world—their locations becoming sites of pilgrimage for millions and causing healings and conversions for centuries.

What most people do not know is that, although only a handful of apparitions have been officially approved—ten by local bishops and sixteen by Rome in some way—there have been hundreds of accounts of Marian apparitions down through the centuries. Sometimes the supposed apparitions generated some local interest, but no investigation was undertaken; sometimes there has been disagreement between diocesan and Vatican authorities. The ongoing case of Medjugorje, Bosnia-Herzegovina, from 1981 to today is a complicated version of this latter case. As of 2020, Rome has approved pilgrimages to the site, but final full approval has been withheld until the apparent visions conclude and the case can be studied in its entirety.

Jesus seems to prefer to speak to the world through His Mother since He went to sit next to the Father in Heaven. The messages she gives are always of prayer and conversion to her Son—and sometimes of warning if we do not do so. Mary also seems to appear at pivotal moments in history to help guide humanity to the best possible path. She has a motherly concern for us and does not want us to be lost to her and to God.

Mary intervenes for us in our earthly struggles. She tells us to avoid sin, to repent, to pray, and to avoid damnation. She talks about the ongoing choices we face and the consequences of our actions. The Christian story is not over. We cannot sit back and just wait for Heaven to be handed to us; we must struggle and fight the good fight. The Marian messages are repeated warnings and encouragement to make the right choices, to win the prize, and to attain the joys of everlasting life.

—Adam Blai, Author, *The Catholic Guide to Miracles: Separating the Authentic from the Counterfeit*

LEGEND

 An apparition recognized by the Vatican

 A visionary recognized as a saint, blessed, venerable, or servant of God

 The pope visited the apparition site and / or gave it special privileges

 An apparition recognized by the local bishop

 An imprimatur or *nihil obstat* granted to the texts of the revelations

 Devotion recognized at the apparition site

 Unusual miracles at the apparition site

 An apparition recognized by the Coptic Church

 An apparition accepted by the belief of pilgrims

THE WORLD OF
MARIAN APPARITIONS

MEXICO CITY

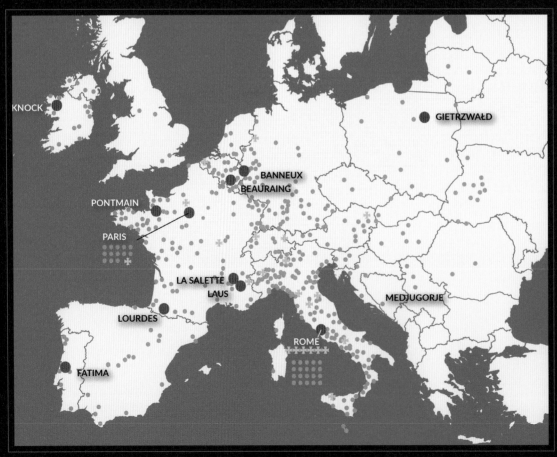

LEGEND

- Recognized by the Vatican after bishop approval
- Approved by the local bishop
- Unconfirmed as supernatural
- ✠ Marian apparitions to future saints

EUROPE

KNOCK

GIETRZWAŁD

BANNEUX
BEAURAING

PONTMAIN

PARIS

LA SALETTE
LAUS

MEDJUGORJE

LOURDES

ROME

FATIMA

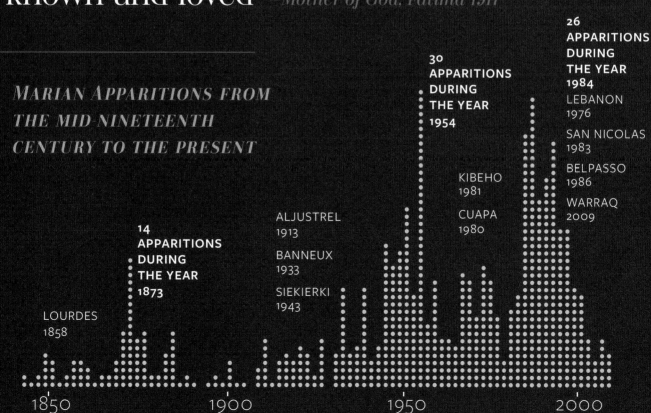

PHILIPPINES

—— KIBEHO

"Jesus wants me to be better known and loved" *—Mother of God, Fatima 1917*

MARIAN APPARITIONS FROM THE MID-NINETEENTH CENTURY TO THE PRESENT

26
APPARITIONS
DURING
THE YEAR
1984

LEBANON
1976

SAN NICOLAS
1983

BELPASSO
1986

WARRAQ
2009

30
APPARITIONS
DURING
THE YEAR
1954

KIBEHO
1981

CUAPA
1980

ALJUSTREL
1913

BANNEUX
1933

SIEKIERKI
1943

14
APPARITIONS
DURING
THE YEAR
1873

LOURDES
1858

1850   1900   1950   2000

THE WORLD OF
MARIAN APPARITIONS

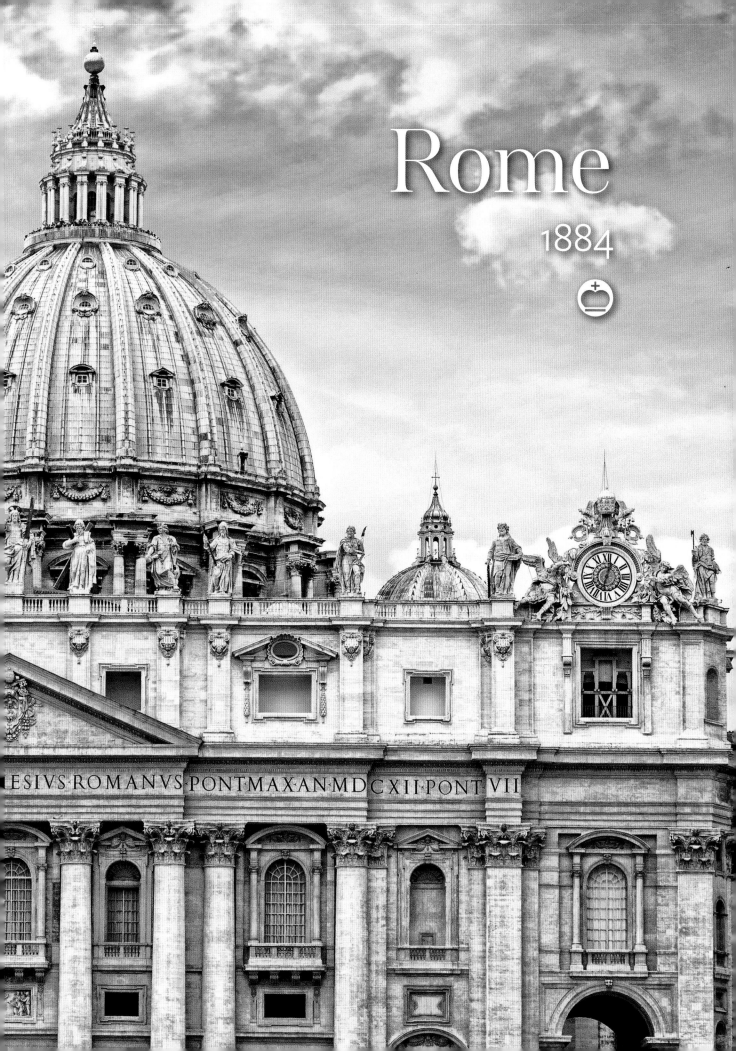

Rome

1884

On February 20, 1878, Gioacchino Pecci became the bishop of Rome, taking the name Leo XIII.

A Vision of the Church's Future

Pope Leo XIII's prophetic vision of the Church's future had a Marian character, not because Mary herself appeared to the Holy Father, but because the terrible events she allowed him to see moved him to promote the Rosary as the key to victory over Satan.

O n October 13, 1884—exactly thirty-three years before the Miracle of the Sun at Fatima—Pope Leo XIII received a chilling vision that left a clear mark on his pontificate and, decades later, became the key to interpreting the many horrors of the twentieth century. After celebrating Holy Mass in one of the Vatican's private chapels, the Holy Father was standing on the steps of the altar when his face suddenly turned gray, and in an instant, he collapsed unconscious to the ground. For five minutes, he lay motionless. Then, upon regaining consciousness, the pope turned to the prelates who had rushed to his side and said, "Oh, what terrible images I have been permitted to see!"

The subject of this apparition was the next hundred years, during which Satan would be allowed free rein over the world. We do not know the details of Leo XIII's vision, but we do know that he saw the grave moral and spiritual damage that would afflict the world and the Church herself in the twentieth century.

> When Leo XIII took the papal throne, he believed that only a carefully targeted re-Christianization of society could heal the wounds of the contemporary world.

> Leo XIII's dedication to Mary throughout his pontificate suggests that she showed him how to win the battle against evil.

LEO XIII'S GREAT PRAYER
Deeply shocked and moved by what he saw, the pope rushed to his office and composed a prayer to St. Michael the Archangel, which all priests would be required to recite at the end of Mass:

ITALY

Rome

St. Michael the Archangel, defend us in battle. Be our protection against the wickedness and snares of the devil. May God rebuke him, we humbly pray, and do thou, O prince of the heavenly host, by the power of God, thrust into Hell Satan and all the evil spirits who prowl about the world seeking the ruin of souls. Amen.

Although the liturgical reforms of the Second Vatican Council removed this obligation, the prayer is still said in some churches after each celebration of the Eucharist. In that moment, at the end of the liturgy, we remember Leo XIII's vision.

The Prayer to St. Michael may seem strange to us today. Its direct references to battles with evil spirits and Satan tend to awaken a sense of unease, yet this prayer is not only an authentic devotion but also an efficacious exorcism, capable of curtailing the devil's destruction and repelling all evil attacks. For evidence, consider what happened when this prayer

▼ *The fruit of the Holy Father's mystical experience turned out to be a prayer to St. Michael the Archangel. To this day, it is recited in some churches at the end of the liturgy.*

A St. Michael
the Archangel,
prince of the
heavenly host and
defender of the
Catholic Church.

A bronze figure
of St. Michael the
Archangel.

was suppressed in 1964. Only a few years later, all kinds of social pathologies and moral distortions had been written into law. Pornography entered the mainstream, birth control use skyrocketed, and abortion became legal in many countries.

A VISION FORETOLD

If St. Michael was the hero of Leo XIII's vision, what was Mary's role? At least three pieces of evidence suggest that she revealed the future to the pope and appointed St. Michael as protector of the Church. The first bit of evidence is the similarity between Leo XIII's vision and the Marian apparitions to Mariana de Jesus Torres y Berriochoa in Quito, modern-day Ecuador, in 1594. Astonishingly, both visions contained the same message: in the twentieth century, a great crisis would afflict the Church, and Satan would be given power over the world.

In Quito, Mary revealed herself as the slayer of Satan and called on St. Michael, prince of the heavenly host, to defend the world against evil. She appointed him commander of the heavenly army, which fights under her banner and with her weapon: the Rosary. In other words, Mary held the key to victory over the atrocities she revealed to Mariana de Jesus and Leo XIII.

THE ROSARY POPE

The second piece of evidence for Mary's role in Leo XIII's vision is the influence she had on his pontificate, both before and after 1884. It is no coincidence that the same pope who saw a vision of Satan's hundred-year rule wrote as many as twelve encyclicals about Mary—more specifically, about the Rosary. In fact, Leo XIII so persistently promoted the Rosary

as the way to God through Mary that he became known as "the Rosary pope."

Leo XIII's first encyclical on the Rosary, *Supremi Apostolatus Officio*, was published on September 1, 1883. A year later, by the time of his vision, he had managed to write another encyclical and an apostolic letter on the Rosary. One gets the impression that these texts opened the way for the pope's vision. The Holy Mother saw in Leo XIII her zealous devotee who—if properly guided—could help save the Church from Satan's attack. Indeed, the texts that the Holy Father wrote after his vision were so edifying and lucid, one might think they were divinely inspired.

Let us dive into the sea of Leo XIII's teachings on the Rosary. In his 1891 encyclical *Octobri Mense*, the pope writes: "By the will of God, Mary is the intermediary through whom is distributed unto us this immense treasure of mercies gathered by God, for mercy and truth were created by Jesus Christ. Thus as no man goeth to the Father but by the Son, so no man goeth to Christ but by His Mother." That is why we must turn to Mary and ask for her help and care. The best way to approach Christ by His Mother is the Rosary because "more than any other means it can impetrate from God the succour which We need," and it "is most opportune for the needs of these times." For this reason, Leo XIII "desired to revive everywhere this devotion, and to spread it far and wide among the faithful of the world."

Additionally, the pope writes, the Rosary—as a means of revealing the mysteries of the Faith—is a pedagogical tool: "The Rosary offers an easy way to present the chief mysteries of the Christian religion and to impress them upon the mind," and it "affords to faithful souls a wonderful confirmation of faith, protection against the disease of error, and increase of the strength of the soul." Contemplating the mysteries of the Rosary dissipates the shadows of ignorance and diminishes our risk of falling into error.

Leo XIII even argues that piously reciting the Rosary can heal the wounds of entire societies: "For [social] evils such as these let us seek a remedy in the Rosary. ... For We are convinced that the Rosary, if devoutly used, is bound to benefit not only the individual but society at large." For this reason, he urges, "With all possible earnestness ... strive by the recitation of the Rosary to aid both yourselves individually, and the Church in her need."

In short, the Rosary strengthens the truths of the Faith in our hearts, remedies the ills of society, and revives our desire to follow the Mother of God,

thereby opening God's kingdom to us. Through the Rosary, we receive what is foretold and promised in the mysteries of faith—eternal life in union with God.

CONCLUSION OF THE HUNDRED-YEAR VISION

The final piece of evidence for Mary's role in Leo XIII's vision is the date given as the end of Satan's extra-ordinary power: 1984. That year, John Paul II consecrated Russia and the world to the Immaculate Heart of Mary, despite Satan's best efforts to the contrary. Immediately, an unexpected transformation occurred in countries possessed by evil. Then, in 1987, John Paul II declared a Marian year, which accelerated the conversion of Russia foretold by Our Lady of Fatima. Two years later, the era of Soviet Communism ended, and within ten years, eighty-seven dictatorial governments collapsed,

▲ *The pope explained how the Rosary is an effective weapon against evil and an invaluable aid on the path toward union with God.*

◄ *Leo XIII's pontificate began during particularly severe attacks on the papacy and the Church.*

the Berlin Wall fell, and Eastern and Central Europe were liberated from Communism.

It's worth noting the uncanny (some would say diabolical) "coincidences" that occurred during the consecration and nearly prevented it from occurring. First was the attempted assassination of John Paul II on May 13, 1981; John Paul himself credited his survival to Our Lady of Fatima. Then, there were the incomplete consecrations of Russia and the world in 1952 and 1982. In 1984, during the complete consecration, the pope's microphone inexplicably failed during the most important moment of the act of consecration recited by him. But he completed the consecration nonetheless, and Sr. Lúcia (who was still alive) confirmed that it satisfied Our Lady's request.

During that time, the media was reluctant to discuss the role of Mary (and the act of consecration) in the transformations that occurred around the world. Journalists focused only on the dramatic events of this period: the rise of Solidarity in Poland, the fall of the Berlin Wall, the Velvet Revolution in Czechoslovakia. Nobody asked about the cause of these miracles, but we know the truth. The great struggle of the twentieth century has been won ... but Mary's battle with the enemy has not come to an end.

San Giovanni Rotondo

1911

In 1997, an image of Padre Pio appeared on this building in Orta San Giulio, in northern Italy.

Padre Pio's
Laughing Madonna

To say that Padre Pio was a Marian visionary is unquestionably an understatement. This holy stigmatic lived in the permanent presence of the Mother of God, whom he called his Mammina. Their relationship was warm and sincere.

➤ *Our Lady not only appeared to Padre Pio but also remained a permanent presence in his life.*

For some saints, meeting Our Lady is no more unusual—and even feels more natural—than spending time with a family member. Padre Pio of Pietrelcina was one such saint. When the future Capuchin was only five years old, Mary began to accompany him through visions that were as real to him as meetings with other people. She consoled him, led him to Jesus, and protected him from evil spirits. In his humility, Padre Pio became convinced that everyone experienced Mary's closeness in a similar way. When he began to suspect that he had been granted a singular grace, he asked Fr. Agostino da San Marco, his longtime confessor and spiritual director, "Don't you see the Madonna?" On receiving a negative reply, Padre Pio said, "You deny it for holy humility!"

Other monks noticed the young saint's closeness with the Blessed Mother. The monastery chronicler noted that two of Padre Pio's confreres asked him jokingly, "Does Our Lady ever come to your cell?"

San Giovanni
Rotondo

ITALY

He looked at them in surprise and replied with a smile, "You should rather ask me if she ever leaves my cell."

In one of his letters, Padre Pio wrote that the Blessed Virgin Mary did not leave him, even when he was celebrating Mass: "With what great attention she accompanied me to the altar this morning. It seemed to me that she had nothing else to think about but me, filling my heart with holy sentiments."

CONVERSATIONS DURING ECSTASIES

The intimate language in which Padre Pio spoke of Our Lady offers another look at their close relationship. Padre Pio called Mary his Mammina, Dearest Mother, Most Holy Mother, Beautiful Mother, Most Blessed Mother, and, interestingly, his Poor Mother. He had many other affectionate names for the Mother of God, which he frequently used during his ecstasies, when he completely withdrew from the world to be alone with her. Thanks to Fr. Agostino, who had the good fortune to address these ecstasies, we have a record of Padre Pio's conversations with Mary. For example, on November 30, 1911, Padre Pio cried out to our Most Holy Mother, "Your eyes are more resplendent than the sun ... you are beautiful, little Mother, I glory in you, I love you ... assist me!" He continued, "Oh, you are so beautiful ... are you laughing? It does not matter ... you are beautiful!"

Let us humbly admit that we do not understand much of this. The holy stigmatic's words are strange, arising from a mystical experience that is inconceivable to us.

A BEAUTY BEYOND THIS WORLD

Like many saints who saw Mary, Padre Pio emphasized that the language with which he described our Most Holy Mother was analogical, used out of necessity. In limiting us to the things of this world, our imperfect human language cannot fully capture the experience of encountering the Mother of God. This is why, although fascinated by Our Lady's beauty, Padre Pio loathed any attempt to describe

In the 1950s, a modern basilica dedicated to Our Lady of Grace was built next to the former monastic church, which was also dedicated to her.

The Sanctuary of St. Padre Pio in San Giovanni Rotondo.

Built to accommodate crowds of pilgrims visiting San Giovanni Rotondo, the shrine boasts impressively modern and original architecture.

Mary's appearance. On hearing one of his confreres singing a Marian hymn with the chorus "You are lovely as the sun, fairer than the moon," Padre Pio cried out, "If Our Lady were only as those words say, I would refuse to go to Paradise."

On another occasion, Fr. Alberto d'Apolito asked the saint to write a short prayer on the back of a picture of Our Lady with the Child Jesus. Handing the picture to Padre Pio, Fr. Alberto improvidently expressed his admiration for the beauty of Mary's face. Padre Pio took the picture, looked at it, and gave it back to him, saying, "They could not have painted an uglier one!"

"I was flabbergasted," recalled his confrere and friend. "I whispered, 'Yes, Padre! You have seen Mary, and that is why the picture seems ugly to you. What does Mary look like?'"

Padre Pio replied, "Who could possibly describe her beauty?"

OUR LADY'S POWERFUL INTERCESSION

Padre Pio eagerly availed himself of every grace he received from the Blessed Mother. To those who asked for his intercession, he repeated, like a refrain, "I shall ask Our Lady." He assured them, "Let us be faithful and persevering, and Our Lady will not be able to remain deaf to her children's prayers." To someone who had journeyed a long way to visit him, Padre Pio said, "My son, the Hail Mary is worth more than your long journey."

Countless people benefited from the great power of Padre Pio's prayers to

A window above the entrance to the monastic church from which Padre Pio often blessed locals and pilgrims.

Home for the Relief of Suffering in San Giovanni Rotondo.

Mary. Among them was Fr. Alberto, who offered the following account:

In the spring of 1963, when I was the superior of the monastery in Pietrelcina, I came down with the flu and caught such a serious thyroid infection that I lay in bed for three months. ... The doctors decided that I ought to be referred to the hospital. At my request, I was taken by car to San Giovanni Rotondo. Before entering the hospital, I went to see Padre Pio, who blessed me and promised to pray to Mary for me.

I was admitted to the Home for the Relief of Suffering ... under the care of Professor Luciano Lucentini, and, over several weeks, lost over thirty-three pounds and felt ever weaker, ever worse, despite the vigorous and intensified medical treatment.

One night, I fell out of bed and injured my head. I did not have the strength to get up. Two patients, who heard my cries for help, helped me back into my bed. The doctor on duty was called and disinfected and stitched my wound.

The next morning, Professor Lucentini came to see me. Worried by the lack of improvement, he said, "Fr. Alberto, we have to take you to Rome as soon as your temperature drops. I'll go with you."

I replied, "Professor, if the illness is serious, I want to remain in San Giovanni Rotondo. Since my time has come, I want to be here, where I was born and where my parents are buried." ... I was fully aware that that my illness was serious, so I entrusted myself to my heavenly Mother and the prayers of our beloved Padre Pio, who was worried about me and gave me to know, through his confreres, that he was close to me and was praying for me. I felt worse, ever worse.

The days went by. I was not able to travel, so Professor Lucentini decided to go to Rome alone in order to consult Professor Cassano.

During his three day absence, my temperature dropped, and I felt slightly better. When Professor Lucentini returned from Rome, he immediately came to see me and was pleased to see that my health had improved. Eventually, after three months, I left the hospital completely healthy. On being discharged from the hospital, I

⋏ *Padre Pio celebrated every liturgy with great reverence. To him, Mass was a real participation in the Passion of Christ. He was always focused, serious, prayerful, and intent on the miracle being wrought.*

immediately made my way to the monastery to thank Padre Pio, who, embracing me, said, "Go and thank Our Lady. She healed you! She is so good to you."

THE STATUE OF OUR LADY OF FATIMA

Our Lady healed not only Padre Pio's friends and confreres but also the visionary himself. In 1959, the pilgrim statue of Our Lady of Fatima was taken to several cities across Italy. Out of respect for Padre Pio, who had been ill for a long time, the statue made a special stop in San Giovanni Rotondo. Though he was very weak, Padre Pio left

his cell in order to welcome the statue. Deeply moved, he kissed the statue and put a rosary in Our Lady's hand.

When the statue was taken to the terrace of the Home for the Relief of Suffering, where it was to be placed in a helicopter, Padre Pio asked to see it again. So he was taken on a chair to a window in the choir of the old church. Paolo Carta, then bishop of Foggia, describes what happened next: "From a window Padre Pio watched the helicopter fly away with eyes filled with tears. To Our Lady in flight Padre Pio lamented with a confidence that was all his own, 'My Lady, my Mother, you came to Italy and I got sick, now you are going away and you leave me still ill.'"

When Padre Pio said this, a sudden shiver shook his body, and he felt completely well. He could stand and walk. Later, he would explain that "Our Lady came here because she wanted to cure Padre Pio."

THE DEVIL'S ATTACKS

In addition to healing her beloved Padre Pio, Mary protected him at times of temptation and weakness, indicating how he could reject Satan, who attempted to attack his weakest points. That is why the visionary humbly repeated, "Our Lady saved me from Hell, to which I deserved to go."

The devil fears no one but great saints. He cannot conquer the soul of one who is devoted to God. Instead, he vents his impotent, infernal rage upon it, too terrified to reveal himself in his hideous form. Lacking access to the soul, he attacks the body.

Padre Pio wrote about these attacks again and again. His confreres often heard strange noises, shouts, and screams coming from his cell. In a letter of January 18, 1912, addressed to Fr. Agostino, Padre Pio stated: "The devil ...can take on many forms. He has been appearing recently with his brothers, all armed with clubs and various metal objects. ... They pulled me out of my bed a few times and dragged me out of the bedroom. However, I am patient."

One night, terrible noises coming from Padre Pio's cell awakened the residents of the monastery. The monks hurried to see what had happened. When they burst inside, they could not believe their eyes. Padre Pio's cell looked as if a tornado had struck it. Nothing was in its place. The furniture was overturned and broken. What could have been torn was torn. What could have been broken was broken. In the middle of the floor lay Padre Pio, who had just been attacked by a legion of enraged demons. His shirt was ripped, and his body was bruised and covered in blood. But one thing

▲ *San Giovanni Rotondo—once a small Italian town—is now visited by millions of pilgrims.*

◄ *The Sanctuary of St. Padre Pio—a monument to this great saint.*

Padre Pio died on September 23, 1968. He celebrated his last Mass the day before his death.

Before his death, Padre Pio said, "Love the Madonna and make her loved. Always recite her Rosary."

did not fit the scene: there was a pillow under his head.

The monks lifted Padre Pio up, pointed to the pillow, and asked: "And that?"

The answer was just as laconic: "The Madonna."

Mary did not prevent Satan from attacking the saint's body. Instead, she taught Padre Pio to gain spiritual benefits from the attacks, both for himself and for sinners. She also gave him a sense of security. After all, since she was permanently with him, nothing fatal could happen to him. Even more, she showed him her motherly tenderness and brought him comfort and consolation.

FINAL TESTAMENT

Two days before his death, one of Padre Pio's spiritual children asked him, "Padre, tell us something."

He replied, "Love the Madonna and make her loved. Always recite her Rosary. That is the armor against the evils of the world today."

These sentences, pronounced on his death bed, epitomize Padre Pio's strong desire to see Mary venerated throughout the world. As he wrote in one of his letters, "I wish I had a voice strong enough to call all the world's sinners to love the Blessed Virgin Mary! But that is beyond me. So I asked my beloved guardian angel to do it for me. ... I would like to reach all people to bid them to love Jesus and Mary."

Padre Pio's cell at San Giovanni Rotondo is preserved as he left it.

St. Padre Pio's body exhibited for public veneration.

Aljustrel

1913

> There was something extraordinary about Lúcia, something that convinced Fr. Cruz, who had come to minister in Aljustrel, that the girl not only knew more about God than other children did but also was as spiritually mature as an adult.

Little Lúcia's
Madonna

Lúcia always desired sanctity. She prayed that Christ might keep her heart pure, as she wanted to offer her purity to Him. Her first confessor noticed that she was unusually mature for a six-year-old. Mary was aware of the girl's maturity, too, as she had a very important task for Lúcia: to receive and promulgate Mary's messages at Fatima between May and October 1917.

All Catholics ask themselves, "What is the key to Christian perfection? What must one do to become a saint?" Perhaps Lúcia dos Santos's path to sanctity can teach us how to reach spiritual perfection.

Like many child visionaries, Lúcia desired sanctity from a young age. The hearts of children are pure, open, and trusting; they instinctively understand that God is present in everyday life.

Her mother, Maria Rosa, was an excellent home catechist. On winter evenings, she told her children about God and His commandments. She based her teaching on the simplest catechism. The children listened to her with great interest and respect.

By the age of six, Lúcia was familiar with the entire catechism. Fr. Pena, who taught catechism classes to the local children, asked Lúcia to stand next to him during

⋏ Lúcia's parents conscientiously instructed their daughter in the Faith.

> Lúcia was born on March 22, 1907, in a village in Portugal. She was the youngest child of António dos Santos and Maria Rosa Ferreira.

request, however, Fr. Pena objected, since she was only six years old. At this, Lúcia put her head on his knees and began to cry. That did not help.

Francisco Rodrigues da Cruz, a popular Portuguese Jesuit, happened to enter the church just as Lúcia burst into tears. He asked the girl what was wrong. Lúcia told Fr. Cruz her story, and the Jesuit urged her pastor to change his mind:

> *"Fr. Pena, you can let this child go to Communion. She understands what she's doing better than many of the others."*
>
> *"But she's only six years old,"* objected the good priest.
>
> *"Never mind! I'll take the responsibility for that."*

Fr. Cruz's determination was surprising. What was so special about little Lúcia? He must have noticed her precociousness and unusual openness to God. He must have sensed that God had great plans for this little girl. Later, he would become a great advocate for the Fatima children.

Though not much is known about Fr. Cruz, his encounter with Lúcia demonstrates that he, too, was a perfect instrument in God's hands. His cause for canonization was opened in 1951, and he currently holds the title Servant of God.

OUR LADY'S SMILE

Fr. Cruz heard Lúcia's confession before her First Holy Communion. When she came out of the sacristy, everyone made fun of her. Her mother said: "My child, don't you know that confession is a secret matter and that it is made in a low voice? Everybody heard you!"

But no one heard what Fr. Cruz had said. The priest took Lúcia seriously, even though she was a six-year-old child.

the lessons so that she might answer questions and assist those who did not fully understand the material.

LÚCIA'S DESIRE FOR HOLY COMMUNION

Given Lúcia's knowledge of the Faith, it is not surprising that she desired to make her First Communion as soon as possible. She longed to be perfectly united with God. When she made her

Image of the Blessed Virgin Mary from Lúcia's family home.

> The little church where the visionaries were baptized and Lúcia received her First Holy Communion.

⋏ The statue of Our Lady that smiled at Lúcia, Fatima parish church.

∨ Baptismal font, parish church.

He gave her remarkable instructions: "My child, your soul is the temple of the Holy Spirit. Keep it always pure, so that He will be able to carry on His divine action within it."

Worried, Lúcia asked what she had to do to keep her heart pure. Again, Fr. Cruz spoke to her as if she were an adult: "Kneel down there before Our Lady and ask her, with great confidence, to take care of your heart, to prepare it to receive Her beloved Son worthily tomorrow, and to keep it for Him alone!"

Lúcia never forgot those words.

After making her confession, Lúcia hurried to the statue of Our Lady of the Rosary. There, she had her first encounter with Mary: the statue smiled at her. The bond between the little girl and Our Lady was forged, never to be severed.

JESUS' PROMISE TO LÚCIA

On the day of her First Holy Communion, Lúcia did what Fr. Cruz had urged her to do. She prayed, "O Lord, make me a saint. Keep my heart always pure, for You alone."

Then, deep within her heart, she clearly heard the following words: "The grace granted to you this day will remain living in your soul, producing fruits of eternal life." That was Lúcia's second personal encounter with the supernatural. From that day on, she would remain on the path to sanctity.

MYSTICAL ADOPTION

Seven years after her First Communion, Lúcia received a singular grace. Our Lady appeared and told her that she was going to adopt the girl: "Henceforth you will be my child." We know of several cases of "mystical espousals,"

but Church history attests to only one "mystical adoption." This is a particularly remarkable feature of Lúcia's spirituality.

The visionary's memoirs and letters show that our heavenly Mother frequently gave her advice and instructions. In a letter of January 9, 1940, Lúcia wrote: "The Immaculate Heart of Mary is my refuge, principally in the most difficult hours, and so I am always saved. ... How much this certainty inspires and comforts me. I find strength and consolation in it."

After they began to see the Blessed Mother, Fr. Cruz told Lúcia and her two cousins, "Be assured, have no fear; it was not a devil who appeared to you but the Holy Virgin." But the care and protection Our Lady promised Lúcia did not end with the Fatima apparitions. Neither did it end with the apparitions the saint would receive in 1925 and 1929 (in Pontevedra and Tui, Spain, respectively). Throughout Lúcia's life, Our Lady would continuously reveal her presence through visions, the last of which occurred during Lúcia's time as a Carmelite nun. Mary would appear through Lúcia's statue of Our Lady of Fatima, which occasionally shed human tears.

⋏ *Loom in Lúcia's family home.*

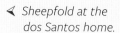

◄ *Sheepfold at the dos Santos home.*

⋏ *Lúcia's bed, dos Santos home.*

Fatima

1917

The Message of Fatima

In October 1917, crowds gathered around three small visionaries. There were believers, doubters, and also those who wished to be healed. They all became witnesses to a miracle, and they all departed changed and filled with grace.

Thanks to Our Lady, a little-known part of Portugal became one of the world's largest Marian pilgrimage sites.

In 1917, the Virgin Mary appeared to three children in Fatima, Portugal, giving them spiritual messages for the world. Mary appeared to the children on the thirteenth day of each month from May 13, 1917, to October 13, 1917.

Experts say that Fatima is the "greatest revelation since apostolic times." The Church has been poring over the contents of the Fatima message for more than a hundred years, but its many truths have not yet been fully explained. The Fatima message is rightly compared with Holy Scripture: the truths of both Fatima and the Bible are without end. The Fatima truths, however, are not in some sort of competition with the Word of God; rather, Fatima is simply a

contemporary reminder, a repetition of the gospel.

Yet only a few details of this extraordinary apparition are widely known. We know of Mary's calls to sacrifice one's desires, to make acts of reparation, to pray the Rosary, to observe the First Saturdays, and to practice devotion to her Immaculate Heart. But few know that Mary expressed a wish to be better known and loved, that she rejected visionaries who were inclined to gossip, or that she spurned the perfumes offered to her.

She chose the youngest children from ordinary Christian families as visionaries. It was as if she wanted to draw attention to the dignity of children, as well as their extraordinary potential for spiritual development. It seems that children are capable of rising to the heights of spiritual maturity, even to the heights of sanctity. During the Jubilee Year 2000

Fatima

PORTUGAL

◁ *"I want you to pray the Rosary daily in honor of Our Lady of the Rosary, in order to obtain peace for the world and the end of the war."*

celebrations, the Church raised the little visionaries to the ranks of the beatified, with the exception of the eldest, Sr. Lúcia, who did not die until February 13, 2005, in the Carmelite convent in Coimbra, Portugal.

Sr. Lúcia was ten years of age when she had her visions in 1917. Her cousins, Francisco and Jacinta, were nine and seven respectively. The children were friends, and they worked together grazing sheep.

ANGELIC PREPARATION

The first apparition occurred in 1915. Lúcia dos Santos, Maria Justino, Teresa Matias, and Teresa's sister Maria Rosa saw a figure, as white as snow, shining in the sun's rays above some trees. Lúcia would have forgotten about the apparition—unlike her friends, who talked about it everywhere they went—were it not for the fact that a year later, when she was grazing sheep with her cousins Francisco and Jacinta Marto, an angel appeared to the children on three occasions.

An angel appeared to the children on three occasions in order to prepare their hearts to receive Our Lady's message.

He taught them several prayers and prepared them to meet Our Lady. During the third and most important apparition, he explained the mystery of the Eucharist, the tangible presence of Jesus Christ in the world.

Yet the Fatima story does not begin with the Marian apparitions in 1917, nor even in 1915, when the eight-year-old Lúcia dos Santos saw the angel for the first time. The Fatima message had its beginnings eight hundred years earlier. Interestingly, it was connected with a special angel: St. Michael the Archangel.

Experts on Fatima state that the first unclear apparition of an angel "wrapped in a sheet" and "white as snow" was of St. Michael the Archangel. If it is true that he initiated apparitions in Fatima on three occasions (in 1147, 1385, and 1917), then these appearances point to a victorious battle, a decisive battle fought under the most adverse circumstances—the battle against demons, who want to rob us of our eternal life.

St. Michael's pre-Fatima apparitions began at a "difficult time," a time when—and historians and theologians are in agreement here—a new era began in human history: the twelfth century, when the world saw the breakup of the prevailing unity of state and religion, of scientific knowledge and theology. At that time, the situation was so dire that even the Church began to rock on her foundation. Divisions multiplied everywhere, the most sinister being the era of controversial popes.

The first Fatima incident did not occur in Fatima itself but in its vicinity. In 1147, during Afonso the Conqueror's siege of Santarém Castle, which was occupied by the Moors, the prince of angels appeared to the Christian knights on their way to do battle. Sword raised, St. Michael led them to victory.

The same day that the Moors surrendered Santarém Castle, the siege of Lisbon began. It, too, ended in the expulsion of the enemy. During this second battle, on August 13, history's first miracle of the sun occurred above the besieged city.

Throughout Portugal, churches, triumphal arches, statues, and paintings were created in honor of St. Michael. During funerals, a banner depicting St. Michael was carried in front of coffins in order to summon his power to protect souls from the power of Satan.

On August 13, 1385, an army under the command of St. Nuno Álvares Pereira (also known as St. Nuno of St. Mary) halted for a rest near the church in the village of Seiça. As the knights rested before the imminent battle, St. Nuno begged the Blessed Virgin Mary throughout the night for the grace of victory.

The next day, the army marched through what is now Fatima. As the soldiers passed through the village, they heard angels singing high up in the sky and saw St. Michael the Archangel in front of them, sword raised, as a sign of victory. The apparition began when St. Nuno later was riding through a valley called Cova da Iria. He jumped off his horse and fell to his knees. Then, divinely inspired, he called out that the ground on which he was kneeling was sacred. It was precisely there that the Fatima children would meet the Mother of God.

PRAYER AND SACRIFICE

The first Marian apparition at Fatima occurred on May 13, 1917. As on any other day, the children were grazing sheep. Lightning suddenly appeared in the clear blue sky. (Storms occur quite frequently in that part of Portugal, and they usually come unexpectedly.) The children began to drive the herd along, looking for a safe place to take shelter. Then there was another flash of lightning, and the children saw a beautiful woman standing on a small rock oak. She was all in white, emanating a light brighter than the sun's rays. The children were so close to Our Lady that they were within the light that enveloped her.

Then they heard a voice say, "**Do not be afraid. I shall not harm you**."

A conversation ensued between Our Lady and Lúcia.

"Where are you from?" asked Lúcia.

"**I am from Heaven**."

"What do you want of us?"

"**I have come to ask you to return here for six months in succession, on the thirteenth day, at this same hour. Later on, I will tell you who I am and what I want. Afterward, I will return here yet a seventh time**."

"Shall I go to Heaven?"

"**Yes**."

"And Jacinta?"

"**Also**."

"And Francisco?"

"**Yes, but he must first say many Rosaries**."

Our Lady asked: "**Are you willing to offer yourselves to God to bear all the sufferings He will send you, as an act of reparation for the sins by which He is offended and for the conversion of sinners**?"

"Yes," replied the children.

"**You will have to suffer a great deal, but God's grace will be your strength**."

On saying those words, Our Lady stretched out her hands. Light streamed out from them, a light so bright that it moved the children to fall to their knees and praise God.

After a few moments of silence, Our Lady said, "**Pray the Rosary every day, in order to obtain peace for the**

▲ *The house where Lúcia dos Santos was born and brought up.*

▼ *The children went to the site of the apparitions on the thirteenth day of every month (except August, when they were imprisoned) until October 1917.*

▲ *In appearing to Lúcia, Francisco, and Jacinta, Our Lady emphasized the dignity of children and their potential for spiritual development.*

▲ *On the last day of the Fatima apparitions, the young visionaries were surrounded by nearly one hundred thousand people.*

world and the end of the war [World War I]."

Then she began to rise toward the east and vanished into the sky.

SUBSEQUENT APPARITIONS

During the next apparition, Our Lady said, "**I want you to come here on the thirteenth of next month, to pray the Rosary every day and to learn to read. I shall tell you what I want later**."

Lúcia said, "I want you to take us to Heaven."

"**Yes, I shall take Jacinta and Francisco soon, but you will remain here for some time yet. Jesus wants to avail Himself of you to make me better known and loved. He wants a devotion to my Immaculate Heart to be established throughout the world**."

"Am I to remain here all alone?"

"**No, my daughter, I shall never forsake you. My Immaculate Heart shall be your refuge and the path that will lead you to God**."

Then Our Lady stretched out her hands, and light streamed out of them. The children saw themselves in the light, as if they were immersed in God. Jacinta and Francisco seemed to be in that part of the light that went up toward Heaven, while Lúcia was in the light that streamed downward. The children saw a heart encircled by thorns in front of Our Lady's right hand. They understood that it was her Immaculate Heart, affronted by the sins of humanity and in need of acts of reparation.

On July 13, Our Lady said, "**I want you to pray the Rosary daily in honor of Our Lady of the Rosary, in order to obtain peace for the world and the end of the war, as she alone can obtain that grace. … In October, I will tell you who I am and what I want. I shall also work a miracle so that all might believe. … Sacrifice yourselves for sinners and constantly repeat, especially when offering a sacrifice: 'O Jesus, this is for love of Thee, for the conversion of sinners, and in reparation for the sins committed against the Immaculate Heart of Mary.'**"

Our Lady stretched out her hands again, and the light they emanated seemed to penetrate the ground. The children received a mysterious vision of Hell. Then, Our Lady commented on that terrifying sight. She spoke of her Immaculate Heart as the last resort for the world and foretold World War II, the persecution of the Church and the Holy Father, and the spread of Communism. But she also spoke of the eventual triumph of her heart, a victory to be effected by the consecration of Russia to her Immaculate Heart and the practice of the Five First Saturdays devotion.

WORD SPREADS

In those days, the government of Portugal fought against the Church in various ways. When the apparitions in Fatima became more and more widely known, the authorities concluded that these events were at the very least an inconvenience. On August 13, in order to prevent an increase of "religious hysteria," the mayor of the district of Vila Nova de Ourém (a Freemason) kidnapped the children at the site of the apparitions. Threatening them with torture and death, he strove to wring information out of them. In the end, having failed to achieve anything, he had to release the visionaries.

August 13 saw the usual prelude to the apparitions: thunder, lightning, and a small cloud over a rock oak tree. The Blessed Virgin Mary arrived for the meeting but did not reveal herself. She spoke to the children a few days later, informing them that Fatima lost many graces due to the conduct of the mayor.

The kidnapping of the children turned out to have an effect that the persecutors of the Church had not anticipated. The press covered the events of August 13 extensively, and tens of thousands of pilgrims came to Fatima.

The last two apparitions were accompanied by strange signs. Here is a testimony pertaining to the September 13 apparition:

> The ground was covered in bushes. There were several small trees and small stone walls that demarcated property boundaries. In order to have a better view, we climbed onto one of the walls, which was between the site of the apparitions and today's church. We could see the people who had gathered below us, but the little shepherds were barely visible. At first, I did not notice anything. It was not until the end of the apparition, when I looked up at the sky, that I saw what seemed like a luminous globe floating above the ground. It moved a little toward the west; then it pulled away from the horizon again, and headed for the sun. We were extremely moved. We prayed fervently. ...Either before or after, but certainly that same day, we—admittedly not everyone—saw falling rose petals

An immense crowd in the Cova da Iria saw the sun revolve around its axis in an amazing spiral dance.

> As requested by the Blessed Virgin Mary, a small chapel was built on the site of the first apparition. Today, it is the heart of a magnificent sanctuary.

or snowflakes. We could not touch them because they vanished before they fell on the ground. That was enough to lead us to believe that the whole incident was God's doing.

During the September apparition, Our Lady told the children, "**Continue to pray the Rosary in order to obtain the end of the war. In October Our Lord will come, as well as Our Lady of Dolors and Our Lady of Carmel. Saint Joseph will appear with the Child Jesus to bless the world. God is pleased with your sacrifices**."

THE FORETOLD MIRACLE

On October 13, 1917, almost one hundred thousand people had gathered in Fatima. The rain poured down. There were puddles and mud everywhere. The children struggled to make their way through the crowd. When the visionaries reached the rock oak, Lúcia, inwardly inspired, asked the

people to close their umbrellas, and it immediately stopped raining. Shortly after, the children saw a light, and Our Lady appeared on the rock oak tree. She said, "**I am the Lady of the Rosary. Continue to pray the Rosary every day. The war is going to end, and the soldiers will soon return to their homes.**" She added, "**The people must amend their lives and ask forgiveness for their sins**."

Sr. Lúcia recalled: "When Our Lady vanished into the infinite distance, we saw St. Joseph with the Child Jesus to the side of the sun, together with the Blessed Mother in white and wearing a blue mantle. It seemed that St. Joseph and the Child Jesus blessed the world, making a sign of the cross. Shortly afterward, that apparition vanished, and we saw the Lord Jesus with Our Lady of Mount Carmel."

At that time, the crowd observed the miracle that had been foretold. One of the witnesses recalled:

It poured down rain on October 13. The sky was covered with heavy, gray clouds. There were people everywhere, as far as the eye could see. Some were praying, others were kneeling deep in thought, yet others were singing. People stood with their umbrellas open (which did not help much), waiting patiently for the children to arrive. ...They appeared five minutes before the appointed time. When Lúcia asked the people to close their umbrellas, it stopped raining, as if someone had turned off the tap in the shower. The children also asked the men to take off their hats. A man who stood next to me did not do so. After a few seconds, the sun appeared. The man humbly took his hat off and said, "I believe it now, as none of us could have done that."

⊻ *A six-ton bronze crown atop the tower of the Basilica of Our Lady of the Rosary in Fatima.*

In answer to Our Lady's appeal, many people began to pray the Rosary again. This form of devotion is particularly beloved by Our Lady.

Many pilgrims walk the penitential path around the chapel on their knees—an unforgettable testimony of faith.

The crowd stood completely silent. Various colors emanated from the sun. People's clothes took on a golden shade and dried immediately. Then the sun began to revolve around its axis in an amazing spiral dance, as if it had detached itself from the firmament, and began speeding toward the earth. Then it returned to its original position.

All those who witnessed the miracle were terrified, shouting, begging God to forgive them their sins. The blind and the handicapped begged to be healed. I saw discarded crutches and those blind from birth who had regained their sight.

After the miracle, the children asked the people to say the rosary daily. Otherwise, the world would be engulfed in a terrible war, and all would suffer greatly.

People thought that the end of the world was imminent. They fell to their knees and begged God for forgiveness. Those who had gone to Fatima to ridicule the apparitions and to "put an end to the farce" were converted.

After a while, the sun returned to its normal position. So ended the Fatima apparitions.

The 1917 message of Our Lady of Fatima has been hugely influential, a guide for successive generations. The Holy See has officially announced that the apparitions are in accord with the teaching of the Church and has urged people to listen to the "message of the century." In 1982, Pope St. John Paul II said that the words spoken by Our Lady in Fatima "seem to be approaching their fulfillment toward the end of the century." He added that the Fatima message is more relevant than ever.

VISIONARIES REJECTED BY GOD

When Lúcia saw an angel above the forest as early as 1915, two years before the apparitions in Fatima, she wrote: "We were on the slopes of Mount Cabeço when we saw something like a small cloud in human form descending from the sky, moving slowly above the trees below us, as if wanting to draw our attention. ... A deep conviction arose in me, which I do not intend to hide: I thought it was my guardian angel."

Interestingly, neither Jacinta nor Francisco—her cousins and best friends—were with her at the time. Instead, Lúcia was with three other friends: Teresa Matias, Maria Rosa Matias, and Maria Justino. These children saw the angel during the first apparition, which was a preparation

for the coming of Our Lady. Except for Lúcia, they all ran to the village to tell everyone about what they had seen. Perhaps God, having put them to a simple test, abandoned His intention to make them His messengers upon seeing that the girls were unable to keep a secret.

Only eight-year-old Lúcia passed God's test. She kept everything she saw to herself. God had to find other companions for her. Francisco and Jacinta, then, were second-choice visionaries. It was to them, together with Lúcia, that the Angel of Peace appeared in order to prepare them to meet the Queen of Heaven a year later.

Teresa Matias, Maria Rosa Matias, and Maria Justino lived pious lives, but the Lord God did not avail Himself of them as witnesses of miraculous events. He did not entrust the Fatima message to them. In this way, God showed us the importance of a beautiful Marian virtue: the virtue of silence.

⌄ *The construction of the Basilica of the Holy Trinity in Fatima ended in 2007. It is the world's fourth-largest Catholic church.*

Basel

1917

The Mystical Wound

Adrienne von Speyr was both a strong woman who faced hardship and a doctor who attracted people—not only because she treated them at no cost but also because she had a healing charism. She hid a secret in her heart: a mystical wound.

▾ Adrienne von Speyr was born in La Chaux-de-Fonds, a Swiss town located on the border with France.

In 1985, a conference took place at the Lateran University in Rome with three of the contemporary Church's luminaries in attendance: the Holy Father, John Paul II; Cardinal Joseph Ratzinger, prefect of the Congregation for the Doctrine of the Faith; and Hans Urs von Balthasar, regarded by some as the greatest theologian of the twentieth century. Their focus was the spirituality of a certain extraordinary woman—a layperson from Switzerland who led a relatively normal life.

Adrienne von Speyr was born in 1902 in La Chaux-de-Fonds, Switzerland. Her early life was like that of any other child born to a typical wealthy Protestant family. When she was fifteen, however, her father died. Everything changed. She and her three siblings were left with a mother who did not love them. Adrienne's mother forced her daughter to attend a commercial school so the girl could find work at a bank.

Once again, God had other plans. Exhausted, Adrienne fell ill with tuberculosis. She had to leave home for three and a half years in order to be treated—first at the home of a relative, who was also a doctor, and then at her uncle's home.

On Adrienne's return home, her mother prevented her from taking her graduation exams. She also tried to dissuade her daughter from studying medicine. Yet she made money by giving numerous private lessons, caught up with her schoolwork, and passed her exams with distinction. She then began university studies and maintained herself by taking on exhausting jobs. She defended her doctoral thesis, got married, and opened her own practice, seeing up to eighty patients every day. Adrienne exercised her charism of physical and spiritual healing as a popular doctor who treated people at no cost and even paid for their medicine. It is said that she convinced several thousand women not to abort their unborn children.

But that stage of her life also had its grim side. Exhaustion led to her having three miscarriages. In 1934, her husband Emil died suddenly and unexpectedly.

Basel

SWITZERLAND

BEAUTY HIDDEN BENEATH THE SURFACE

Although a seemingly ordinary woman, Adrienne was blessed with a priceless spiritual treasure: mystical encounters with Mary. At age fifteen, she had a vision of the Blessed Mother in the company of angels. She described the experience as follows: "That morning, I woke up very early and saw Our Lady. I had never seen such beauty. I did not feel any fear at all. On the contrary, I was filled with a new joy, overwhelming and benign at the same time. She left a very vivid impression on me—a wonderful mystery. I then found, In a certain sense, a refuge. From that time on, I have had a great affection for the Mother of God. I knew that I ought to love her."

So wrote a young girl who was brought up in the Protestant tradition, in a family where Our Lady was certainly not venerated—a family that was religiously indifferent. The young Adrienne began to follow a path unknown to Protestants, a path that would eventually lead her to the Catholic Church.

The experience left a visible mark on Adrienne. Ever since the apparition, to the end of her life she had a mystical wound under her left breast. It is probably the only case in the history of apparitions that the Blessed Virgin Mary inflicted a mystical wound on anyone.

A MEETING WITH THE MASTER

Adrienne sought the truth about the Mother of God in philosophy, theology, and literature. As she studied, she began to understand the meaning of suffering. She also discovered that "if one wants to come to a synthesis of God and the world," one has to love with all one's might. That synthesis "between Heaven and the world" was very frequently emphasized in her visions and inspirations.

▼ *Adrienne, a seemingly ordinary though very ambitious and hardworking woman, hid in her heart a secret whose fruits still await the world's appreciation.*

⋀ *Lithograph depicting the cathedral in Basel.*

The apparitions in Basel are examples of private apparitions, the contents of which we shall never fully know.

When the girl was fifteen years old, her life changed unimaginably.

She then met a man who would soon become a beacon that led many to the truth. Hans Urs von Balthasar was a Jesuit priest and theologian who, during their first discussion, showed Adrienne the way: "I explained ... that in saying 'Thy will be done,' we do not offer up all our works to God, but our readiness to fulfill His will in steadfast commitment." The visionary wrote the following about that discussion: "It was as if I had leaned on a switch, which suddenly turned on all the lights." Fr. Balthasar wrote that from then on, she began to "continuously and completely renounce herself, forget about herself, and abide in openness to the Word of God."

When she was baptized, a veritable explosion of mystical experiences followed. As she wrote, no sooner had her "reserved affection in regard to the Mother of God" come to an end than a familiar intimacy began. Apparitions of the Blessed Virgin Mary multiplied.

They occurred almost every day, so that Adrienne von Speyr and Our Lady became very close. Adrienne began to live more "there" than "here."

Adrienne's other charisms soon became evident. She experienced ecstasies, bilocated, and received the stigmata. Beginning in 1941, Christ allowed her to share in His Passion during Holy Week. "That which Adrienne experienced," wrote Fr. Balthasar, "was worse than Hell; she experienced the sense of losing God forever."

During ecstasies, she dictated essays to von Balthasar on the Holy Trinity, the Blessed Virgin Mary, the communion of saints, and many other topics. In 1945, Adrienne von Speyr and Hans Urs von Balthasar founded the *Johannesgemeinschaft* (Community of St. John), the aim of which is "to be at God's disposal and do whatever He asks."

Adrienne von Speyr is an example of a true mystic, to whom the Blessed Virgin

Mary was of the utmost importance. The visionary's family and friends kept repeating that Adrienne had "a virtually unimaginable intimacy with the Blessed Virgin Mary." There is no authentic Christian mysticism without an openness to Mary. The fact that the Blessed Virgin Mary was at the heart of Adrienne's life is clearly evident in her writings. According to von Balthasar, her famous book *Handmaid of the Lord* is essential reading if one wants to become familiar with the mystic's spirituality.

In her mystical writings, Speyr referred to the Blessed Virgin Mary as "a wedding ring that the Father gave to His Son as a sign that the work of salvation would end successfully." She said, "the Mother of Our Lord is the Church," and said "the Church was Mary from the very first moment of its existence." In this way, God's Bride became the Church, and because we are the Church, Mary's seal of election is imprinted on all of us. As Speyr wrote: "Whatever God did for His Mother, He had the Church in mind."

The Blessed Virgin Mary also revealed to Adrienne that prayer was part of Mary's nature and an expression of her orientation to God. It was always so, even when she was still unable to pray vocally, even before she came to know God through her reason. She looked at everything in God's light, and everything spoke to her of God.

Hence, the life of the Blessed Virgin Mary was in everything a journey toward God. Mary went toward Him step by step, and each step was infallible. Her life was without that which virtually all of us experience—the necessity of a radical reorientation, a need for conversion. She lived with her eyes fixed on Heaven the whole time.

A WORK STILL UNRECOGNIZED

In September 1967, when Adrienne was dying, she referred to the Blessed Virgin Mary's first apparition. That wonderful meeting with the Blessed Virgin in 1917 led her to write: "I had never seen such beauty." On the day of her death, she called out, "How beautiful it is to die!"

One year after her death, Hans Urs von Balthasar wrote that although Adrienne dictated more than sixty volumes (of which thirty-seven have been published), no one had yet taken her writings seriously. To this day, the situation has not changed much. And yet von Balthasar has declared that "her works were much more important" than his and that their joint work "cannot be separated."

⌄ *"I had never seen such beauty," said Adrienne, recalling her first meeting with Our Lady.*

Radzymin

1920

The Anti-Bolshevik
Mother of God

Miracle on the Vistula is not just a stirring battle scene but also a symbolic view of that which determined the course of the skirmish. When painting this work, Jerzy Kossak could not forget Our Lady, the quiet heroine of the battle who kept watch over her children.

The heroic priest Ignacy Skorupka, who was killed during a skirmish, became a symbol of the Battle of Warsaw.

History tells us that Our Lady has appeared on battlefields on numerous occasions and that those miraculous events have had a bearing on the outcome of wars. There have been many such apparitions, but one of the most important occurred in 1920 near Warsaw, Poland, on the feast of the Assumption of the Blessed Virgin Mary.

The Miracle on the Vistula (or the Battle of Warsaw) was the fruit of an ocean of prayers to Our Lady. It is a Marian miracle clearly connected with the Fatima apparitions, during which Our Lady warned of "Russia's errors" and promised to help if people would pray and do penance. At the Warsaw-Praga cathedral on June 13, 1999, Pope St. John Paul II said, "It was a great victory for the Polish Army. It was so great that it was impossible to explain it in a purely natural way. Hence, it was called the Miracle on the Vistula, which was preceded by the nation's fervent prayers."

The Holy Father pointed to two things, the supernatural help from Heaven and the prayers that procured it—the prayers not only of tens of thousands of individuals but of a whole nation, which occasioned an apparition of the Blessed Virgin Mary and changed the course of history.

EXAMPLE FROM POLAND

The apostolic nuncio to Poland, who was in Warsaw when it was under threat from the Red Army, saw the Miracle on the Vistula in the same way that John Paul II did. He knew that the victory, which he called "Mary's victory," was the fruit of the nation's earnest prayers and acts of penance. The nuncio was so impressed that, on being elected pope (taking the name Pius XI), he had a scene depicting the Battle of Warsaw painted on a wall in Castel Gandolfo, the papal summer residence. Convinced that the Battle of Warsaw attested to God's intervention in the course of history, he wanted to encourage the faithful to pray.

Communism took power in 1917, the year of the Fatima apparitions. It oppressed the people of Russia, but that was just a starting point for its conquest of Europe and the world. Our Lady of Fatima warned that plans had been made "to spread Russia's errors throughout the world."

In November 1918, a revolution broke out in Germany. The country was proclaimed a republic, and local labor movements prepared to take over. The Bolsheviks began to think about quickly reaching the German border in order to help overturn the order that had existed there for generations.

Similar sentiments also prevailed in other countries, as the Communist International became more and more active. The Red Army marched on the West. Commander Mikhail Tukhachevsky summarized the aims of the Bolsheviks in his famous directive of July 2, 1920: "The way leads over the corpse of Poland to a universal conflagration. ... On to Wilno, Minsk, and Warsaw—forward!"

"And everything is ready for the conquest of the world," wrote the Polish bishops to episcopates throughout the world. "There are whole hosts already organized in every country just waiting for the battle cry. ... It is not us alone who are in danger. Poland is but a stage toward the conquest of the world. ... Poland, in the Bolshevik march on the world, is the last barrier to it, and should she collapse, it will flood the world with waves of destruction."

The Vatican understood that "presently, not only the Polish nation's existence is in danger, but the whole of Europe is under the threat of the horrors of another war," as Pope Pius XI wrote in a letter to Cardinal Pompili five days before the Miracle on the Vistula.

AN EASY VICTORY?

Moscow's plans quickly unfolded. A Polish bishops' letter of July 1920 describes what came as Bolshevism advanced: "Murders, slaughter ... burning villages and towns come in its wake. But in its blind envy it primarily seeks to destroy healthy social ties, every leaven of true education, every healthy system, all religions, and the Church."

On July 23, 1920, the Provisional Polish Revolutionary Committee, which was to be a puppet government for the

POLAND

⌃ *The cemetery chapel doubles as a monument commemorating the Battle of Radzymin.*

Polish Soviet Republic, was established in Smolensk. A week later, the committee announced that it was going to take over Poland. Its members, including Felix Edmundovich Dzerzhinsky and Julian Baltazar Marchlewski, followed the Soviet divisions advancing on Warsaw in a special train. Eventually, the train reached Wyszków, where the committee prepared to seize power after the Red Army had taken the Polish capital.

Toward the end of July, the Polish forces were pushed back to the Curzon Line (the Bug River), and on August 10, 1920, the front line was in the vicinity of the Polish towns of Przasnysz, Wyszków, Siedlec, and soon Działdowo. That day, Red Army commander Mikhail Tukhachevsky issued his directive to take Warsaw. Everything had already been planned to the last detail. The day of entry into the capital of Poland was announced: August 15.

The Red Army soldiers marched on Warsaw certain that they would easily take the city, where, they were assured, "chocolate lay on the streets" and the shops were full of clothes, shoes, and all sorts of goods. In a homily given in the Warsaw cathedral during a thanksgiving service for the city's deliverance, Archbishop Józef Teodorowicz recalled that "the enemy sent telegrams around

the world declaring that Warsaw had been taken."

So far, the Red Army's success was complete. Nothing at all pointed to its imminent and total defeat, especially as political successes began to accompany its military conquests. Workers in England, France, Czechoslovakia, Germany, Austria, Belgium, and Italy believed that a true democracy had arisen in Russia and that the idea of social justice was beginning to be realized. It may well surprise us today, but Western countries looked upon the Red Army's advance with indifference and perhaps even sympathy. The British prime minister, David Lloyd George, even believed Great Britain's cooperation with Soviet Russia would yield significant economic benefits.

THE CHURCH'S APPEAL

In the face of danger, the Polish bishops called the Poles to unite. They warned that before God they were still not a nation, despite having regained independence. In the face of an inevitable defeat, the Church called everyone to forget about themselves for the sake of the homeland: "Sacrifice all your partisan jealousies for her, any desire to rule over one another, all the venomous acids that eat into her soul and her organism. ... Be selfless in the

General Tadeusz Rozwadowski's order of August 14, 1920.

◄ *View of Radzymin, destroyed by shelling, in 1920.*

service of the homeland, because it is only through great sacrifices that you will retain your freedom."

The Polish people took heed of the bishops' appeal. A time of great national prayer began, as only God could rescue Poland. The people begged for a miracle—and one had, in fact, been promised.

Over forty years earlier, on Good Friday 1872, the Blessed Virgin told a Polish mystic, Wanda Justyna Nepomucena Malczewska: "**When Poland regains her independence, her former oppressors will soon arise in order to strangle her. But my young army, fighting in my name, will defeat them, drive them far away, and force them to make peace. I will help**." The Blessed Virgin Mary had even announced the day of victory. On the feast of the Assumption, in 1873, Our Lady declared: "**Today's feast day will become a national feast day for you Poles, because on that day you shall gain a great victory over your enemies, who were intent on your destruction**."

Poles understood that great promises and prophecies would not be fulfilled without their cooperation. They understood that God would ask them one day: "What did you do in order that the prophecies might be fulfilled?" During the summer of 1920, the Poles did a great deal, enough for God to work a miracle. They became a nation, putting aside personal interests.

They fell to their knees before God and took heed of the bishops' appeal: "Let us pray; let us persist in prayer, and we shall be triumphant, victorious."

A spokesman for the Warsaw clergy recalled that the faithful also undertook "good and penitential deeds capable of procuring God's mercy, like fasting and alms." Henryk Przeździecki, the bishop of Podlasie, wrote: "My dearly beloved, God has shown His mercy toward us so many times, and now He will show us His kindness. He will spare us imminent misfortune if He sees that we are not selfish, egoists, or cowards." Accordingly, on August 12 and 13, when the Soviets reached Radzymin and began shelling

⌄ *Polish emplacement during the battle in August 1920.*

▲ *Headquarters of one of the Polish regiments that fought the Soviets.*

▼ *Burial place of soldiers who fell at the Battle of Radzymin.*

formed, bearing the relics of two patrons of Poland, Andrew Bobola and Ladislas of Gielniów.

One eyewitness said that the city was "transformed into one huge church, filled with many thousands, praying and singing. Even Warsaw had never seen such an assemblage of people. That day, August 8, there was a supplicatory service in the Jesuits' church in Rome. The whole Catholic world prayed for Poland, as it was understood that by fighting against Bolshevism, Poland was defending the whole of Christianity."

In addition to Masses, processions, litanies, and acts of consecration, the great national prayer of 1920 saw churches open day and night and filled with people holding rosaries and singing supplications. Every home became a house of prayer, and people prayed on their knees at roadside statues.

A testimony from that summer recalls that "a crowd stretched from the Church of the Gracious Mother of God (the Patroness of Warsaw) in the Old Town, to the Church of the Holy Cross. People kept vigil day and night, praying to their patroness and queen. They prayed ceaselessly before a statue of the Blessed Virgin Mary located in an open space on Krakowskie Przedmieście, reminding the capital's patroness that she had once rescued Warsaw from the Black Plague. People begged her to choke the red plague and prevent the spread of the bloody Bolshevik terror—not only in Poland but also throughout Europe."

Praga (a district of Warsaw), thousands of people, in an act of humility and penance, lay down in the form of crosses in the square in front of the monastery in Jasna Góra.

PRAYER CALENDAR

According to the metropolitan archbishop's instructions, novenas were offered up twice a day in Warsaw churches, "together with expositions of the Most Blessed Sacrament, litanies to the Sacred Heart of Jesus, as well as acts of consecration." Poland was officially consecrated to the Sacred Heart of Jesus with the participation of the highest Church and state authorities, including the head of state. In Jasna Góra, the nation was reconsecrated to Mary, Queen of Poland, to whom a supplicatory novena was said from August 7 to August 15: the day that victory came.

On Sunday, August 8, twenty-four-hour adoration of the Blessed Sacrament took place in all the churches, without exception. Afterward, each church held a procession to St. John's Cathedral, where one supplicatory procession was

PROVIDENTIAL EVENTS

Cardinal Aleksander Kakowski wrote that something extraordinary must have happened, as the Polish forces "crushed the invading forces, which outnumbered them ten to one. And in driving them

Polish line of defense near Radzymin.

first station was out of commission because it was being relocated. A Warsaw transmitter was quickly tuned into the second, active Soviet radio station and began jamming the Minsk transmitters. So, when Tukhachevsky issued an order to the Soviet Fourth Army to turn back southeast and engage a Polish army at Nasielsk, only the Poles heard his transmission. Then, for two days, Warsaw continuously transmitted Holy Scripture on the frequency.

Another "miracle" that changed the course of the war was the heroism of Fr. Ignacy Skorupka. The editor of the Warsaw Archdiocese News wrote that his brave deeds and valiant death were "of a providential ordinance, a turning point. … That sacrifice of the first of Warsaw's priests saw a victory of astonishing rapidity and magnitude. … The more one looks at this significant day, when the Queen of Poland fulfilled the Polish episcopate's request in Jasna

Polish soldiers near Stara Miłosna in 1920. It was understood that by fighting against Bolshevism, Poland was defending the whole of Christianity.

off, one can boldly say, saved Poland, even the whole world, from inevitable destruction."

It was a miracle, one prayed for by the nation.

In fact, there were several strange coincidences—or providential events. The first "miracle" was Stalin's decision not to strengthen Mikhail Tukhachevsky's position, despite orders issued by Sergey Sergeyevich Kamenev, commander in chief of the Red Army, and Leon Trotsky, the war commissar. Reinforcements from the southern army eventually set off north after a delay of ten days, but they arrived too late to participate in the Battle of Warsaw.

Another remarkable event was the capture of the Soviet Fourth Army's headquarters in Ciechanów, including one of two Bolshevik radio stations that received orders from the Minsk headquarters. The Poles knew that the

Góra, it becomes clear that this quiet and pious priest ... was called to fulfill Joan of Arc's mission at a turning point in our history."

He added, "God demanded that he [Fr. Skorupka] become a reparatory sacrifice for the nation, because great things are not achieved without great sacrifices."

A MARIAN MIRACLE

The Queen of Poland fulfilled the request of her nation. Spectacularly,

she herself appeared on the battlefield to support the Polish forces. Cardinal Kakowski mentioned this apparition in the context of Fr. Ignacy Skorupka's heroism. He wrote in his diary: "Young, wounded soldiers told me about the details of Fr. Skorupka's death when I visited them in the hospital. The wounded, captured Bolsheviks told me that they saw a priest in a surplice, a cross in his hand, and the Mother of God above him. They said that they could not shoot at the Mother of God, even though she was against them."

Apparently, Fr. Skorupka had a vision of the Mother of God, Queen of Poland, after which he rallied soldiers to counterattack—the soldiers being students who had volunteered only days before to defend their homeland under impossible odds. Fr. Józef Bartnik, S.J., an expert on the Miracle on the Vistula, wrote:

> Our Lady appeared as the Gracious Mother of God, the Patroness of Warsaw. ... She appeared in the sky before dawn, a monumental figure who filled the whole of the still-dark sky. She was dressed in a wide, flowing mantle, which protected the capital, and was in the company of Polish hussars who, at the Battle of Vienna, drove off the pagan hordes in all directions, under the slogan "In the Name of Mary." The Mother of God held something akin to a shield that protected the city entrusted to her care.

> The apparition of Our Lady was seen by dozens, or rather hundreds, of Bolsheviks attacking Polish units in the battle over access to the capital. That apparition caused fear among

The Jesuit Church of the Gracious Mother of God in the Old Town was one of many places where the inhabitants of Warsaw gathered to pray.

the soldiers, terror and panic that would be impossible to describe.…

The Mother of God, surrounded by light, was clearly visible against the backdrop of the night sky! The Bolsheviks, at the sight of Our Lady, fled in extreme terror, leaving Radzymin behind, which seemed to have been in their hands for good! The Bolsheviks retreated in panic. They fled in all directions, across the country, across the fields. Vehicles broke down; horses collapsed, and the roads were strewn with them. Soldiers fled despite the fact that desertion meant a court martial—a firing squad.

A similar miracle occurred near Włocławek, where Our Lady prevented the Russians from crossing the Vistula River.

Events began snowballing. On August 16, 1920, there was a counterattack. The larger part of the Soviet forces made a disorderly retreat as Polish forces chased them farther and farther to the east.

Poland was saved, and prayers of thanksgiving were raised throughout the country.

A LESSON FROM HISTORY

The Miracle on the Vistula, though uncomfortable for subsequent governments, who have distorted and pushed it to the margins of historical events, is still remembered by the nation. It tells us what is most important: to stay faithful to God and to strive for national unity. When "For God and country!" once again becomes a thunderous call, anything will be possible. As Cardinal Kakowski said, "God but awaited the Poles' consent to stop feuding, for them to be at one in loving their homeland, in order that He might show them the power of His mercy."

As God and His decrees are unchangeable, we can be certain that the slogan of 1920, "Ut unum sint" (That they may be one), embodied in religious and social life, will change the face of Poland.

⬥ *Praying before an image of the Gracious Mother of God, people implored her to save them from God's wrath yet again and to deliver Poland from the Bolshevik terror.*

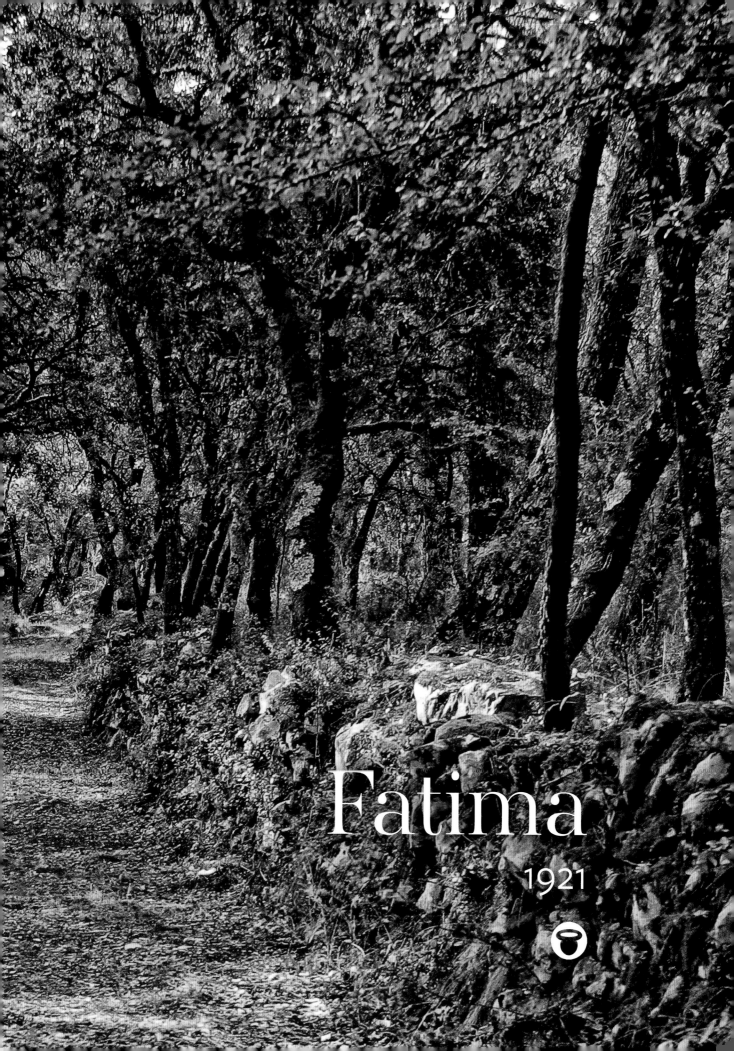

Fatima

1921

Mother of Obedience

The Church represents God's authority on earth. Obedience to her authority is obedience to God. Mary asked for obedience during the very mysterious seventh apparition at Fatima. Lúcia obeyed the local bishop, although his will was contrary to her own.

▲ In her humble observance of Church precepts, Lúcia's life was a beautiful testimony of obedience to the will of God.

There are many ways to holiness. The way of Fatima entails offering to God all the difficulties of daily life. The Blessed Virgin Mary told the children, "**Offer God all the suffering that He might send in reparation for the sins that offend Him and for the conversion of sinners**."

God sends us many opportunities to make reparation for the world's sins, just as He sent them to Sr. Lúcia and her mother. In the spring of 1921, the parish priest informed Maria Rosa dos Santos that she and her daughter had to go to the small town of Olival, where they were to meet the vicar general of their diocese. Initially, Lúcia's mother refused to go. It was a long way, and she was not in good health. Because she did not want to displease the vicar general, however, she eventually agreed.

After some reflection, Maria Rosa decided to divide the journey into three stages. On the first day, she intended to reach the village of Soutaria, where they would spend the night with their friend Dona Emilia. The next day, she planned to be in Olival, and after meeting the

vicar general, she would return to Soutaria, spend another night there, and then set off at dawn to her home in Aljustrel. A three-day journey awaited the sick woman. But Lúcia's mother said she would "bear the hardship out of love for God, and then perhaps He might help me."

What was the journey like? Sr. Lúcia recalled: "Maria Rosa set the day of departure, and both of us set off on foot along roads and stony paths, crossing mountains, fields, and quiet hills, where we heard only the sound of our own voices reciting the Rosary. From time to time, we sat down on a rock beside the road in order that my mother might rest a little." When some friends offered them hospitality, Maria Rosa declined, saying that she had undertaken the hardship "out of love for God."

Incidentally, the vicar-general spoke on behalf of the bishop. He enjoined Lúcia not to go to Lisbon or Santarém, the two cities where the family was considering sending her to school. The bishop wanted the visionary to go to Porto, in order to study at a school run

PORTUGAL

Fatima

◄ *Maria Rosa,
despite being ill,
accompanied her
daughter on an
exhausting journey
to Olival.*

by nuns. Lúcia's mother did not like the idea. Accommodation for Lúcia in Lisbon and Santarém had already been arranged. The cities were familiar and the people friendly. Porto seemed foreign and distant. That was precisely why the bishop chose to send Lúcia there: no one would recognize her.

Again, after putting forth human arguments, Maria Rosa invoked her faith. She said, "Since the bishop himself wanted it and was willing to take responsibility ... I agreed."

And what did fourteen-year-old Lúcia think? "I preferred to go to Lisbon, but in order to do what His Excellency the bishop had asked and to comply with what my mother said, I decided to go to Porto." She then explained her difficult decision to her mother, who agreed, "because the bishop represents God."

Going to Porto was another way for Lúcia to make a sacrifice for God. How could she not take advantage of this opportunity?

As it later turned out, her consent had been written into God's plan. He would allow her stay in Porto to bear great fruit: the Fatima apparitions were approved by the Church largely because the bishop had the opportunity to get to know the visionary better and ascertain the authenticity of her testimonies.

The return trip was such a great effort for Lúcia's mother that she was bedridden for two days afterward. But that journey set in motion the most mysterious of the Fatima apparitions, the so-called seventh apparition.

THE SEVENTH APPARITION

During the first apparition in May 1917, Our Lady of Fatima shared her intention to continue meeting with the young visionaries. She said: "**I have come to ask you to return here for six months in**

▲ *The idea of going to
Porto, distant and
foreign, aroused
many fears in Sr.
Lúcia. But it turned
out that her stay
there contributed
to the recognition
of the authenticity
of her testimony.*

As her personal physician, Dr. Branca Paul accompanied Sr. Lúcia during the last years of her life.

Sr. Lúcia was faithful to the Fatima message to the very last apparition, when the Blessed Virgin Mary appeared at the moment of her death.

"The Immaculate Heart of Mary is my refuge, especially in very difficult moments."

succession, on the thirteenth day, at this same hour. Later on, I will tell you who I am and what I want. Afterward, I will come yet a seventh time."

For ninety years, we knew nothing about the mysterious seventh apparition. Then, on the evening of April 30, 2007, there was a meeting at the Shrine of the Most Blessed Sacrament in Hanceville, Alabama, with Fr. Robert Fox and Dr. Branca Paul among the participants. Dr. Paul was Sr. Lúcia's personal doctor during the last fifteen years of the visionary's life and was present at her death, making her an important witness. During the meeting, Dr. Paul mentioned that she had discovered Sr. Lúcia's notes. Among them was a personal diary that Lúcia began to keep when she was at the school run by the Sisters of St. Dorothy in Porto. An entry dated June 15, 1921, described the seventh apparition, which took place after the deaths of Francisco and Jacinta. There was no longer any trace of the oak tree at Cova da Iria (pilgrims had cut it up into small pieces for relics), but there was a little chapel, which to this day is a witness to the prayers of the devotees of Our Lady of Fatima.

Not long after returning from Olival, the young Lúcia had gone to Cova da Iria to seek advice and comfort in the Rosary. She hoped to find light from Heaven and consolation from the Immaculate Heart of Mary. She was confused upon hearing that the bishop wanted her to leave Fatima and go to faraway Porto, in order to hide from people who constantly sought contact with her, wanting to know all the details of the Fatima apparitions.

The description of the apparition is short: "I then felt a friendly, affectionate, motherly hand touch me on my shoulder. I looked up and saw Our Lady of Fatima, who said: "**Here I am for the seventh**

time. Go, follow the path which the Bishop wants you to take, this is the will of God."

In this brief apparition, Our Lady simply leaned toward Lúcia and enjoined her to obey the bishop. That was certainly an important sign for Sr. Lúcia's long and complicated life. From the spring of 1921, the Fatima visionary always willingly obeyed her superiors, who represented God. She knew that in doing so, she was showing obedience to her beloved Holy Mother, who had asked her to listen to the Church. This was certainly a key element in her rapid growth in sanctity. Sr. Lúcia obeyed the Church even when her whole being rebelled, as in the case of the instructions to keep a diary and to write down the contents of the third secret of Fatima.

Fatima

1921

The Seventh
Fatima Apparition

"I have come to ask you to return here for six months in succession, on the thirteenth day, at this same hour. Later on, I will tell you who I am and what I want. Afterward, I will come yet a seventh time."

▲ *Dr. Branca Paul took care of Sr. Lúcia during the last fifteen years of the visionary's life.*

Mary announced that she would appear to the Fatima visionaries seven times. The first six times, she would appear on the thirteenth of every month, from May to October 1917. The apparitions would occur at the same time (noon), and in the same place: Cova da Iria.

Our Lady of Fatima spoke differently about her seventh visit. This apparition would take place at some unannounced future time. The clear distinction between the first six apparitions and the seventh suggests that the latter was particularly important to a later era. Generations closest to the apparitions were given messages to convert Russia, to spread the First Saturday devotions, and to dedicate themselves to the Rosary, but other generations received an additional "seventh sign." This sign was for our generation.

➤ *The entrance to the Shrine of the Most Blessed Sacrament in Hanceville, Alabama.*

A NINETY-YEAR-OLD PROBLEM

Until May 2007, the seventh apparition was a troublesome issue. The authors of certain works on Fatima chose to omit any mention of it. This, among other reasons, led to the general acceptance that the Fatima apparitions ended in October 1917 and consisted of only six visitations of the Blessed Mother with Lúcia, Francisco, and Jacinta. If there was a seventh, it was surmised to have taken place in Pontevedra in 1925, or four years later in Tui, Spain. After all, the Blessed Mother announced in July 1917, "I shall come to ask for the consecration of Russia to my Immaculate Heart and the Communion of Reparation on the First Saturdays." The former request was made at Tui, and the latter at Pontevedra.

The identification of the seventh apparition with the Pontevedra event continued for decades, but in 2007, new information came to light that disproved this hypothesis. Fatima once again surprised us.

AN EXTRAORDINARY DISCOVERY

On April 30, 2007, an amazing discovery was revealed. Dr. Branca Paul, Sr. Lúcia's personal physician, had found a short note about the mysterious seventh apparition in the visionary's diary. She shared this information during a meeting at the Shrine of the Blessed Sacrament in Hanceville, Alabama, whose attendees included Fr. Robert Fox, the founder of the Fatima Family Apostolate. On May 13, the American priest published the information Dr. Paul gave him about the apparitions and announced that extensive excerpts of

their conversation would appear in the June–July issue of his newsletter, *Fatima Family Messenger*. However, when that issue was published, it did not mention the seventh apparition. Most likely, the Holy See had decided to place an embargo on Sr. Lúcia's notes.

When news of Dr. Paul's historic discovery reached the media, it sent a wave of excitement through regions associated with Fatima. That is not surprising; the information disclosed in Sr. Lúcia's notes was proof that the Holy Mother had fulfilled her promises and had come to Cova da Iria a seventh time. "What did Mary say?" the faithful wondered. Why didn't Sr. Lúcia reveal the message of this apparition? Was the message supposed to be discovered only after her death because it was intended for later generations?

Fatima

PORTUGAL

◄ *There was a note concerning the seventh apparition of Our Lady of Fatima in Sr. Lúcia's private records.*

FATIMA

▲ *The Shrine of the Most Blessed Sacrament in Alabama.*

➢ *The seventh apparition took place on June 15, 1921, after the deaths of Francisco and Jacinta.*

Admittedly, Dr. Paul did not reveal much about the seventh apparition, but the facts we know so far match the "puzzle" found in Sr. Lúcia's cell. It won't be long before the Church will finish reviewing the seventh apparition and Sr. Lúcia's notes. Fr. Luciano Cristino, archivist of the Sanctuary of Our Lady of Fatima, will conclude the review and officially provide access to some of the notes related to this topic. But the restriction may also be an important sign that Mary appeared at Fatima to bring a message to today's world.

The revelation was waiting for Lúcia on the evening of June 15, 1921, in the same place where the previous apparitions had occurred, in Cova da Iria. Young Lúcia was supposed to leave her beloved region the next morning. She was leaving for Porto, a city in northern Portugal. To her, it seemed like a journey to the end of the world.

That day, Lúcia set out on a farewell journey to her beloved places. She visited the locations of the apparitions of the Angel of Peace in Loca do Cabeço. She stopped by Valinhos, where the Virgin Mary appeared in August 1917, and finally, she went to Cova da Iria. There she took out a rosary and knelt. She prayed as the angel taught her, on her knees, face down. It was supposed to be her goodbye prayer. However, her journal reveals something more. Lúcia was praying for strength. She felt lost when she heard that the bishop had ordered her to leave her hometown of Fatima. She did not want to go to the distant city of Porto, where she was supposed to hide far away from people she knew, forbidden to have contact with her family.

The decision to leave for Porto was made in the spring of 1921. The pastor informed Lúcia's mother that she was to take her daughter with her and go to the town of Olival. That's where the vicar-general of the diocese wanted to meet with her. He was the one who delivered the bishop's decision for Lúcia not to travel to Lisbon or to Santarém, where the family was planning on sending her. The visionary was supposed to go to the border of Portugal and be educated at a school run by nuns. Her mother reluctantly accepted this decision.

After visiting Olival, Lúcia suffered greatly. She agreed to leave, but deep down, she was opposed to it. At that time, Lúcia was still far from sainthood. We know through documents disclosed by Fr. Antonia Martinsa that young Lúcia still had a lot of pride, selfishness, and what may be called youthful immaturity.

THE MEANING OF THE APPARITION

The day when Lúcia visited Cova da Iria to find comfort and strength, she found Our Lady of Fatima. Mary came to say goodbye to her and to give her advice—something the visionary truly needed.

The apparition was brief and Lúcia summarized it with fitting brevity. Here is the first page of her journal: "In my loneliness, once again I fell to the ground, and then I felt your helping hand and maternal touch on my shoulder. I looked up and saw you. It was you, the Blessed Mother, giving me a hand and showing me the way; your lips opened and the sweet timbre of your voice restored light and peace to my soul: **'Here I am for the seventh time. Go, follow the path the Bishop wants you to take, this is the will of God.'**"

Fr. Luciano Cristino revealed these facts, but did not add to her words.

OBEDIENCE ABOVE ALL ELSE

The subject of the message was obedience to Church authorities, who represent God. According to the latest conversations with the vice-postulator of Sr. Lúcia's cause for beatification, the call to obey the Church was an important factor in her long and difficult life. Sr. Lúcia kept repeating, "I have to be obedient; that's what Our Lady of Fatima wants of me." This is a common entry on all the pages in her notes, which means she lived it every day.

Now we know why from the year 1921 the Fatima visionary always, willingly, and without any opposition showed obedience toward her superiors, even though her nature and simple

⋀ *"Here I am for the last time. Go, follow the path the bishop wants you to take; this is the will of God."*

The Blessed Mother asks for faithful obedience above all else.

human judgment rebelled against their decisions. She knew that by being obedient, she was showing loyalty to the Blessed Mother, who asked her to listen to the voice of the Church. The vice-postulator is convinced that obedience was one of the key elements that allowed Lúcia to grow rapidly in holiness. As Pope St. John Paul II taught, "One makes greater progress in a short time of obedience and submission to Mary than he makes over years of personal effort based solely on his own endeavors." Sr. Lúcia was obedient to the Church even when she felt sharp opposition, such as when she was instructed to write down on a piece of paper the content of the third secret of Fatima.

AN APPARITION FOR US

The seventh apparition of Fatima perhaps immerses us in God's divine plans. They are unclear to us now, but maybe someday, after the fact, they will become obvious to us, and we will understand.

What does the apparition tell us? It gives us the most important guidance for our times and for our lives: advice from Heaven on how to save ourselves, for as Lúcia wrote a few years before her death, "we are living in end times." We must be obedient—often going against ourselves, against our judgment—and follow what the Church says.

A civilization free of authority is growing among us. This domain of unlimited freedom is boundless, without any respect for experts. The crisis of authority has affected every sphere of life, including the Church.

And then comes the apparition from Fatima—an apparition for the first decades of the twenty-first century. It is radical: it calls for blind obedience regardless of our own logic, our own desires. Like Sr. Lúcia's, our nature challenges obedience, and yet Mary tells us, "Go the way the Church shows you. At the end is my victory."

Obedience is a difficult virtue that decides our whole future. It allows us to take part in the eternal victory of Mary, announced at Fatima. Her victory will take place in the Church, not outside of it. It won't present itself in our plans, in our ambitions, in our wisdom and intellect. The Church will be the source of this culmination, for Mary works through the Church, within which her Immaculate Heart will triumph. We must persevere with the Church until the end. Cardinal Stefan Wyszyński never ceased to remind us of this. The slogan *Poland semper fidelis*, which the cardinal repeated with pride, expresses the dedication of the Polish faithful that allowed Poland to emerge from Soviet control without bloodshed.

Obedience is a most difficult task, one we all must face. The seventh apparition of Fatima is a powerful reminder that there is no other way to victory than faithful obedience.

⅄ *The pastoral center of Paul IV at the shrine of Fatima is named after the first pope to go on pilgrimage to Fatima.*

Pontevedra

1925

The Contemplative
Mother of God

At Fatima in 1917, the Mother of God foretold that Jesus desired to entrust a special task to Lúcia: a devotion to the Immaculate Heart of Mary, which Christ wished to make known throughout the world. Lúcia learned the true meaning of this devotion eight years later.

⋏ Lúcia left Fatima in the summer of 1921. After spending four years in Porto at a school run by the Sisters of St. Dorothy, she entered the novitiate of the Congregation of the Sisters of St. Dorothy in Pontevedra, Spain.

Who has not heard of Sr. Lúcia, the visionary from Fatima? She was the main witness to the apparitions of the Virgin Mary in 1917, when she was ten years old. In 1924, she joined the Congregation of the Sisters of St. Dorothy, and in 1948, she entered the Carmelite Order. She resided at the Carmelite convent in Coimbra until the age of ninety-seven. Some people think that God wanted to keep her on earth until the Church had responded to all the requests made at Fatima. But Our Lady had made another request: to spread the Five First Saturdays devotion throughout the world.

In 2005, the First Saturdays devotion began to spread throughout the Church following two major deaths: those of Sr. Lúcia and Pope St. John Paul II. In October of that year, moreover, the Pontifical Council for the Laity recognized the World Apostolate of Fatima as an international association of the faithful.

ENCOUNTERS WITH A BOY
The course of the Pontevedra apparitions was unusual. The actual apparition occurred in between two encounters with a small boy.

The first encounter took place in the autumn of 1925, when Sr. Lúcia was taking out the trash for her convent. As she later wrote:

Several months before [the apparition], I met a boy and asked him if he knew the Hail Mary. He said that he did. However, he did not know the beginning. So I said the prayer with him three times. When we had finished, I asked him to say it himself. But he was silent. I asked him if he knew where the Church of Our Lady was. He said that he did. So I asked him to go there every day and say the following prayer: "My heavenly Mother, please give me Jesus, your Son." I taught him the prayer and returned home.

There was apparently nothing special about the encounter. The pious novice talked to a small child. She taught him a prayer and urged him to visit a church. As far as Sr. Lúcia knew, there was nothing out of the ordinary.

Pontevedra

SPAIN

◀ *The Immaculate Heart of Mary, encircled and constantly wounded by the thorns of blasphemy and sin, is the essence of the apparitions in Pontevedra.*

A MEETING WITH MARY IN PONTEVEDRA

A few weeks passed by behind the walls of the convent in Pontevedra. Sr. Lúcia, overwhelmed by daily tasks, forgot about the apparently chance encounter with the boy. She continued the ordinary life of a novice. On December 10, 1925, however, her peaceful way of life was disrupted. For the Blessed Virgin Mary appeared to Sr. Lúcia in order to entrust her with a task: mankind was to renew its veneration of her Immaculate Heart and begin to practice the First Saturdays devotion.

Sr. Lúcia wrote in a letter of May 18, 1941, that Mary asked her to establish the devotion on two occasions: once on December 10, 1925, "and on another occasion, but I do not remember the date." Here are the events of the first apparition, as recorded by Lúcia herself:

> *On December 10, 1925, the Most Holy Virgin appeared in Pontevedra, with the Child Jesus, borne by a luminous cloud, beside her. The Most Holy Virgin put her hand on my shoulder and showed me her Heart surrounded by thorns, which she held in the other hand. The Child Jesus said,*

▼ The Mother of God wants mankind to practice the First Saturdays Devotion and thereby renew its veneration of her Immaculate Heart.

"*Have compassion on your Most Holy Mother's heart, covered with thorns, which ungrateful men keep piercing, and there is no one to make an act of reparation to remove them.*"

Then the Most Holy Virgin said, "*Look, my daughter, at my heart, surrounded with thorns with which ungrateful men pierce it at every moment by their blasphemies and ingratitude. You at least try to console me and say that I promise to assist at the hour of death, with the graces necessary for salvation, all those who, on the first Saturday of five consecutive months, shall confess, receive Holy Communion, recite five decades of the Rosary, and keep me company for fifteen minutes while meditating on fifteen mysteries of the Rosary, with the intention of making reparation to me.*"

In one of Sr. Lúcia's letters, she elaborates on the theme of the Five First Saturdays devotion:

We shall be happy in giving our beloved heavenly Mother this proof of love, which, as we know, she expects of us. As for me, I must admit I never felt happier than when the first Saturday came. Is it not true that our greatest happiness lies in being all for Jesus and Mary; to love them exclusively, unconditionally? This is clear in

the lives of the saints. ... They were happy because they loved, and ... we have to try to love as they did, not only to enjoy Jesus' company, which is the least important thing (if we do not enjoy His company here, we shall enjoy it there), but to console Jesus and Mary by loving them. If we do that, many souls shall be saved.

ANOTHER ENCOUNTER WITH THE BOY

Mary and Jesus' request had been conveyed. The time came to realize it. First, Sr. Lúcia herself began to practice the new devotion. She also felt called to propagate it, all the more so as the request from Heaven turned out to be insistent.

It was the middle of February 1926. Two months after the apparition, Sr. Lúcia came across the same child whom she taught to pray to the Blessed Virgin Mary. As she recalled:

On February 15, 1926, I was very busy, and I did not give [the propagation of the First Saturdays devotion] much thought. I went out to throw the garbage away at the same place where I came across a boy several months previously and asked him if he knew the Hail Mary. ... I saw him again and asked him if he had asked Our Lady for the Child Jesus. The boy turned to me and said: "Have you propagated that which Our Lady requested?" On saying that, light radiated from him. I realized that it was Jesus.

TIME FOR ACTION

The propagation of the Five First Saturdays devotion turned out to be a difficult task. Sr. Lúcia's confessor

Lúcia heard the words, "Have compassion on your Most Holy Mother's Heart, covered with thorns."

demanded confirmation through a second apparition. He asked for signs, maintaining that the new form of devotion was unnecessary, as many people were practicing the Fifteen Saturdays devotion, which was associated with the fifteen mysteries of the Rosary.

Regarding the charge that the devotion was unnecessary because the Church already had a similar devotion, Jesus replied in an apparition to Sr. Lúcia: "**I prefer those who practice the Five First Saturdays Devotion as an act of reparation to the Immaculate Heart of Mary to those**

⋏ *Chapel, formerly Sr. Lúcia's room.*

➤ *Church of the Pilgrim Virgin in Pontevedra—part of the façade crowned with two towers.*

◄ *Sr. Lúcia was unaware that persons from Heaven had again entered her mundane monastic life.*

▼ *A statue in the chapel of the Congregation of the Sisters of St. Dorothy.*

who practice the Fifteen Saturdays **unfeelingly and indifferently**."

Sr. Lúcia's mother superior was prepared to propagate the new devotion, but her confessor declared that "she would not cope on her own," and that "she could do nothing on her own to make it more commonly known."

Jesus also reacted to this charge: "**It is true that the mother superior cannot do anything alone, but with my grace she could do anything**."

What do these Fridays mean? Christ answered this question, too:

My daughter, the motive is simple. There are five kinds of offenses and blasphemies uttered against the Immaculate Heart of Mary: Blasphemies against the Immaculate Conception; blasphemies against her perpetual virginity; blasphemies against her

Divine Maternity, in refusing at the same time to recognize her as the Mother of men; blasphemies of those who openly seek to foster in the hearts of children indifference or scorn, or even hatred for this Immaculate Mother; the offenses of those who directly outrage her in her holy images. Here, then, My daughter, is the reason why the Immaculate Heart of Mary causes Me to ask for this little act of reparation and by means of it, moves My mercy to forgive those souls who have had the misfortune of offending her. As for you, try without ceasing, with all your prayers and sacrifices, to move Me to mercy toward those poor souls.

Tui, Spain

1929

On June 13, 1929, Lúcia received a special task from Heaven—not for herself, but for the highest Church authorities. The fate of mankind depended on the fulfillment of this mission.

Patroness of
Russia's Conversion

▼ Statue in the convent chapel in Tui.

At times, the tasks that Mary sets before us seem to be difficult, if not impossible, to carry out. More than fifty years went by before Pope St. John Paul II responded to Mary's call at Tui for Russia to be consecrated to her Immaculate Heart.

Most of us are familiar with Our Lady's call for the consecration of Russia, but only a few are aware that it was in the Spanish town of Tui—not Fatima—that Mary made this request. In fact, when John Paul II gave a sermon on the significance of the Fatima apparitions, over half of the text was about Tui.

One might think of the Fatima message as spanning three different apparitions: Fatima (1917), Pontevedra (1925), and Tui (1929). These events are related not only because they involve the same visionary, but also because Our Lady promised at Fatima that she would continue meeting with Lúcia. Specifically, in July 1917, she said, "**I shall come to request**

Tui

SPAIN

the consecration of Russia to my Immaculate Heart."

The apparition in Tui didn't end the Fatima apparitions, but it was the last major apparition connected with Fatima. After 1929, Lúcia had many "minor" supernatural encounters that are unknown to us. They are important, however, for without them we would not have come to know the contents of the apparitions at Pontevedra and Tui.

During one of the so-called minor apparitions, Our Lady said the time had come for Lúcia to promulgate the call for Russia's consecration to her Immaculate Heart. In response, the visionary wrote an account of her meeting with Mary in Tui, Spain, on June 13, 1929. "I asked my superiors and my confessor for permission to celebrate a holy hour every Thursday to Friday night from eleven to midnight," she wrote. "One night I was alone. I knelt down by the bannisters in the middle of the chapel to say the Angel's Prayer. I was tired, so I stood up and continued to pray with my arms raised. Suddenly the whole chapel was illumined by a supernatural light."

VISION OF THE HOLY TRINITY

Sr. Lúcia continued her account of the events in Tui as follows:

A cross of light that extended to the ceiling appeared on the altar. In a brighter light, the face of a man and the top half of His body were evident on the upper part of the cross. There was an equally luminous dove on His breast and the body of another man nailed to the cross. Just below the waist, a chalice and a large host were suspended in the air, upon which dripped blood from the face of the crucified Man and from a wound in His breast; the blood trickled over the host into the chalice. The Blessed Virgin Mary stood under the right arm of the cross as Our Lady of Fatima, her Immaculate Heart in her left hand, without a sword or roses, but with a crown of thorns and a flame. There were large letters of crystal-clear water running down over the altar under the left arm of the cross, forming the words "Grace and Mercy."

*I understood that the mystery of the Most Holy Trinity had been conveyed to me. I received an inspiration as to the mystery, which I am not free to reveal. Then Our Lady said: "**The moment has come when God shall instruct the Holy Father, together with all the bishops of the world, to consecrate Russia to my Immaculate Heart, promising to save it by this means. Countless souls are damned through God's justice for sins committed against me; so I have come to ask for reparation. Offer yourself as a spiritual sacrifice for this intention and pray**."*

Our Lady disclosed to Sr. Lúcia a secret pertaining to the Holy Trinity during this apparition. Sr. Lúcia was not permitted to reveal that secret, but the rest of the apparition's contents are known.

◀ *Plaque commemorating Sr. Lúcia's novitiate in the Congregation of the Sisters of St. Dorothy in Tui.*

▲ *The Tui apparition, like the one in Pontevedra, was an echo of the events of Fatima. Our Lady promised she would return to ask for the consecration of Russia.*

△ John Paul II and
a statue of Our
Lady of Fatima.

Lúcia, Our Lady lamented that her call had not been answered and that, as a result, evil continued to increase throughout the world. The delay in fulfilling Our Lady of Fatima's request saw Russia's errors take on other forms, creating new threats capable of instilling a "culture of death" throughout the world. The need to carry out the consecration was now more urgent than ever.

CONSECRATION OF RUSSIA

Consecrations were performed in 1942 and 1952 by Pius XII and again in 1964 by Paul VI. But none of these consecrations fulfilled the requirements set down by Our Lady of Fatima, primarily because they were not performed collegially—that is, in union with all the bishops of the world.

In 1978, John Paul II was elected pope. He prioritized the "collegial" consecration but was badly wounded by an assassin's bullet on May 13, 1981. While in the hospital, he familiarized himself with all the Fatima documents. He realized the urgency of Mary's call at Tui and decided to carry out the consecration exactly as she had requested.

A year after the attempt on his life, John Paul II performed the consecration, stating: "I am here, united with all the Pastors of the Church in that particular bond whereby we constitute a body and a college." Unfortunately, it was discovered that not all of the bishops had received the Vatican's instructions for the consecration, and so it was not performed collegially.

Finally, on March 25, 1984, the consecration was successfully completed. John Paul II entrusted Russia and the world to the Immaculate Heart of Mary. Furthermore, he begged Heaven to put an end to the "other dangers" besieging

Our Lady's request was simple yet difficult. The Holy Father was to consecrate Russia to the Immaculate Heart of Mary—not alone or with a group of bishops, but "collegially"—that is, in union with all the bishops of the world. On a given day, all the bishops were to unite spiritually with the Holy Father and carry out the same act of consecration.

For fifty years, the Church was unable to fulfill Mary's request. According to Sr.

Western civilization: consumerism, materialism, egoism, and contempt for life.

The consecration had an immediate effect. Within a year, signs of unexpected transformation began to appear in Central and Eastern Europe, and as foretold by Our Lady of Fatima. The slow process of Russia's conversion began. In the Soviet Union, the reformer Mikhail Gorbachev came to power. In his homily during the first Russian pilgrimage to Fatima, Archbishop Tadeusz Kondrusiewicz said, "There has been a tremendous momentum in the transformation of Russia since 1987—from the Marian Year!" Two years later, Soviet Communist rule came to an end. As John Paul II wrote in his apostolic letter *Tertio Millennio Adveniente*, "In the unfolding of those events one could already discern the invisible hand of Providence at work with maternal care."

◄ *In 1948, with special permission from Pius XII, Lúcia left the Congregation of the Sisters of St. Dorothy and entered the Carmelite Order.*

∀ *Statue of Our Lady of Fatima in Red Square, Moscow.*

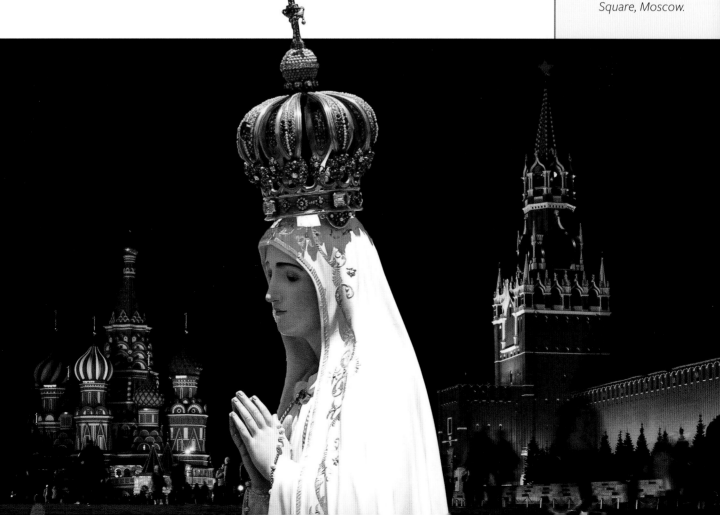

Łagiewniki, Vilnius, and Płock

1930s

Intercessor for Mercy

⌄ *Sr. Faustina in the company of those closest to her during a visit to her family home in Głogowiec.*

Daily contact with Jesus, frequent meetings with Mary, conversations with saints...the numerous apparitions Sr. Faustina experienced pervaded her life.

Sr. Faustina Kowalska's everyday life was so focused on Heaven that she could write: "Though I see and feel that but a thin veil separates me from the Lord, I desire to see Him face to face."

Faustina was able to enter that world because she lived "under the Virgin Mother's mantle." The visionary wrote: "She watches over me, teaches me. I am at peace beside her Immaculate Heart. I snuggle up to her heart like a little child."

This Marian devotion accompanied Faustina at every stage of her spiritual life. She understood that true children of God have a special love for the Blessed Virgin Mary. Jesus Himself instructed her to ask His Mother for help. And she did. The Blessed Virgin then led Faustina along the path to sanctity; she also revealed the plan that God in His mercy had for the world.

IN MARY'S SCHOOL

We know that Sr. Faustina endeavored to be alone with Our Lady as frequently as possible. She sensed that meetings with the Mother of God required a special intimacy: peace and quiet, detachment from worldly affairs, and an openness to spiritual profundity. At such times, when Faustina sought union with her heavenly Mother and opened her heart to her, Our Lady appeared.

Mary explained many things to Faustina. For example, Faustina wrote: "When I was alone with the Blessed Virgin, she taught me about the interior life. She told me that '**the soul's true greatness lies in loving God and in humbling oneself in**

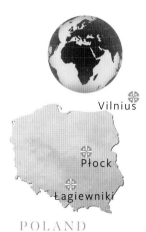

His presence, completely forgetting oneself and believing oneself to be nothing, for the Lord is great. He takes pleasure in the humble alone and opposes the proud.'"

Gradually, Faustina's supernatural encounters with Mary began to merge with her everyday life. She wrote: "Like a good mother, she is always with me, aware of all my tribulations and endeavors."

In her diary, known as *Divine Mercy in My Soul*, she wrote:

> *I saw the Blessed Mother. She was inconceivably beautiful. She said:* "**My daughter, at God's command I am to be your Mother in a special and exclusive way, while I want you to be my child in a special way too. My beloved daughter,**

◁ *Faustina's family home, now a small museum housing objects that once belonged to the Kowalski family.*

▷ *Faustina's birthplace.*

◁ *A small, modest plaque in a Łódź park recalls the memorable day when Christ appeared to Faustina.*

practice the three virtues that are dearest to me and most pleasing to God. The first is humility, humility, and once again humility. The second virtue is purity. The third virtue is love of God. As my daughter, you in particular must manifest these virtues." Then Our Lady pressed me to her heart and vanished.

PERSONAL MEETINGS WITH OUR LADY

In addition to receiving visions and interior inspirations containing spiritual advice, Sr. Faustina experienced many apparitions that could be considered personal meetings.

When she was halfway through her novitiate, Faustina had serious doubts about her salvation. Then she was visited by Our Lady and the Child Jesus. Faustina wrote: "My soul was filled with joy, and I said, 'Mary, my Mother, do you know how much I suffer?' She answered: '**I know**

how much you suffer, but do not be afraid. I share your suffering with you, and I always will.' She smiled warmly and disappeared."

Months passed. The young nun trusted in God, hoping against hope. Then she had a strange vision in which Our Lord called her to stand at the altar of her

> "Like a good mother, she is always with me, aware of all my tribulations and endeavors," said the future saint about the Blessed Mother.

> Nuns making bread. Faustina's duties included work in the convent kitchen.

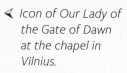

◄ Icon of Our Lady of the Gate of Dawn at the chapel in Vilnius.

from her heart, some turned toward Heaven while the others covered our country."

In 1933, in Jasna Góra, Poland, Faustina had another special meeting with Our Lady. For six hours, the visionary prayed unceasingly before the image of the Black Madonna of Częstochowa. This was no ordinary prayer. Faustina wrote: "The Mother of God told me many things. ... I felt that I was her child, and that she was my Mother. She did not refuse any of my requests." We have a similar testimony (unfortunately incomplete) from 1935.

MARY'S ROLE IN DIVINE MERCY

The Blessed Virgin Mary did more than lead Sr. Faustina along the path of virtue by her motherly care. Our Lady's presence in the visionary's life had another dimension: the revelation of Mary's role in Divine Mercy. It was through apparitions that Faustina received the message of Divine Mercy, which she was to convey to the world.

In Faustina's notes, we discover an apparition that aptly illustrates Mary's role in Jesus' work of mercy. Our Lady and the Child Jesus appeared to Faustina and her confessor. Because Faustina was talking to Jesus, she paid little attention to what Our Lady was saying to the priest. She recalled: "I heard a little of what the Mother of God told him, that is: '**I am not only Queen of Heaven, but also the Mother of Mercy and your Mother**.' She then stretched out her right hand, in which she held her mantle, and covered him with it."

According to Faustina, the message of Divine Mercy glorifies both Mother and Son: "I once saw the Divine Mercy image in a small chapel, and all at once the chapel became an enormous, beautiful

⋀ Fr. Michał Sopoćko, Faustina's confessor and spiritual director, during his stay in Vilnius.

convent's chapel. She saw a large crowd gathered there, asking for graces. Faustina heard Jesus' voice: "**Do whatever you wish. Distribute graces as you will, to whom you will, and whenever you will**." After a while she heard words that indicated her path to sanctity: "Try to unite yourself in prayer with My Mother. Pray wholeheartedly in union with her."

Faustina also heard the Savior ask her to say a novena. Her fulfillment of that request bore fruit in a significant apparition. "I saw the Mother of God between Heaven and earth, clothed in a bright robe. She was praying with her hands crossed on her bosom, her eyes fixed on Heaven. Fiery rays emanated

> *Praying before the miraculous image of Our Lady of Częstochowa, Faustina felt Mary's exceptional closeness and loving care.*

▲ *Window of the cell in the Łagiewniki convent where Faustina died.*

church, wherein I saw the Mother of God with the Child Jesus in her arms."

The Divine Mercy has many devotees throughout the world, and yet many don't know that Mary was present when Jesus revealed certain aspects of the message. In October 1934, in Vilnius, Jesus and Mary appeared to Faustina. With His silent Mother as His witness, Our Lord declared that He was the King of Mercy and that the first Sunday after Easter was to be the feast of Divine Mercy.

JUSTICE TRANSFORMED INTO MERCY

On the first Friday of September 1936, Sr. Faustina had a vision of Our Lady of Sorrows, who "was shielding us from God's terrible punishment. For God wants to inflict terrible punishment on us, which He cannot do because the Mother of God is shielding us." Faustina had a similar vision a year later: "I saw the Lord Jesus, like a king in great majesty, looking down upon our country with great severity. But at His Mother's request He prolonged the time of His mercy." Our Lady's intercession, she said, moved the King of Mercy and protected the world from God's just chastisement.

About her vision of Our Lady of Sorrows, Faustina wrote: "A terrible fear seized my soul. I prayed ceaselessly for Poland, for my dear Poland, as she is so ungrateful to the Mother of God. Were it not for the Mother of God, all our efforts would be of little use."

Our Lady had stressed the connection between herself, Divine Mercy, and Poland in an apparition on the Feast of the Assumption in 1934. Our Lady told Faustina: "**My daughter, I want you to pray, pray, and once again pray, for the world, but especially for your country**." Our Blessed Lady enjoined Faustina to pray continually as an act of reparation, "**for one can pray ceaselessly in spirit**."

On November 15, 1935, on the last day of the novena in preparation for the feast of Our Lady of the Gate of Dawn in Vilnius, Sr. Faustina "saw the Child Jesus stretching out His hands toward His Mother," who became lifelike. "When the Mother of God was speaking to me," recalled the visionary, "Jesus stretched out His little hands toward the congregation." As devotion to the Divine Mercy continues to spread throughout the Church, the faithful may hope that its Marian aspects will also be made known to the world.

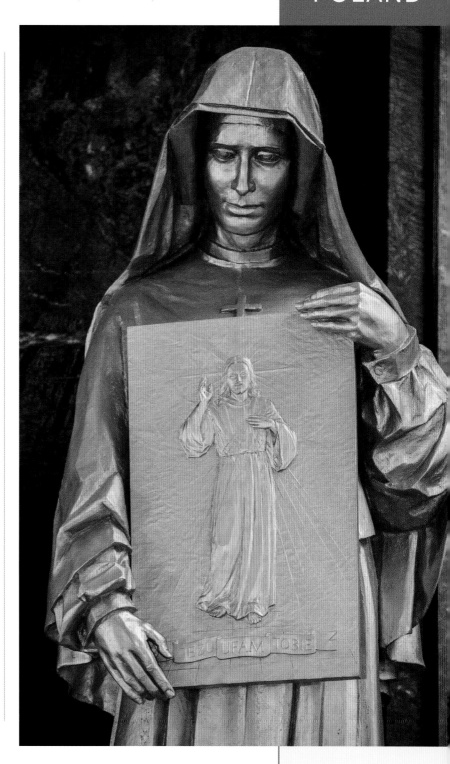

⋏ Statue of St. Faustina at the Basilica of Our Lady of Sorrows, Queen of Poland, in Licheń.

Beauraing

1932

Madonna with the Golden Heart

"I will convert sinners," said Mary in Beauraing, a small Belgian village. These words, entrusted to five children, broke through the noise of atheist propaganda. The message reached many who had turned away from the Church and had abandoned the Faith. Mary's words gave them hope and comfort.

Numerous supernatural phenomena occurred in Belgium during the years 1932 and 1933. Claims of Marian apparitions spread throughout the country, drawing both awe and ridicule, but also changing lives and inspiring conversions. Two sets of apparitions have been officially confirmed by the Church. One is in Banneux; the other is in Beauraing, where Mary appeared thirty-three times to a group of children.

Fifteen years had passed since the apparitions in Fatima, and the Blessed Mother's prophecies were beginning to be fulfilled. Soviet Russia had begun to build a global empire. In Italy, Mussolini was attacking the Church, and in Germany, Hitler was rapidly climbing the rungs of power. Across Europe, communists and fascists exacerbated the social unrest caused by the global economic depression. Plagued by unemployment, the peoples of Europe joined long breadlines. Influenced by atheist propaganda, the dire economic and political situation, and the Church's failure to pay attention to their suffering, many formerly devout Catholics left their Faith.

It is easy to accuse these people of ill will, but as Mary revealed at Beauraing, Heaven appealed to them with great love and mercy. God chose these religiously indifferent people to receive an important message from His Mother.

VISIONARIES

Like their contemporaries, the families of the five Beauraing visionaries had little to do with faith. They didn't know any faithful Catholics except for Mrs. Degeimbre, a widow who sometimes attended Mass. But the Voisins did not think about God at all. The only reason Hubert Voisin sent his thirteen-year-old daughter Gilberte to a school run by the Sisters of Christian Doctrine was that "the child had no appetite, and we knew that the sisters could make children eat."

It was Gilberte's studies at the Catholic academy that gave the Blessed Mother an opportunity to appear to her and four other children: Gilberte's siblings,

Beauraing

BELGIUM

fifteen-year-old Fernande and eleven-year-old Albert, as well as the Degeimbre sisters: Andrée and "Little Gilberte," who were fourteen and nine, respectively. Every evening, the four of them met Gilberte at the academy and walked home with her.

DISTANT SIGNS

On November 29, 1932, the four children were on their way to the academy. They entered through the gate of the convent garden, which was enclosed by a low iron fence. On the left, they could see a railroad embankment with a tall viaduct. Across from the viaduct was a grotto of Our Lady of Lourdes.

The children rang the doorbell and waited, stomping their feet in the cold. Then Albert turned toward the viaduct.

"Look!" he called out. "The Blessed Mother dressed in white is walking above the viaduct."

The other children thought he was joking. "Those are car lights," said one of the girls, without looking at the viaduct.

But Albert wasn't joking. His face, so full of delight, made everyone turn toward the embankment. Indeed, there was a woman walking on a white cloud.

The terrified children began banging on the door. At that same moment, Gilberte and the porter appeared. The girl looked in the direction the excited children were pointing.

"Oh!" she exclaimed. The porter saw nothing.

"The figure can't move by itself," she said, thinking the children were talking about the statue of Our Lady of Lourdes in the grotto.

The visionaries ran home as fast as they could. Nobody believed their story. When another vision occurred the following day, Mrs. Degeimbre became convinced that someone was misleading the children. She decided to expose the prankster. Armed with a heavy stick,

*"**Pray. Pray a great deal**," said the Blessed Mother.*

The economic situation, atheist propaganda, and the failures of the Church herself caused Belgians to abandon their Faith en masse.

she went to the academy building. Five adults accompanied her.

That evening, the Blessed Mother appeared four times: first, on the main path leading through the garden; next, halfway between the convent and the grotto of Our Lady of Lourdes; then, once again between the grotto and the gate; and finally, under the hawthorn bush growing by the fence. Mrs. Degeimbre did not see anyone, but the children did. At the sight of the Holy Mother under the hawthorn bush, they fell to their knees and began to recite the Hail Mary in thin, peculiar voices.

VISITATIONS AND CONVERSATIONS

The next evening, the gate to the convent was closed and fierce dogs let loose. The mother superior had decided to put an end to the farce. Yet Mary appeared again under the hawthorn, as she would for all subsequent visits. She wore a long white dress that radiated a blue glow. Her hands were folded in prayer. She had a beautiful smile and blue eyes. She looked very young.

Upon seeing her, the children knelt on the cobblestone path. Finally, the children spoke to her.

"Are you the 'Immaculate Virgin'?" asked Albert.

The woman nodded.

"What do you wish?"

"**For you to be good always**," said the Blessed Mother in her first words to the children.

On December 6, Mary appeared with a rosary. From then on, the children prayed the Rosary while waiting for the visitations, and during them, they continued praying.

The Blessed Virgin Mary instructed the visionaries to come on December 8,

⋏ *The child asked: "What do you wish?" "**For you to be good always**." These were the Blessed Mother's first words to the visionaries.*

the feast of the Immaculate Conception. A crowd gathered in anticipation of a miracle or special sign. The apparition was extraordinary, but the crowd didn't realize what was happening until they saw the children fall into ecstasy. After the apparition, Fernande confessed: "I saw nothing—not the hawthorn, fence, trees, or people. I only saw the Blessed Virgin Mary, who was smiling at us."

Those gathered around the visionaries began testing them. They burned them with matches and pricked them with needles, but the children didn't flinch. They shined flashlights in their eyes, but their pupils didn't even dilate.

When the apparition ended, the children bore no sign of having been injured. "Just think, Dad," said Gilberte to her father. "They wanted me to believe that they pricked and burned me with fire."

GOLDEN HEART

On December 17, the Holy Mother asked for a chapel to be built. Four days later, she told the children: "**I am the Immaculate Virgin**." When asked why she revealed herself, she answered: "**So that people may come here on pilgrimages**."

On December 28, she announced that she would soon be coming for the last time. The next day, as she said goodbye to the children, a golden heart surrounded by rays of light appeared on her breast. Fernande saw it first, followed by Gilberte and Andrée. Mary said: "**Pray. Pray a great deal**."

On the last day of the year, all the children saw the Immaculate Heart. The next day, Gilberte heard the Blessed Mother say: "**Always pray**," and on January 2, Mary announced: "**I will speak to each one of you separately**."

THE LAST MEETING

January 3 was the day of the last apparition. First, the Blessed Mother appeared to all the visionaries except for Fernande. She entrusted them with a secret. To Gilberte, she passed on a promise: "**I will convert sinners**." Along with a personal secret, she told Andrée: "**I am the Blessed Mother and the Queen of Heaven. Pray always**."

Before she departed, she showed the children her Golden Heart once more. While the four visionaries went to the convent, the distraught Fernande remained under the hawthorn and continued to pray the Rosary. Suddenly she heard a loud bang, like a lightning bolt, and saw a fireball on the bush. She wasn't the only one to perceive it. Many people heard the loud noise and saw a strange fire.

These dramatic events seem to indicate that Mary wanted to bring special attention to her last meeting with Fernande. The conversation was short yet important:

"**Do you love my Son**?"
"Yes."
"**Do you love me**?"
"Yes."
"**Then sacrifice yourself for me**."
Then Mary showed Fernande her heart and said: "**Goodbye**."

MIRACLES MULTIPLY

Our Lady of Beauraing has performed many miracles. Ten-year-old Pauline Dereppe had been suffering from bone disease for three years. On December 4, Albert asked the Blessed Virgin Mary to heal her. Seeing Mary's smile, the boy was convinced Pauline would be cured

⋏ *On the breast of the Holy Mother, the children saw a golden heart surrounded by rays of light.*

miraculously. He was right. On February 15, after a prayer was said under the hawthorn bush, Pauline was instantly healed of her illness.

Fewer than six months later, Maria Van Laer was healed of tuberculosis, which had deformed her spine and caused necrosis in one of her legs. Lying on a stretcher under the hawthorn, the sick woman was able to move for the first time in many years. The next morning, she woke up completely healthy.

The most important miracles in Beauraing, however, were the conversions. In 1945, the Holy Mother converted the editor of *Le drapeau rouge*, a communist

▼ *Sanctuary of Our Lady of Beauraing.*

newspaper. As the man stood under the hawthorn tree, something threw him to the ground. He said: "I tried to support myself on my legs and I fell. ... For a long time, I saw nothing but the figure of the Blessed Virgin among the leaves of the hawthorn. It totally changed me."

But the most-publicized "miracle" also did great harm to the reputations of the original visionaries. After his alleged recovery from spondylitis in June 1933, a fifty-eight-year-old man named Tilman Côme claimed to have seen the Blessed Mother. He said this meeting was the continuation of Mary's apparitions to the children. Allegedly, the Virgin told him: "I came to the glory of Belgium. ... Show yourself among the people. Your requests will be heard."

Côme gained a huge crowd of supporters, leading to a flurry of suspicions about the authenticity of earlier events in Beauraing. Dozens of similar pseudo-mystical events took place across Belgium around this time.

What ultimately proved the authenticity of the apparitions in Beauraing was the children's humility. While Tilman Côme and his followers strove to attract crowds and gain approval, the children stepped into the shadows. They did not seek attention. Rather, they focused on Mary's call to be good and pray always.

In May 1935, a special commission began investigating the apparitions in Beauraing. Their work was interrupted by World War II, but it resumed shortly after the liberation of Europe. On July 2, 1949, Bishop André-Marie Charue announced that the "events have supernatural characteristics." He wrote, "We give thanks ... to God and to the Most Holy Virgin: we are able in all serenity and prudence to affirm that the Queen of Heaven appeared to the children of Beauraing during the winter of 1932–1933, especially to show us in her maternal Heart the anxious appeal for prayer and the promise of her powerful mediation for the conversion of sinners."

The statue of Our Lady of Beauraing was blessed and canonically crowned on Aug 22, 1946, on the feast of the Immaculate Heart, later to be called The Queenship of the Blessed Virgin Mary. Pope St. John Paul II visited Beauraing on May 18, 1985, which in itself is a sign of Vatican recognition for a miraculous event.

MESSAGE

During these apparitions, Mary used not only words but also gestures to communicate with the children. In Beauraing she did not speak about her Immaculate Heart: she showed it to the children. Interestingly, the

visionaries followed Mary's example of silent witness. They all started families and lived quiet lives. As one theologian said, "Perhaps Our Lady has recognized that in our time it is of the utmost importance to set an example of a truly Christian family life."

The Holy Mother also described herself using several titles. Above all, she called herself the "**Immaculate Virgin**." From the Miraculous Medal apparitions (1830) to the Marian visits at Lourdes (1858), Pabianice (1904), Fatima (1917), Tui (1929), and Beauraing, Mary persistently emphasized her Immaculate Conception.

Mary also emphasized that Christians cannot love Christ without also loving His mother. Hence her two questions: "**Do you love my Son**?" and "**Do you love me**?" We can't love Mary without loving Jesus. As Paul VI put it, "Christian means Marian."

⋀ The children, in anticipation of another visit with the Holy Mother, prayed the Rosary together.

⋖ Of the many purported Marian apparitions in Belgium, only those in Beauraing and Banneux were officially recognized by the Church.

Banneux

1933

⋀ *Mariette Beco, the oldest of seven children.*

Our Lady of the Poor

*In Banneux, Mary presented herself using a remarkable, previously unheard title: "**I am the Virgin of the Poor**," she said to little Mariette. She didn't ask for much. Rather, she promised to bring relief to the suffering. Soon after, at the spring chosen by her, the first healings took place.*

⋎ *The figure of Our Lady of the Poor above the miraculous spring, which she indicated to the visionary at the time of the apparitions.*

S ome apparitions, such as those at Guadalupe and Fatima, are infused with drama—full of signs, miracles, and unexplainable phenomena. Others come like whispers. The apparitions in Banneux, Belgium, are in the latter category.

The apparitions began on January 15, 1933. Most of the townspeople of Banneux were at home. Traffic was light. It wasn't just because of the cold: widespread unemployment and inflation

had devastated the economy of Europe, including that of tiny Belgium.

Mariette Beco was sitting by a window, watching over a sick baby and looking after her ten-year-old brother. Suddenly, she saw someone standing in the vegetable garden where her father grew onions and cabbage. The girl rubbed her eyes. She saw a beautiful woman in a glowing white dress and a sky-blue sash. The raised hem of the robe revealed her foot, which was decorated with a

Banneux

BELGIUM

◄ *The Chapel of St. Michael the Archangel, located on the grounds of the sanctuary in Banneux.*

golden rose. In her right hand the figure was holding a rosary that shone like diamonds. She nodded at Mariette and smiled encouragingly.

The girl thought she was seeing a reflection of the lamp on the table. She moved it aside, returned to the window, and once more lifted the curtain. The figure was still there.

"Mother, there's a beautiful lady in the garden," Mariette cried. "She's smiling at me!"

Louise Beco looked out the window. For a moment she thought she saw a white light that resembled a human figure.

"Maybe it's the Virgin Mary," she joked, and then she went about her business.

Mariette got a rosary and began praying. She said several decades, during which the lips of the Mother of God also

moved in prayer. Then Mary raised her right hand and motioned, summoning Mariette. The girl grabbed her hat and coat, but her mother was faster. She turned the lock and in a sharp tone told her daughter to stay inside. By the time the disappointed girl returned to the window, the vision had ended.

The next morning Mariette went to school and told her best friend, Josephine Léonard, everything. Josephine laughed. After a moment, however, she changed her mind, for Mariette had started to cry. When school was over, Josephine dragged her friend to the pastor to tell the story. He didn't believe her, either.

"WHERE ARE YOU GOING?"

Three days passed. Those who knew Mariette couldn't believe the changes

▲ *The Shrine of Our Lady of the Poor is surrounded by a picturesque forty-acre park.*

The road where Mariette walked under the Holy Mother's guidance during the apparitions on January 18 and 19 and February 11 and 20.

On the grounds of the sanctuary, there are numerous statues and chapels commemorating the unusual events in Banneux.

in her behavior. She was diligently preparing for religion lessons, she didn't miss classes, and she listened to her teachers. What's more, you could find her in church in the morning before school!

On Wednesday, January 18, a powerful instinct told Mariette to go to the garden at seven in the evening. Her father wasn't a religious man, by any means, and yet he followed her out.

Mariette knelt down and began praying the Rosary. Suddenly she held out her hands as if greeting someone. A woman in white came down from the horizon toward her. The beautiful woman floated above the ground on a gray cloud. "It was like smoke," Mariette later explained.

Julien Beco didn't see the Holy Mother joining his daughter in prayer and leaning over her in a gesture of maternal tenderness. But what he saw in the eyes of his eldest child deeply moved him. He thought, "Fr. Jamin should see this."

Because he couldn't find the pastor, he brought the family's neighbor, Michel Charlesèche. They arrived just as

Mariette was leaving the yard. With her head bowed, she walked swiftly down the road. The girl passed them as if she didn't see them at all.

"Where are you going? Come back!" cried Julien in a frightened voice.

"She is calling me," Mariette answered calmly, without stopping.

The men followed her. Three times the floating figure stopped for a moment, and Mariette fell on her knees. Shortly after, Mariette stepped off the road and headed toward a small spring.

"**Plunge your hands into the water**," said the Blessed Mother. "**This spring is to be dedicated to me**." Then she said goodbye, assuring the girl that she would return.

That night Julien Beco spoke with the pastor, trying to convince him that his daughter had seen the Mother of God. The priest dismissed him. "Holy Mary is not seen so easily."

Also that evening, Fr. Jamin had told a Benedictine monk that he would like Heaven to give him a sign—"for example, to convert Mariette's father." To the pastor's amazement, the next morning Mariette's father went to confession and received Holy Communion.

AN AMAZING TITLE

Mariette saw the Holy Mother the next day and the day after. Each apparition began the same way, at the same time: seven in the evening. On Thursday, eleven people witnessed Mariette's meeting with Mary. On Friday, there were more than twenty.

Mariette asked: "Who are you, madam?"

The woman answered: "**I am the Virgin of the Poor**." Mary gave herself a title that no litany had ever named.

◄ *In accordance with the wish expressed by the Blessed Virgin Mary, a small chapel was built at the site of the apparitions.*

Again Mary led the girl to the spring. "**This spring is reserved for all the nations ... to bring comfort to the suffering**," Mary explained.

Mariette did not fully understand the Blessed Virgin's words. Later Mariette asked her father in private what "***Je viens soulager la souffrance***" meant. She did not understand French and asked Mr. Beco to translate the Blessed Virgin's words into the Walloon language.

The next day the Virgin of the Poor expressed her wish: she wanted a "small chapel" to be built in Banneux. Then she placed her hands on the child's head in a gesture of blessing. She made the sign of the cross and left. The girl fainted.

"BELIEVE IN ME; I WILL BELIEVE IN YOU"

Every evening Mariette went out to the garden, knelt on a sack, and prayed two or three Rosaries; sometimes she did this as many as seven times. But the Mother of God did not appear for three weeks.

Finally Our Lady of the Poor came to Mariette on Saturday, February 11: on the seventy-fifth anniversary of the apparitions in Lourdes. She again led the visionary to the spring and asked her to dip her hand into the icy water. "**I come to relieve suffering**," she repeated at the end of her visit.

When Mary appeared again on February 15, Mariette exclaimed: "Holy Mother, the priest told me to ask for a sign." In response, the Immaculate Mother only smiled. She had already given a sign.

The girl repeated the request. Mary told her, "**Believe in me. I will believe in you**."

Five days later Mary appeared again. She brought Mariette to the spring and said: "**My dear child, pray. Pray very much**."

Two weeks later, on March 2, the final apparition took place. It was raining. One of the women held an umbrella for the visionary. As the girl prayed the second decade of the Rosary,

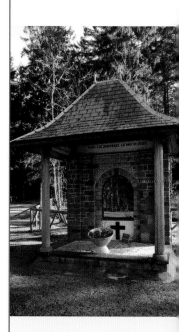

▲ *Shortly after the apparitions ended in Banneux, the first healings began.*

A modest chapel was built next to the visionary's home, where Mariette first saw the Blessed Virgin Mary.

In 1942 public devotion to the Virgin of the Poor was approved.

the heavy rains stopped and a star appeared in the sky. In the middle of the third decade, Mariette stood up, reached out, and fell to her knees again. Mary assured the girl that she was the "**Mother of the Savior, Mother of God**," and she blessed her. She added: "**Farewell — until we meet in Heaven**." The visionary understood that she would not see Mary again on earth.

ACKNOWLEDGMENT OF THE APPARITIONS

In January 1935, Cardinal Jozef-Ernest Van Roey, the primate of Belgium, set up a commission to investigate the Marian apparitions that were multiplying in the country. The local diocese assembled a committee to examine Mariette Beco's claims. The visionary was so tired of being questioned that she confessed, "If I knew what awaited me, I wouldn't tell anyone a single word. I would build the small chapel in the garden myself."

As a matter of fact, the chapel was finally built by the lay people covering the expenses. It was consecrated on August 15, 1933, only five months after the apparitions ended. Because it was small and its decor and construction were inexpensive, devotees of Our Lady of the Poor built hundreds of copies around the world.

At the site of the apparitions, miracles began to occur. A woman called Mrs. Goethals, a mother of four children, had been critically injured in a car accident. Her jaw and the bones of her temples were crushed. She became completely deaf and lost the ability to eat solid foods; she was in constant, unbearable pain. On May 21, 1933, the woman traveled with her entire family to Banneux to beg the Virgin of the Poor for help. After drinking a few drops of the water from the Marian spring, she felt worse. The pain that pierced her face was intolerable. Her husband helped her rest in the shade. After a few minutes, the woman said she could open her mouth without pain. Her deformities were healed. She could eat, and her hearing was restored.

Such miracles occurred at least twenty times during the first five years after the apparitions. Certainly, these wonders were strong arguments for the validity

◄ *"I come to relieve suffering,"* said Mary, once again pointing to the miraculous spring.

of the apparitions. Yet the bishop of Liège, Louis-Joseph Kerkhofs, did not recognize the apparitions in Banneux until August 22, 1949, on the feast of the Immaculate Heart of Mary.

Over the years the Vatican has shown its support for the authenticity of these apparitions in various ways. On August 14, 1956, Msgr. E. Forni, the Apostolic Nuncio to Brussels, solemnly crowned the statue of the Virgin of the Poor. In 1985, Pope St. John Paul II went to Banneux and had an audience with Mariette at the sacristy. More than a decade later, on July 31, 1999, the Vatican issued a letter to the Bishop of Liège to commemorate the fiftieth anniversary of the apparitions; similarly, on May 31, 2008, the Vatican sent a special envoy from Pope Benedict XVI to the celebrations marking the seventy-fifth anniversary of the apparitions of the Virgin of the Poor.

Mariette lived to age ninety. Unlike other visionaries, she didn't feel called to monastic life. She married a restaurateur, but their relationship was not completely successful. You could often find Mariette praying in her family garden, where the Virgin of the Poor met her and brightened her life with heavenly radiance.

▼ In 1949 Louis-Joseph Kerkhofs, the bishop of Liège, officially recognized the apparitions in Banneux.

Heede

1937

Queen of the Poor Souls in Purgatory

The Blessed Mother came to Heede shortly before World War II. She came to warn and admonish. She called repeatedly for conversion and prayer. She revealed the arrival of what her Son called a "minor judgment," and she said that those who answered the call would have a chance to petition God for His mercy.

▲ *Jesus' message to Greta:* **"Humanity ... disregarded the voice of the Most Holy Mother when she revealed herself at Fatima and admonished them to do penance. Now I myself have come to warn the world; the times are serious!"**

I n the age of dictators, the idea that the Church had authority over souls was unacceptable. Every aspect of human life was to be under the full control of the State. Any attempt to appropriate even the smallest degree of power was immediately met with severe reprisal. So when the Blessed Mother appeared in Nazi Germany, the Gestapo quickly intervened. That is why, of the hundred apparitions that took place in Heede, we know the stories of only a few. But those we know of are truly extraordinary.

In 1937, on All Saints' Day, four girls were passing by a cemetery for soldiers who had died in World War I. The names of the girls were Anna Schulte, Greta and Margaret Gansferth, and Susanna Bruns. Suddenly they saw a beautiful woman radiating an unusual light and smiling at them. She held a baby in one hand and a globe with a cross in the other. Mother and Son wore shining crowns. The girls immediately recognized the figures as the Virgin Mary and the Child Jesus. The children said that Mary was smiling

because she was embracing them with her light. She put them at the center of God's presence.

A TIME FOR PRAYER

Like the residents of other apparition sites, the people of Heede, a small town located in Lower Saxony in northwestern Germany, received the news with skepticism, even mockery. But significant changes began to take place in the ridiculed visionaries. All four girls gave up comfort, pleasure, and entertainments. Instead, they spent time on long and ardent prayers, waiting impatiently for the hour when the vision would return.

The children's radical conversion, along with the miraculous healing of a sick rector, finally convinced everyone that something extraordinary must have happened. As word spread that the Blessed Mother had appeared in Heede, crowds came from surrounding cities and villages.

The Gestapo were quickly ordered to put an end to what was called "superstitious nonsense." The children were arrested and placed in an asylum. Nonbelievers justified the regime's cruelty by saying the children suffered from an intellectual disorder. Pilgrimages to Heede were strictly prohibited, and when the children were sent back to their families after a month, they were banned from visiting the site of the apparitions.

If there were no visionaries and no pilgrims, the authorities thought, they could stem the apparitions. No matter: Mary began to appear to the children in secret.

"THE TIMES ARE SERIOUS"

In her messages to the children, she asked for conversion and prayer, especially the Rosary. She asked to be invoked with the words of the Litany of Loreto. She also entrusted the visionaries with prophecies, solemn messages, and a secret for the pope. Mary gave the children a vision of future disasters and warned of some terrible events, which she called a "minor judgment."

In a later apparition, Jesus Himself gave a stern warning:

Humanity ... disregarded the voice of the Most Holy Mother when she revealed herself at Fatima and admonished them to do penance. Now I myself have come to warn the world; the times are serious! May the people finally do penance for their sins; may they distance themselves from evil with all their heart and pray, pray much that the indignation of God be calmed! May they especially recite often the Holy Rosary: this prayer is powerful with God.

Jesus also told the children, "**Mankind finds itself in a worse state than**

Heede

GERMANY

⌄ *Heede became a place of pilgrimage and prayer. Pilgrims can visit two Catholic churches and the cemetery where Mary appeared.*

before the Deluge. Mankind is
suffocating in sin. Hatred and greed
rule their hearts. This is the work of
the Devil."

Thus Heede became the first
apparition after Fatima with an
apocalyptic message. Mary announced,
**"The world is about to drink the
dregs of the chalice of divine wrath
for their innumerable sins which
wound the Sacred Heart of Jesus.
Pray, ... pray a great deal, especially
for the conversion of sinners."** She
added another request: **"I wish to be
invoked as Queen of the Universe
and as Queen of the Poor Souls."**

The second title is especially striking,
given that the first apparitions occurred
in a military cemetery. Thousands of
people who died violent deaths were
buried there. The children had been
walking to the church to obtain an
indulgence for the suffering souls in
Purgatory. Mary reminded the visionaries
that she has power over Purgatory:
she can take many souls from there
to Heaven, if only we will beg her as
Queen of the Poor Souls. Additionally,
this title may have been a reference to
the violent, sudden death that awaited
millions of people in the coming disaster.

The Marian apparitions in Heede
lasted three years and ended on
November 3, 1940. That day the children
saw the Blessed Mother for the last
time. Mary appeared in the same
cemetery where the visionaries had first
seen her. Before leaving, she said, **"Be
good. Surrender to the will of God.
Pray often, especially the Rosary.
Now farewell, my children, until we
meet in Heaven!"**

The children shouted, "Mother, thank
you!" Then Mary left, never to appear
again to any of the visionaries.

THE NEXT CHAPTER: GRETA GANSFERTH

Almost five years later, Jesus began
appearing to Greta Gansferth. When
these apparitions began, Greta received
the stigmata. On the recommendation
of her spiritual director, she kept a
diary where she recorded her mystical
experiences. Greta met regularly with
the Savior and the "Angel of Justice,"
but she never saw the Blessed Mother,
although she heard Mary's voice
coming from a bright light.

⌃ *The miraculous
meetings with the
Blessed Mother
filled the girls'
hearts with faith
and piety.*

⌃ *Mary said to the four
visionaries: "**I wish to
be invoked as Queen
of the Universe and
as Queen of the Poor
Souls.**"*

▲ *Mary appeared in Heede as Queen, confirming her participation in the reign of her Son.*

What did Jesus say to Greta? His message was purely apocalyptic. The Son of God announced, "**I am near. The earth will tremble and suffer. It will be terrible: a minor judgment. For those who are not in a state of grace, it will be frightful. The angels of My justice are now scattered all over the world. Men do not listen to my voice. They close their ears, resist my graces, and refuse my mercy, my love, and my merits**." He added: "**This generation deserves to be annihilated, but I desire to show myself as merciful. Tremendous things are in preparation. That which is about to happen will be terrible as never before since the foundation of the world**."

Then Jesus said, "**All those martyrs who in these grave times have suffered so much form the seeds for the renovation of the Church**." He added: "**With a few faithful I will build up My kingdom**."

Christ also spoke of Mary's intercession:

In these times, the Blessed Virgin Mary and the angels will intervene. Hell will believe that victory is theirs, but I will seize

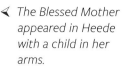

THE COMING OF THE LIGHT

During His conversations with Greta, Jesus referred to the former apparition of the Mother of God, who had appeared in a bright light at Fatima. He spoke the same words that Sr. Lúcia had written in her diary: "**The light was God**." Then, Jesus announced:

I will come with my peace. As a flash of lightning, this kingdom will come—much faster than mankind will realize. I will give them a special light. For some, this light will be a blessing—for others, darkness. The light will come like the star that showed the way to the wise men. Mankind will experience my love and my power. I will show them my justice and my mercy. My beloved, the hour comes closer and closer. Pray without ceasing!

Greta Gansferth died in 1996. Pilgrims who have received graces through her intercession visit her grave.

CHURCH APPROVAL

Given the "undeniable evidence regarding the seriousness and the authenticity of the manifestations," the diocese of Osnabrück confirmed the supernatural character of the events in Heede. A particularly strong argument for the authenticity of the apparitions is their congruence with the events of Fatima: Mary's request for prayer, and especially the Rosary, her warning of disaster, and her promise of a new era when souls will reject Satan's power. Both Heede and Fatima announced the victory of the Immaculate Heart of Mary and the advent of a time of grace. Another strong emphasis of both apparitions is the focus on the suffering souls in Purgatory who are waiting for our prayers.

it from them. Many blaspheme Me, and because of this, I shall allow all kinds of misfortunes to rain down upon the earth, for through this, many will be saved. Many expiate all they can for those who curse me now. My beloved, the hour is near. Pray incessantly and you will not be confounded. I will gather My chosen ones. They will come together, and they will glorify Me. I come. Blessed are those who will be prepared. Blessed are those who hear Me.

▲ *Pilgrims visiting the grave of Greta Gansferth talk about the graces they have received thanks to her intercession.*

▲ *The message of Heede strongly highlights the need for earnest prayer, especially the Rosary.*

Siekierki

1943

Holy Mother
Teacher of Youth

▲ *The Holy Mother Teacher of Youth Sanctuary.*

▲ *A chapel was built on the site of the apparitions in 1946.*

A page from Władysława Papis's diary from 1943.

In those days, Siekierki was a small village near Warsaw. Because it didn't even have a church, it rarely appeared on maps. Yet even though the nearest shrine was two miles away, the residents of Siekierki weren't far from God. Heaven confirmed their holiness by sending the Queen of Heaven and Queen of Poland.

The village of Siekierki consisted of a few simple families leading simple lives. The villagers earned their livelihood by breeding livestock or extracting sand from the Vistula River. These simple people felt a particularly strong devotion to the Blessed Mother. During the month of May, Marian hymns could be heard from every home. "For many years during the evening hours in May," recalled Władysława Papis, "the residents of Siekierki gathered together at the crosses, especially the youth and children, to worship God and the Mother of God with the words of songs and the Litany of Loreto."

Daily life was difficult, but the people worked hard to raise their standards of living. Władysława's parents, Józefa and Jan Fronczak, bought a small plot and put all their savings into building a house. Their existence was stable, if modest, until World War II broke out on September 1, 1939. The German army attacked Warsaw, burning down almost all of Siekierki. When the exiled population returned, many people—including the Fronczaks—found their homes in ruins.

For years after, Poland suffered under German rule. As Władysława wrote, "People's lives were getting harder every day."

For the sake of her family—and despite the harsh winter and lack of warm clothes—Józefa took her husband's small salary and went to the village near Dęblin to sell a little bit of food. She slept in train stations and, not having much money, was forced to sell potatoes and wholemeal flour to a bakery in Siekierki. Despite her diminutive frame, she carried her produce by hand: up to ninety pounds at a time. Her earnings were small; only a few potatoes, one kilogram of flour, and a little bit of milk could be spared for the family. It didn't matter to her that it was a long way from the streetcar at Czerniakowska Street to Siekierki.

Warsaw
Siekierki

POLAND

◄ *The Holy Mother,
Teacher of Youth.*

▲ **"Ask and you will
receive. ... Pray,
dear children,
and I will cover
you with my
maternal cloak."**

MADONNA OF THE CHERRY BLOSSOMS

Władysława was twelve when the Virgin Mary first appeared to her. As she later recalled, "The day of May 3, ... after coming back from the cross [where the litany was sung], I sat by the window to look at the beautiful view that was unfolding." She remembered that "the silence of the twilight set the mood for prayer." But Władysława was in low spirits:

> I did not like to see people tease each other. I would watch with sorrow when someone was getting hurt and I couldn't help them. Several times, on the streets of Siekierki, I met a mentally ill boy. Other boys would pour buckets of water on him and make fun of

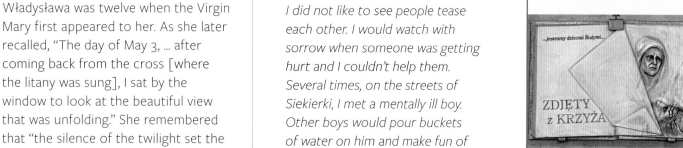

▲ *One of the Stations
of the Cross in
the sanctuary in
Siekierki.*

him. There was also another boy who I felt sorry for. He was a Jew who escaped from the ghetto and lived in Siekierki for several weeks. Women gave him food. He was most likely killed by Commandant Herman in the fields near Siekierki.

Sitting by the window, I thought of him, and knowing no other prayers besides the common prayers, I said a Hail Mary. I took one last look at the orchard covered in flowers, and I was about to leave to go rest. My eyes stopped, however, on the cherry blossom tree growing closest to our window. On this tree, where the stump branches off into boughs, a figure stood. She was dressed in a trailing, fluorescent dress the color of fog or white clouds. She wore a veil, slightly shorter than the dress, which covered her hair. Her dress was fastened with a thin blue sash, which was tied at the front. She wasn't standing directly on the tree. Under her feet was a hill-shaped cloud.

Then, Władysława recounts:

> *I began to pray—not for myself but for the whole world. When I finished, the Holy Virgin looked at me, and I sensed that I forgot to pray for something. I started thinking, trying to remember, and my conscience told me, Pray for your sick uncle. And then I said: "For my uncle to recover." The Holy Mother still looked at me. And then I said: "And if he doesn't recover, please take him into Heaven, beside you, dear Mother." When I said that, the Holy Mother turned right three times, rose up, lowered herself into the original position, and disappeared.*

REJECTING SATAN

More apparitions followed, which Władysława carefully recorded:

> The residents of Siekierki were chosen by Mary; they were to be a **"life raft for the world."**

⌃ *In the year of the apparitions, a chapel was hung on the cherry tree.*

> *I forgot that I was at home. The window and the floor where I was kneeling disappeared. There was only the wonderful Mother of God. I reached out my hand to her to lessen the distance that separated us. I didn't know how to pray. I was kneeling without moving, and with all my being, I was absorbing her beauty. After about fifteen minutes, she left, and I once again saw the window, floor, ceiling, and walls.*

A photographer captured an image of her outstretched hands.

Then, Władysława's visions took a darker turn:

> *[On] May 7, I prayed by the window, waiting for the Holy Mother, but I had to lie down with my aching, longing heart because the Holy Mother did not come. At night I*

woke up, and as I lay on the bed, a glowing light struck the side of the window, lighting up half the room. I sat down, and outside the window I saw the Holy Mother by the cherry tree. Delighted that she came to me, I asked the Holy Mother for blessings on the whole world.

Then, to the left, an old man in red clothes appeared. He had long hair and a long gray beard. He showed me some gold toys, trying to tear me away from the Holy Mother. But how could I look at that man when I saw the Holy Mother, whom I wanted to be with always? He wasn't able to tempt me because I asked the Holy Mother for help. The Holy Mother smiled; he disappeared, and the Holy Mother stayed.

THE IMMACULATE CONCEPTION

More apparitions occurred. Mary appeared in the guise of Our Lady of the Immaculate Conception. She dictated a litany and a chaplet in honor of the Immaculate Conception. Remarkably, she also taught Władysława a song. She sang in a "beautiful, gentle soprano" a "song of welcome." As the visionary wrote: "The voice of the Mother of God is different from a human's voice. The human voice is feeble. … However, the voice of the Mother of God pervades all human beings. This voice is heard with the entire soul."

She sang, "**Hello, hello, beautiful Dawn, Immaculate Virgin Mary. Welcome, welcome, only Mother. Let your cause save us**." This song can be heard in Siekierki to this day. It is the only phenomenon of its kind in the history of Marian apparitions, when Mary communicated with music.

Siekierki is unique for yet another reason. In past appearances Mary repeatedly encouraged visionaries to pray the Rosary, but she had never taught it. In Siekierki she taught that

▲ *Another page from Władysława's diary from 1943.*

▼ *A view of Siekierki.*

prayer to the children, speaking of the Rosary as being made from "her pearls."

Mary's messages were full of rich and colorful symbols, many of which were indecipherable at first. The Roman numeral X appeared at Mary's side, which is believed to symbolize the Ten Commandments. Birds sang and danced midair in her honor; seven mysterious brown birds fell to the ground like stones and then suddenly dissolved. Three large stars and twelve small stars appeared around her. Władysława also saw a chapel and a church, three nuns, and a mountain that people were climbing like ants without reaching the top.

Mary called the villagers to honor her with the title Our Lady of Youth. On September 2, Władysława wrote, "The Most Holy said she chose this day as the feast day of Our Lady of Youth. The Holy Mother also said: '**My Son died young. Therefore, mothers whose children have died, pray and ask today, because today is your feast**.'"

A year after this appeal, the Warsaw Uprising broke out. During that time, Catholics began to widely invoke the Virgin under her new title Our Lady of Youth.

The Holy Mother said that she had chosen the people of Siekierki to be a "**life raft for the world**." This small group of several dozen villagers was chosen to represent the whole world in begging God to rescind His punishment. Their prayers and acts of penance were to change the course of history.

A MESSAGE FOR THE WORLD

From the very beginning of the apparitions, Władysława's reaction to the sight of Jesus was very different from her response to Mary. She commented, "I didn't know how to pray and how to speak to Jesus. I started singing, but I couldn't. I called out to Jesus using simple words, as if I were speaking to my father. I felt very small—like a tiny ant—in the face of such great majesty." Mary assured her, "**Three hearts love me; three hearts cherish me; three hearts want the world to convert. Come to me and my Son**."

Mary also stated her purpose for the Siekierki apparitions: "**I came to you, so you can see that when you follow in my footsteps, you will not die**." She told Władysława, "**I will walk the land; I will visit villages and cities; I will knock on your doors**." Cardinal Stefan Wyszyński, the famed Polish primate and close friend of Pope St. John Paul II, said during his 1970 visit to Siekierki: "If not me, then my successor will build a sanctuary here so the Mother of God can receive the glory she deserves."

Władysława admitted that when the Holy Mother revealed her title, she said the word teacher. However, thinking she misheard, the girl didn't write the word in her diary. For her, "a teacher was a woman teaching at a school, and after all, Mary didn't teach at school."

That part of her title was "rediscovered" by Cardinal Józef Glemp, Cardinal Wyszyński's successor as primate of Poland. Without knowing the detail just mentioned, he was inspired to call Our Lady of Siekierki "Holy Mother, Teacher of Youth."

In 1994—just as Wyszyński had predicted—Cardinal Glemp consecrated a new church in Siekierki. Three years later, he declared it the Holy Mother Teacher of Youth Sanctuary.

"Come to me and my Son."

Balazar

1944–1955

Mother of Light

Alexandrina — bedridden, in pain, tormented by agonizing convulsions, and yet cheerful and smiling. How was this possible? Everything she experienced came from Christ, and she accepted these difficult gifts. She offered herself in reparation for souls trapped by sin. Mary gave her yet greater strength.

▲ *A figure of St. Joseph.*

Alexandrina da Costa was born on March 30, 1904. She was the second child of pious, hardworking Portuguese villagers. From the beginning, her life was difficult. Shortly after she was born, her father died. She grew up in a humble home with her older sister, Deolinda, who later became her caretaker and secretary.

Alexandrina dreamed of a life she couldn't find in this small, poor village. She often wandered around the old church in Balazar, contemplating the beautiful statues of Our Lady of the Rosary and St. Joseph. Their rich, magnificent garments fascinated her. She wanted to become like them one day. She wanted to be dressed the same way, to be respected, to be "someone." She wanted to be a saint.

She went to school for only a year and a half and, when she turned nine, was sent to work. Three years later, her employer tried to sexually assault her. She resisted, and by some miracle, her frail fists turned out to be so powerful that the man fell to the ground. Alexandrina fled. For a long time afterward, she kept a rosary in the hand that had dealt the blow. She was certain Mary had saved her.

Alexandrina didn't return to work, but the Holy Spirit was working in her. He awakened a love for the Blessed Sacrament in the girl's heart. Soon, Alexandrina fell ill with typhus and was near death. When her mother gave her a crucifix to kiss, Alexandrina shook her head, saying: "This is not what I want, but Jesus in the Eucharist."

She recovered from the typhus but never regained her full strength. The family decided the girl would make a living from sewing. Together with Deolinda, she learned her new profession. She often did her sewing at home, alone.

All the while, her former employer had been stalking her. He attacked her a second time, trying to enter the house while Alexandrina was alone. The door was unlocked, so the girl grabbed her rosary — her most effective weapon — and waited. To her surprise, the door wouldn't open. Not even a strong blow from her assailant, which nearly shattered the frame, could open it. Finally, the man left. Alexandrina understood that she had witnessed another miracle. Once again, the Holy Mother had saved her.

In March 1918, the man showed up at Alexandrina's home for the third time.

Balazar

PORTUGAL

◄ *The pain Alexandrina experienced allowed her to understand the need for redemptive suffering, that is, suffering united to Jesus' Passion.*

Two other young men accompanied him. Perhaps they knew that Alexandrina was home with her sister and another girl. Once they managed to get inside, they broke down the door on the second floor, which the girls tried to barricade with a heavy sewing machine. The two men grabbed Deolinda and her friend. The original assailant blocked Alexandrina's escape route, but the girl did not give up. She jumped out the window.

The thirteen-foot fall was terribly painful. Despite this, she clenched her teeth, grasped a stout piece of wood, and ran back inside the house. Bruised, scratched, and shocked by the force of Alexandrina's attack, the intruders fled. The girls were saved.

But Alexandrina's life completely changed. The fall had caused irreversible damage to her spine. Over the following months, her pain increased. In 1923, she was told that she would eventually be completely paralyzed. On April 13, 1924, Alexandrina rose from her bed for the last time. For the rest of her life, she was bedridden.

PRAYERS FOR A MIRACLE

Alexandrina believed in healing. She thought the Holy Mother would help her again. The girl's comfort in suffering was prayer, especially the evening Rosary, which she recited with lighted candles and a figure of Mary. The rector of the local church lent her a statue of the Immaculate Heart of Mary during the month of May. Alexandrina liked it so much that she saved every penny and bought one of her own. Before long, she had polished it with her kisses.

Alexandrina persisted in asking Heaven for help. She made many promises, including a vow to devote herself to missionary work. She asked again and again, begging with great faith, confident that she would be heard.

As months went by, the girl slowly accepted her doctor's assessment that she would never walk again. Her desire to heal gradually faded, and she resigned herself to being bedridden, although she didn't willingly accept her cross.

One day while praying, she had a breakthrough. Her mind went to the Blessed Sacrament, and suddenly a thought struck her: *Jesus in the tabernacle is a prisoner, too.*

Alexandrina began to understand. She visited the tabernacle repeatedly in spirit. She remained in front of it, in union with Mary, who (she said) became her teacher. Mary taught her to look at Jesus with perpetual love, console the Sacred Heart, and obtain grace for the conversion of sinners.

⋏ *Mary was Alexandrina's teacher. Above all, she taught her about loving Jesus.*

A DISCOVERY

Alexandrina began to meditate for many hours on the spiritual crisis spreading throughout the world and spoke often of the need for redemptive suffering—that is, suffering offered in union with the Passion of Christ for the same intention: to save people from condemnation and to secure their salvation.

Alexandrina said that every Christian receives a call from God for the reparation of his own sins and those of others. Each of us is tasked with living in a spirit of reparation, offering sacrifices, accepting suffering, and praying not for our own consolation but to open Heaven for others.

▼ *Paralyzed and bedridden, Alexandrina agreed to suffer for the salvation of souls.*

She believed that she now understood her role. She was to joyfully embrace the path of suffering. That's why every extant photograph shows her smiling from ear to ear.

Years later, Alexandrina began to have mystical experiences. Starting in 1931, she sometimes fell into ecstasy. Three years later, the first visions appeared—not of Mary, but of Jesus. Alexandrina heard His words: "**Love, suffer, and make reparation**." From then on, she begged Jesus for the strength and patience to endure the suffering He had destined for her.

FATIMA

Jesus came with a specific request: the promulgation of the message of Fatima. It was the only time in history that the Lord chose someone to be an apostle for an apparition that had ended many years earlier.

One morning, after she received Holy Communion, the Lord told Alexandrina she was to convince the pope to consecrate the world to the Immaculate Heart of Mary:

> "*Through the love which you have for my Blessed Mother, tell your spiritual director that as I asked Margaret Mary [Alacoque] for devotion to my Divine Heart, so I ask you to urge the consecration of the world to the Immaculate Heart of my Mother.*"

In 1935 Alexandrina received from Jesus a series of messages warning that another war would occur as punishment for the sins committed by humanity. Consecrating the world to Mary's Immaculate Heart was the only possible way to prevent the war. Jesus asked Alexandrina to pray, intercede with the pope through her confessor, and offer her suffering for this most important intention.

Alexandrina offered everything. The act of consecration had a high price, which Jesus made clear she would have to pay: "**As a sign that it is my will that the world be consecrated to the Immaculate Heart of my Mother, I will make you suffer my Passion until the Holy Father has decided to implement this consecration**."

In September 1936 Alexandrina's confessor, Fr. Mariano Pinho, conveyed to Cardinal Eugenio Pacelli Alexandrina's request for the consecration of the world to the Immaculate Heart of Mary. Fr. Pinho wrote: "If the world is converted, she [Mary] will reign, and through her, victory will be obtained."

Three years later, Cardinal Pacelli was elected pope. He took the name Pius XII, and in 1942 he fulfilled the request of Our Lady of Fatima, made known to him in letters written by Alexandrina and by Sr. Lúcia, the living visionary of Fatima. (The two women also corresponded with each other.) Pius himself cited both women as inspirations for his decision to move forward with the consecration.

On the morning of Good Friday, Alexandrina heard Jesus announce: "**Glory to Mary! The world will be consecrated to her. It belongs to Jesus and to the Mother of Jesus**."

On October 31, 1942, Pius XII consecrated the world to the Immaculate Heart. Significantly, he used titles the Savior had revealed to Alexandrina: "Queen of the Universe," "Queen of the Holy Rosary," "Refuge of Mankind," and "Victor in All God's Battles."

That same day, Alexandrina called out to Jesus and Mary: "Oh my eucharistic love, I cannot live without You! O Jesus, transform me into Your Eucharist! Mother, my dearest Mother, I wish to be of Jesus."

In response she heard: "**You will not take food again on earth. Your food will be my Flesh; your blood will be my Divine Blood; your life will be my life. You receive it from me when I unite my heart to your heart**."

For the next thirteen years, Alexandrina received nourishment only from the Eucharist.

QUEEN OF SORROWS

Although by age ten Alexandrina was already having mystical conversations with Jesus about the apparitions in Fatima and their role in the history of the world, she did not see Our Lady until age forty. When the Blessed Virgin

▲ *Alexandrina received a specific mission from Jesus: to spread the message of Fatima.*

◄ *Alexandrina frequently clutched a rosary. She repeatedly experienced its power.*

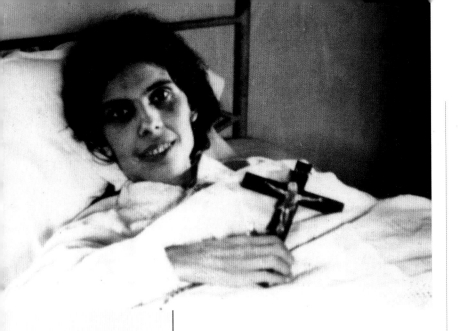

*Jesus said to a simple Portuguese girl: "**Thousands have been saved by your terrible sufferings**. ... **I appoint you a protectress of mankind. You will be powerful with the All-Powerful**."*

In 1942, Pope Pius XII fulfilled the request of Our Lady of Fatima, made known to him in letters written by Alexandrina and Sr. Lúcia. The pope consecrated the world to the Immaculate Heart of Mary.

appeared to her for the first time on December 2, 1944, she confirmed the words of Jesus, who had, the previous day, made Alexandrina His mystical bride. The Lord had said: "**Accept my holy mantle. With it you can cover the whole world. It is enough for everyone. Accept my crown; you are queen**."

It soon became apparent that the mystic suffered terrible torture when someone said the word *sin* or *sinners*. Even during the Hail Mary, at the words "Pray for us sinners," Alexandrina experienced a sharp pain. The mere mention of sin's presence in the human soul caused her suffering, which had salvific value. People came to Alexandrina, spoke about sin, and were cleansed by her suffering.

A well-known incident occurred on December 26, 1938. A doctor tried to compel Alexandrina to sit in a chair. "He forcibly tried to get me out of bed," recalled the mystic. However, the doctor couldn't lift the paralyzed woman.

Then the doctor ordered Alexandrina to say the Hail Mary. When she said the entire prayer, without trembling during the words "Pray for us sinners," he grasped her chin and whispered: "I caught you. You didn't begin trembling when you said the word *sinner*."

At that very moment Alexandrina twitched with terrible convulsions. The doctor failed to hold her down, and he was thrown to the floor. When he got up, he dusted himself off and went to the neighboring room, where Fr. Pinho was waiting for him. The priest explained that this strange phenomenon didn't occur when Alexandrina spoke of sin, but only when others did. The mystic didn't suffer for herself, he said, but for us.

A VISION

One morning Alexandrina asked the Blessed Mother to prepare her soul to receive Holy Communion. Suddenly a supernatural peace overwhelmed her, and she saw the following vision:

*My eyes were open. I saw a crowd of angels forming a huge arch. Opposite stood a throne radiating bright rays of light. Our Lord explained that He revealed this vision to me to show that my prayers are heard in Heaven: "**It was the Virgin and my angels, cherubim and seraphim, who came down to prepare your soul. They have thanked and praised me as in Heaven. I am on a throne inside you**."*

THE BEGINNING OF A NEW MISSION

Thousands of people visited Alexandrina, and she told them about Fatima: "Make reparation to Our Lord in praise of the Blessed Eucharist. Penitence! Penitence! Penitence! Pray the Rosary devoutly every day! Practice the First Saturday Devotions! Don't sin! Sin no more — never again!"

Jesus promised to save many sinners through Alexandrina:

Thousands have been saved by your terrible sufferings. If anyone should invoke your name when you are in Heaven, they will never do so in vain. I appoint you a protectress of mankind. You will be powerful with the All-Powerful. After your death, I will make your name widely known; I shall see to it myself. Many sinners will come to your tomb and be converted. Find souls who will love me in my Sacrament of Love to take your place when you go to Heaven. Invite the world to prayer and penitence, that it will be set on fire with love for me.

"ALL IS LIGHT"

Alexandrina's last days came. On October 2, 1955, she told her sister: "Today is the feast of the angels. I felt someone touch my arm this morning and say: '**Who will sing with the angels? You, you, you! In a little while, in a little while**.'"

The evening before her death, Alexandrina whispered: "How right you were! What light there is! What light! The darkness is no longer here! All is light!"

At daybreak on October 13, 1955, she kissed the crucifix and the medal of Our Lady of Sorrows. Her last words were a message to the lost modern world: "Do not sin. The pleasures of this world are worth nothing. Receive Holy Communion daily. Pray the Rosary. This sums up everything." That evening, she died.

Alexandrina's appeal to sinners can be found on her grave. The first words are taken from the Fatima message: "Do not offend God anymore, for He is already too greatly offended." It is written:

> *Sinners: if the dust of my body can be of help to save you, approach; if necessary, walk over it, trample it until it disappears. But never sin again.*
>
> *Sinners: there's so much I want to tell you. This vast cemetery could not contain everything I would like to tell you. Do not offend our dear Lord anymore. Convert yourselves. Do not risk losing Jesus for all eternity. He is so good.*
>
> *Enough with sin! Love Him! Love Him!*

Pope St. John Paul II, who beatified Alexandrina on April 25, 2004, said: "The example of Blessed Alexandrina, expressed in the trilogy 'suffer, love, make reparation,' helps Christians discover the motivation to make 'noble' all that is painful and sad in life."

⋀ *Alexandrina was chosen as an apostle for an apparition that had ended many years earlier.*

◁ *The church in Balazar.*

Ghiaie di Bonate

1944

Queen of Families

During the apparitions in Ghiaie di Bonate, which are sometimes called Fatima's epilogue, Mary appeared many times, surrounded by various figures. Among them were saints and angels, but it was the presence of the Child Jesus and St. Joseph that drew attention to the main theme of this Marian message: family.

A simple seven-year-old girl could not have imagined that millions of people would hang on her words.

Surrounded by crowds, Adelaide went to meet with the Blessed Mother.

Ghiaie di Bonate is located within the diocese of Bergamo. This small, quiet town was hit especially hard by the violence of World War II. And yet, on May 13, 1944—the anniversary of the first Fatima apparition—the Queen of Families appeared in Bonate.

The parallels between Fatima and Bonate are striking. Both took place in the late afternoon. Both took place a year before the end of a war. In both Fatima and Bonate, Mary came with a message of hope and peace, proclaiming the family's role in increasing the holiness of the Church. Finally, both apparitions involved a solar miracle. For these reasons, the apparitions in Ghiaie di Bonate are called "Fatima's epilogue."

Interestingly, however, the Bonate apparitions followed a different pattern. In Fatima the Virgin Mary appeared on the thirteenth of the month for six months, but in Bonate her apparitions occurred in two parts, for a total of thirteen days. The first part lasted nine days (May 13–21), and the second only four days (May 28–31).

A DIFFICULT ROAD

The Holy Mother prophesied to seven-year-old Adelaide Roncalli: "**You will suffer a lot, but do not weep, because then you will come with me into Paradise. In this vale of tears, you will be a little martyr.**" The visionary quickly discovered the truth of these words.

When the apparitions stopped, the girl was isolated, bullied, and mentally tortured. In the autumn of 1945, a comprehensive document was published. By twisting the facts, it called the authenticity of the apparitions into question. Adelaide tried to respond to the allegations and to convince Church authorities of the validity of the apparitions, but she was unsuccessful. In 1948, the bishop of Bergamo, Adriano Bernareggi, issued a decree that there were no supernatural elements in Adelaide's experience and banned any form of devotion based on the message of Bonate.

The author of the 1945 document was a young priest named Luigi Cortesi. Fr. Cortesi was a promising lecturer in philosophy at the seminary in Bergamo. On May 17, he broke the bishop's ban (the diocese had forbidden clerics to visit the place of the apparitions) and arrived in Bonate, where he began a private investigation. After four days he sent an insightful report to the bishop, who didn't scold him but in fact praised his work. Shortly thereafter, Fr. Cortesi obtained formal permission for his investigation and took matters into his own hands.

After the apparitions ended, Adelaide was taken away from Bonate, and Fr. Cortesi gave the order that nobody could approach the girl without his explicit consent. Then, the priest subjected the child to what can only be called psychological torture. Eventually, he forced her to "admit" that she had lied.

On September 14 he dictated to her the following words: "It's not true that I saw the Blessed Virgin Mary. I told lies because I saw nothing. I didn't have the courage to tell the truth, but then I told everything to Don Cortesi. Now I regret telling so many lies."

How did it happen, really? Adelaide wrote an account in her diary.

> *In a room of the Ursuline convent in Bergamo, Don Cortesi, after closing the door, dictated what I should write on a piece of paper. I remember perfectly that because of the moral violence I was being subjected to, I started writing, but I stained the page with ink. He gave me another and patiently forced me to write it again, in order to reach his goal. That's how the betrayal was carried out.*

Meanwhile many people saw what the wicked priest was doing to the child. More and more protests began reaching the bishop, and finally he ordered Fr. Cortesi to cease all contact

Ghiaie di Bonate

ITALY

◄ *With every day that passed, the crowds surrounding Adelaide grew larger. Nearly three hundred fifty thousand people were present during her last meeting with the Mother of God.*

with Adelaide. The girl was returned to her family and, on July 12, 1946, she wrote a statement: "It is true that I saw the Blessed Virgin Mary." The document was signed by seven people, including a rector and four nuns.

A world-famous psychiatrist and psychologist, Fr. Agostino Gemelli, questioned everything Fr. Cortesi proclaimed, but the theological commission investigating the apparitions in Bonate took the young lecturer's conclusions as its starting point. As a result, on April 30, 1948, Bishop Adriano Bernareggi announced,

Ghiaie, may have granted special graces and extraordinary recoveries, thereby rewarding their devoutness." However, by the power of the commission's decree, "every form of devotion to the Madonna of Ghiaie di Bonate remains forbidden, in compliance with the canonical laws."

This negative evaluation, however, was not final. According to the bishop, the authenticity of the apparitions was not proven — but neither was their inauthenticity. (Thirty years later, the local bishop, Clemente Gaddi, allowed individuals and groups to visit the site

⌃ *The house where the Roncalli family lived in 1944.*

⊲ *Adelaide caught up in ecstasy.*

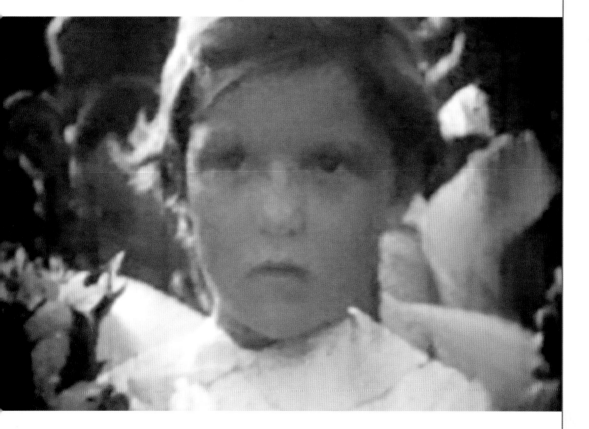

"We do not acknowledge the reality of the apparitions of the Blessed Virgin Mary to Adelaide Roncalli in Ghiaie di Bonate in May 1944." He added: "We hereby declare that it is not our intention to exclude that the Madonna, faithfully invoked by those who in good faith believed she really appeared at

of the apparitions and pray there to the Mother of God. And in 2019 the bishop of Bergamo, Francesco Beschi, authorized devotion to Our Lady, Queen of Families. He did not, however, officially recognize the apparitions as supernatural.)

⊲ *The Mother of God holding two black doves in her hand. The image was painted by Giovanni Battista Galizzi according to suggestions made by the young visionary.*

The apparitions in Ghiaie di Bonate were accompanied by numerous miracles and healings. News of them drew crowds of sick people who wanted to meet with the young visionary and witness the apparitions in hopes of being healed.

TESTIMONIES

Spiritual fruits and testimonies brought about a renewal of interest in Bonate, especially since two popes were involved in the history of the apparitions. The first was Pope Pius XII, who granted Adelaide a private audience in 1949. The girl told the pope a secret that the Holy Mother had entrusted her with on May 17, 1944. It's worth remembering that at the time of the audience, the local bishop's decree denying the authenticity of the events in Bonate had been in effect for a year. For many people, the fact that the Holy Father granted a private audience to the visionary was a clear acknowledgment of his faith in the authenticity of the apparitions.

The second pope associated with Bonate was Pope St. John XXIII. In a letter of July 8, 1960, he encouraged the bishop of Faenza, a personal friend, to investigate the veracity of the apparitions. The pope wrote in the confidential letter: "What's important in *subiecta materia* is the visionary's testimony and the authenticity of what she still maintains at the age of twenty-one, consistent with her first testimony filed at the age of eight, and withdrawn on account of the threats and fears of Hell somebody [Fr. Cortesi] used. It seems to me that the terror of those threats still persists."

Likewise, St. Padre Pio, upon seeing pilgrims from Bonate at his monastery in Pietrelcina, said: "What are you doing here, you who have Our Lady of Bonate in your town?"

There's also the testimony of Fr. Candido Maffeis, whose vocation Adelaide prayed for during one of the apparitions: "These last forty years, instead of losing faith in the Mother of God, who appeared in Ghiaie, there turned out to be a thread ... which

sustained the belief that Mary alone will lead everything to the end, because people have gone astray and destroyed other people, ideas, messages, and personal zeal. ... Using human and sectarian criteria, they crushed and smeared the luminous event in Ghiaie."

What was the content of these apparitions that they should have provoked such fierce and polarizing opinion?

THE FIRST APPARITION

Adelaide Roncalli, following the trend of the times, kept a diary, where she wrote down everything that seemed important and interesting to her. In her entry for May 13, 1944, she noted:

I gathered flowers to bring before the image of the Holy Mother, which hangs halfway up the stairs in our house. I also picked some daisies and arranged them in a wheelbarrow made by my dad. I saw a beautiful, large flower, but it was too tall for me to reach. I stood admiring it, when suddenly I saw a golden point descending from above and slowly approaching the ground. As it approached, it became bigger, so that I could make out the figure of the beautiful lady with the Child Jesus in her arms, standing to the left of St. Joseph. The three figures were wrapped in three oval circles of light and remained suspended in the air. The lady, beautiful and full of majesty, was dressed in a white dress and blue mantle. On her right arm hung a rosary with white beads. On her bare feet there were two white roses. Her dress was decorated with a string of pearls, all equal size, bound in gold and in the shape of a necklace. The circles surrounding the three persons were bright with shades of golden light.

At first I was scared and wanted to run away, but the lady called me in a sweet voice. She said: "Do not run; I am the Virgin Mary!" I stopped, gazing at her, but I was still a little afraid. The Blessed Virgin Mary looked at me and added: "You must be good, obedient, respect others, and be honest: pray well and come to this place for nine evenings, always at this time." The Holy Mother observed me for a few

The Blessed Virgin Mary appeared to Adelaide in two phases: from May 13 to 21 (nine apparitions) and from May 28 to 31 (four apparitions).

Adelaide on the day of her First Communion, May 28, 1944.

saw a bright point, which came closer and changed into the clear, full, and majestic form of the Holy Family. They smiled at me, and then the Holy Mother repeated what she told me the previous day: "**You have to be good, obedient, honest, pray well, and respect others. Between your fourteenth and fifteenth year, you will become a Sacramentine nun. You will suffer greatly, but do not weep, because then you will come with me into Paradise**." Next she began to move away slowly, and she disappeared the same way as the previous day.

Together with her friends, Adelaide headed toward the parish center. Halfway there, she met Candido Maffeis — "a good boy, who started questioning me," as she wrote in her diary. When he heard that Adelaide had spoken with the Mother of God, he nervously asked: "Go back and see if she appears once more, and try to ask her if I will be able to become a priest and give her my life."

The children returned to the place of the apparition and looked up at the sky. After a few minutes, the Mother of God reappeared. When the visionary asked Candido's question, she heard words full of motherly warmth: "**Yes, when the war is over, he will become a Missionary Father according to my Immaculate Heart**." Then Mary disappeared.

Tugging at the girl's apron, Candido began asking insistently what Mary had said. When he heard the good news, he rushed home to share the joyful news with his mother.

The next day, a hundred locals joined the children. The day after that, there were one hundred fifty pilgrims. Then

moments; then she slowly began to move away, without turning away from me. I stared at her with intensity until a white cloud took her from my eyes. The Child Jesus and St. Joseph didn't speak; they only looked at me amicably.

A PROPHECY ABOUT THE VISIONARY'S CALLING

On May 14, Adelaide wrote in her journal:

I was with my friends in the parish recreation center, but when six o'clock began to approach, an overwhelming desire to run to the place where the Holy Mother invited me awakened within me. When I arrived, I instinctively looked up and saw two white doves, and then above them I there were three thousand, seven thousand, ten thousand, and then thirty thousand. On the last day, a crowd of three hundred fifty thousand people stood around Adelaide.

The number of people accompanying Mary also changed. On May 27, instead of Jesus and St. Joseph, eight angels appeared. During another apparition, two saints stood beside Mary. The last apparition was once again of the Holy Family.

A NEW FATIMA

The first miracle of Bonate took place on May 20. A woman named Dr. Eliana Maggi described it under oath: "That Saturday was rainy. At the beginning of the apparition, a ray of sunlight appeared above the girl's head. I raised my eyes to the sky, and I saw a break in the sky in the shape of a cross. For a minute, maybe two, rain consisting of gold and silver specks fell from the sky. Everyone talked about a miracle."

Interestingly, Fr. Luigi Cortesi—the priest who had forced Adelaide to recant—wrote:

Someone saw a strange stream of light falling on the child. ... Others noticed the sun taking the shape of a cross; others saw the solar disc spinning, forming a ring not larger than half a meter. In the lower layers of the atmosphere, some people saw a rain of gold stars, small yellow clouds in the shape of hoops, so thick and near the earth, that some tried to catch them. Different colors appeared on hands and faces, among which yellow prevailed. You could also see hands shine with fluorescent light.

On May 21, another solar phenomenon occurred. Witnesses testified:

Around six o'clock, the sun came out from behind the clouds, swirling and projecting beams of yellow, green, red, blue, and purple light in all directions. They colored the clouds, fields, trees, and the crowds of people. After a few minutes, the sun stopped, to repeat the extraordinary spectacle in a moment. Many saw that the solar disc had turned white like a host, and the clouds seemed to be lowering down on the people. There were those who noticed a rosary in the sky; others saw the lady full of majesty, in a dress that reached the ground. Yet others

A triptych of the Holy Family of Nazareth standing near the Chapel of the Apparitions in Ghiaie di Bonate.

Fr. Luigi Cortesi did much to discredit the visionary

> After many years, Adelaide returned to pray in the place where she once saw the Queen of Heaven.

> People climbed trees and poles to see the visionary, even just for a moment.

saw facial features of the Holy Mother in the sun.

These phenomena were visible not only in Bonate but also in many other places, even Tavernola and Bergamo, where many people saw the sun "fading and radiating all the colors of the rainbow in all directions. A wide yellow ray of light falling on Ghiaie was also observed. ... Seeing these unusual phenomena, people were running out into the streets."

At the same time, more than three hundred people were miraculously healed of severe illnesses. Thousands were converted in a single day.

A "FILM" ABOUT FAMILY

The apparitions in Bonate have one theme: family. As Adelaide recalled:

This revelation was also preceded by the doves, and then on the bright point the Holy Family appeared. [Mary] was dressed as she had been on the previous day, but she stood inside the church. From the side of the main doors there was a gray donkey, a white sheep, a white dog with brown spots, and an ordinary black horse. The animals knelt and moved their lips in prayer. Suddenly the horse got up, walked past behind the Holy Mother's back, and left through the open door, then took off on the only road, leading to the lily fields. However, he failed to trample as many lilies as he wanted because St. Joseph ran after him to catch him. As soon as the horse saw St. Joseph, he tried to hide behind a low wall, which surrounded the lily field. He gave up and was submissively captured. Led by St. Joseph back to the church, he knelt down and returned to prayer.

That day I explained this vision, saying that the horse was a bad person, who wanted to destroy good people. I can now reveal my feelings that accompanied me during the vision. I imagined the horse as an important person, angry and demanding power. Abandoning prayer, the horse wanted to destroy the lilies in the wonderful field, trampling them and destroying their freshness, simplicity, and beauty. When the horse saw St. Joseph, he abandoned his destructive work, and he tried hiding behind a low wall surrounding the field. St. Joseph came to him with a gentle look of reproach and led him back to the house of prayer. When the horse wreaked havoc, the other animals didn't stop their prayers.

The four animals represent the inherent virtues that make up the Holy Family. The horse—the leader—must not stop praying because when he is far from prayer, he can only introduce chaos and destruction. In this way he rejects the patience, gentleness, and family harmony symbolized by the other animals.

The two doves, said Adelaide, represent "harmony," a virtue "which must be present in married couples so that in the presence of the Holy Mother, they can become happy families. Mary also teaches that a blessed family cannot exist without a trusting devotion to the maternal hands of the Mother of God."

In her own record, Sr. Lúcia wrote: "In the Church's pastures, flowers always grow." The vision of Bonate carries a similar message: the flowers of goodness grow in spite of the opposition of the world. And yet the easiest way to destroy them is by destroying the family—a lesson the modern world knows all too well.

The memory of the apparitions in "Italian Fatima" remains alive in the hearts of many Italians.

A humble chapel remains in Ghiaie di Bonate, where faithful visitors gather in prayer.

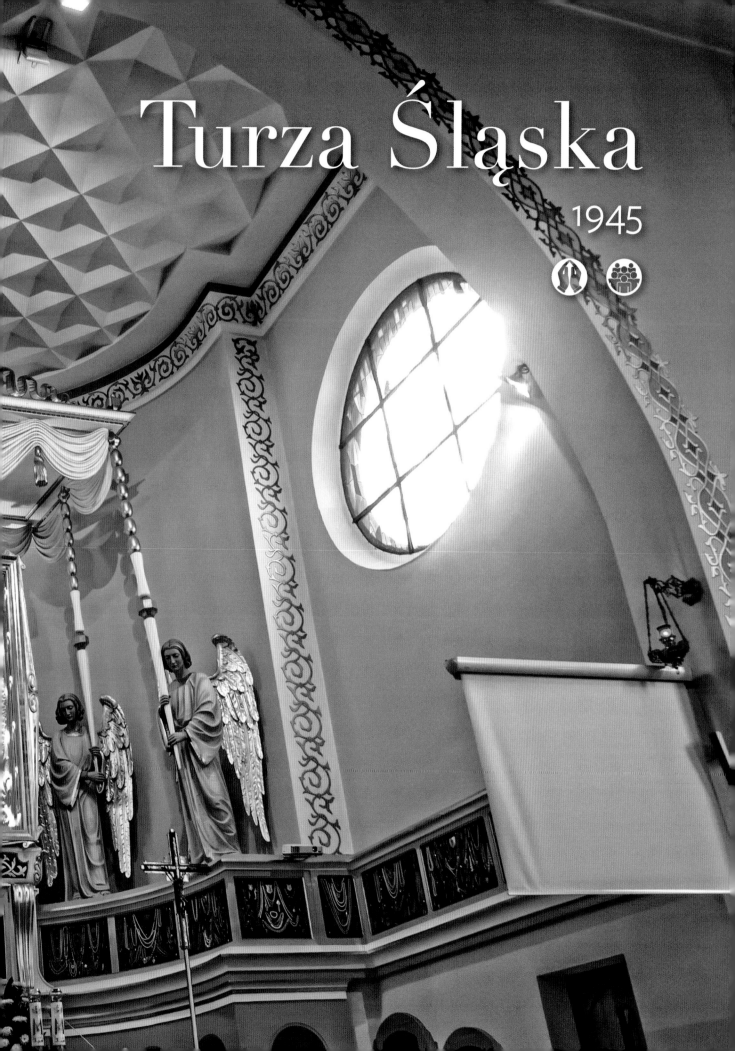

Turza Śląska

1945

Sorrowful Mother of the Battlefield

▲ *Sanctuary of Our Lady of Fatima in Turza Śląska (photo by Maria Brachmańska).*

➤ *Turza Śląska is a small Polish sanctuary, where in response to the Fatima message, people ask for the grace of change and conversion in front of the White Madonna.*

Behind the splendor of the sanctuary in Turza Śląska, an image is hidden inside the chancel. The focus of this devotion is a little-known painting, which serves to heal the tragic events suffered in the region.

Those who are close to Our Lady of Fatima may wish to visit the small church in Turza Śląska. It is indisputably the oldest sanctuary of Fatima in Poland, founded May 13, 1947. This small parish chapel quickly became a hub for prayer, penance, and sacrifice for the Silesians. It had been said for many years that the globe crowning the tower was a prophetic sign that this place would become important for the whole world—as it is today.

Some call Turza Śląska a "night sanctuary." It is best known for its monthly vigils: pilgrims begin their vigil with the all-night devotions that take place from the twenty-ninth to thirtieth of each month. There are those who are there every month for the nighttime meeting with the Blessed Mother. Like the nun who came every month for ten years, offering her sacrifices and prayers for the pontificate of Pope St. John Paul II. That's 120 vigils! Her pilgrimages were cut short by old age.

Turza Śląska is located near the border between Poland and the Czech Republic, two hours from Krakow. The sanctuary

Turza Śląska

POLAND

◄ *Faithful visitors
gather around an
image, not a statue,
at the oldest
Fatima sanctuary in
Poland.*

is in an isolated area, away from the town, tucked away in lush and silent greenery.

A HIDDEN IMAGE

When entering through the main door of the church, you are immediately drawn to the magnificent chancel. Under a large canopy, wonderfully decorated by the 2004 papal crown, four angels hold a painting of Our Lady of Fatima.

But there's another painting hidden behind the first. This second image is the subject of the veneration of those angels towering over the chancel. The miraculous image is usually kept hidden, revealed only during religious services, prayers, and adoration.

The second image is strange. It seems as though it has nothing to do with this place. It is not the work of a talented artist, but something about it attracts

⋏ On June 13, 2004, Archbishop Józef Kowalczyk—in the presence of bishops, priests, and many believers—set the papal crown on Our Lady of Fatima.

attention. In the picture, a teenage boy is laid out on the ground with his head held on the knees of a young mother. You can't see her face, but her whole figure illustrates immeasurable pain and despair. This is a mother mourning her son, who was killed during a battle in 1945. She finds him and embraces his body. This is a present-day Pietà, a sorrowful mother, one of us. And before this simple woman, heaven opens, a cross appears, and under it the Holy Mother, who says: "Do not weep. I too lost my son." The Mother of Sorrows takes the hand of this soldier's mother and comforts her. We look and we ask: Should we offer our suffering for the salvation of sinners? We already know the answer and understand the charisms of Turza Śląska.

The image is based on a true story. It happened on the grounds of the Sanctuary of Our Lady of Fatima. This apparition preceded the local devotion to Our Lady of Fatima, and its painted representation is now kept behind the White Madonna. The focus of the Fatima devotion, the White Madonna, painted in 1947, shows Mary from the first apparition in Fatima. At the bottom of the image, hidden under an oval frame and unable to be seen today, are two scenes that illustrate the main themes of the message: war and the Holy Father.

On the left side of the Holy Mother, a difficult battle is taking place, with armed forces and aviation. (The young soldier was killed here, at the Battle of Gross Thurze. We even know his last name: Szymke.) History is being created by the rulers of the world. But the fruits of it are bitter. On the right, there's the

Basilica of St. Peter in the Vatican. It would seem that nothing is happening there unless one considers that on the right human history is changed through silent prayer, penance, sacrifices that are invisible to people and their fruits are rich. The Holy Mother calls for such actions in her apparitions, as in this little-known apparition in Turza Śląska.

What does the hidden apparition of the Mother of God teach us? Mary not only brings comfort to the distraught mother. In her appeal she says, "Do not weep," and following those words she says she too lost her Son. There is a hidden invitation for the Silesian woman, in her deepest motherly sorrow, to follow the example of the Mother of God. Mary communicates that she didn't give in to despair when Jesus, her Son, died. We know what the Church says and what the entire Christian tradition tells us. The Holy Mother offered her Son for the salvation of humanity, attaching her suffering to His saving Passion. By following the Redeemer, who gave Himself up for us as a sacrificial offering, she herself becomes a small sacrificial victim, thus giving her suffering an eternal dimension.

Under the cross, Mary is perfectly united with Jesus. The Holy Mother appears to say: "Do not cry. Suffering is inevitable in this world. Since it is among us, use it well. Give it to God and He will bring salvation closer to you, and in this vale of tears there will be less weeping and wailing and tears. Do not despair. Help us save the world."

⌄ Turza Śląska is sometimes called the "night sanctuary" because of its monthly prayer vigils that last from dusk till dawn.

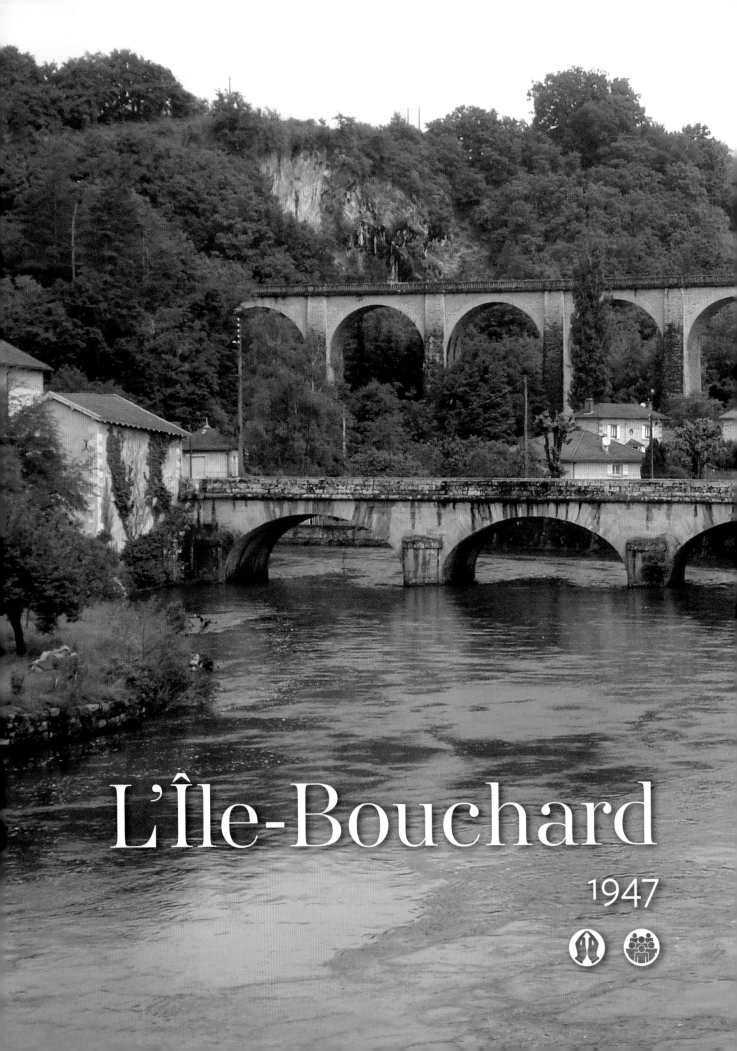

L'Île-Bouchard

1947

The Mother at the Annunciation

On the Feast of the Immaculate Conception of the Virgin Mary, the "Heavenly Mama" appeared to four girls. The Mother of God not only allows them to call her that, but she herself addresses them using words full of tenderness. What's more, she wants to kiss their hands. And she does so, leaving luminous signs on them.

L'Île-Bouchard is a small town near Tours, too small to be marked on most maps. Yet it was here, between December 8 and 14, 1947, that the Annunciation was reenacted before the world—and, in particular, four little girls between the ages of seven and twelve.

The Mother of God set a specific date to meet with these visionaries: the Feast of the Immaculate Conception. Mary appears with archangel Gabriel, who was kneeling as he was during the Annunciation in Nazareth. Since everything in eternity has a present dimension, this scene is truer than we think: the Annunciation in L'Île-Bouchard is the very presence of that singular event in the modern history of the world.

A COMMUNIST FRANCE?

A lot happened in France in 1947. As announced in Fatima, Russia spread its errors across the world. Soviet spies succeeded in infiltrating the governments of the United States, England, and France. France also had a large and popular Communist Party, which won nearly 30 percent of the vote in the 1946 election, taking the most seats of any party. It seemed that everything was in the communists' favor.

North of the Seine, the war completely ruined the economy. The harsh winter of 1946 destroyed a large part of the harvest. The price of gas and electricity increased by 50 percent. Train tickets rose by 250 percent. Due to the lack of grain, bakeries were open only three days a week. Government-held gold reserves were running out.

The leader of the French Communist Party, Maurice Thorez, called for strikes to be organized on October 2, 1947. Shortly thereafter, strikes spread across the entire country and numerous acts of sabotage paralyzed segments of the economy. France stood on the brink of civil war. So far everything was going according to the plan of the Communist International, whose members were in session in September 1947 in Poland.

The leaders of nine Communist parties met there: Soviet, Bulgarian, Hungarian, Polish, Romanian, Czechoslovakian, Yugoslavian, French, and Italian.

On the morning of December 8, Marthe Robin, a mystic and stigmatist, declared: "The Virgin Mary is going to save France by the prayers of little children." In a few hours, in the tiny town of L'Île-Bouchard, near Tours, four small girls were about to meet the Mother of God. But no one would hear about the intervention from Heaven just yet. Another breaking development grabbed the headlines.

After the apparitions were over, the evening news reported that the strikes had ended and that the strike committee decided to call on workers to work. Peace returned to France. To this day, many Frenchmen attribute the sudden reversal of fortune to Our Lady's appearance at L'Île-Bouchard.

THREE CHILDREN, MARY, AND AN ANGEL

On the Feast of the Immaculate Conception, at one o'clock in the afternoon, the three children, twelve-year-old Jacqueline Aubry, her seven-year-old sister, Jeanette, and their cousin, ten-year-old Nicole Robin, were coming home from school. Jacqueline proposed stopping into the church for a moment. She had been brought up by an elderly lady named Grandin, a neighbor of her family's; her own parents were nonpracticing Catholics. "When I was very little," Jacqueline recalled later, "she took me on walks. On the way there and back, we always stepped inside the church to pray. I learned to pray by watching the old woman pray." (There's a lesson here for grandparents!)

⬥ *One of the stained-glass windows decorating the interior of the church in L'Île-Bouchard.*

In L'Île-Bouchard, the Holy Mother appeared to four girls: Jacqueline, her sister Jeanette, their cousin Nicole, and their friend, Laura.

The children entered the church and knelt at a side altar of the Mother of God and began to pray a decade of the Rosary. They were in the middle of reciting their Hail Marys when Jacqueline lifted her eyes and saw before her a beautiful lady dressed in a white robe, with hands joined in prayer, clasping a rosary. To her left, an angel knelt, immersed in contemplation. He was holding a white lily. Moments later, the other girls saw the same vision. Mary smiled at the children. Then Jacqueline whispered that they had to tell people about what happened in the church. The girls ran out of the sanctuary and soon stumbled upon their schoolmate, eight-year-old Laura Croizon, and her thirteen-year-old sister, Sergine.

A SILENT ANNUNCIATION

Now there were five children. But only four saw the Virgin Mary. Sergine, the oldest girl, saw nothing special. The altar, in front of which the children were kneeling, looked like it always did: on the left, a stained-glass window depicting Our Lady of Lourdes, and above the altar, a statue of Our Lady of Victory. Sergine watched in amazement as her friends looked with delight at the corner between the window and the altar. They saw the Virgin Mary standing in a rocky grotto. A golden light surrounded her. Her gown, tied with a blue sash, was brilliant white. On her head she wore a veil that was a white of a different hue, and she held a white rosary in her hand. Her blond hair flowed loosely and seemed to reach all the way down to her feet. The Mother of God's eyes were pure blue. But what attracted their attention the most was the smile of the Madonna: a motherly smile, full of peace.

The angel remained in contemplation, having entered Mary's "little room." He knelt down on his right knee. He was wearing a pink-and-white robe hemmed in gold. The angel's white wings, also trimmed with gold, trembled as if there were a slight breeze, which the children could not feel. He had the same characteristics as Mary: the same color eyes and hair. In his left hand he held a white lily; his right hand was pressed to his heart. "He is brighter, much more heavenly," says Jaqueline. It's not surprising. As the *Catechism* says, angels are "purely spiritual." But that he would pay homage to someone who seems to be lower in the hierarchy of creatures: a spiritual-corporeal being! This may surprise us, but Mary's dignity is greater. Her destiny is more glorious and her union with God deeper.

A thread of understanding exists between the angel and Mary. Human purity meets angelic purity; a human's obedience and the obedience of an angel. The white lily is a gift that God gives to the Holy Virgin. Divine Motherhood will not violate the maidenhood of the Blessed among women.

PURITY

Why so many references to purity? Maybe because today purity is no longer regarded as a virtue. Pope St. John Paul II said, "Faced with the cynicism of a certain contemporary culture, which too often seems not to recognize the value of chastity and degrades sexuality by separating it from personal dignity and God's plan, the Virgin Mary holds up the witness of a purity that illumines the conscience and leads to a greater love for creatures and for the Lord." The less

▲ *Twelve-year-old Jacqueline Aubry, the oldest of the visionaries.*

the virtue is valued, the more heaven calls for it! That's how it was in L'Île-Bouchard.

The children also saw the Blessed Virgin standing on a rectangular block of rock decorated with a garland of five pink roses, with this inscription below: "O Mary conceived without sin, pray for us who have recourse to you." A strangely familiar invocation. We remember it from another Marian

The Feast of the Immaculate Conception December 8, 1947, is the date the apparitions in L'Île-Bouchard began. They lasted seven days.

apparition. One hundred seventeen years earlier in Paris, the Holy Mother had given these words to St. Catherine Labouré. This is the first message from L'Île-Bouchard: We are to recall the apparition of the Miraculous Medal of Rue du Bac. What does the garland of five roses mean? It is the biblical symbol of a wedding. The Annunciation is the scene of Mary's espousal to God the Holy Spirit.

As soon as the children described everything they saw to Sergine, the Mother of God disappeared.

EVIL BEARING GOOD

Now began the unsuccessful attempt to persuade others that the Holy Mother appeared in the church. Typical of Marian apparitions, at first no one believed the visionaries. The parish priest, Fr. Clovis Ségelle, announced that Jacqueline had only experienced double vision. Indeed, the girl wore thick glasses and suffered from very poor eyesight and chronic conjunctivitis; she rubbed her sore eyes constantly.

But the "scientific" explanation was easily refuted. After all, the other children saw the same vision. The girls were questioned separately, and the same account was heard from each of them. Jacqueline spoke to the principal of the school, who made fun of her and said that if the Mother of God was so beautiful, the girl should reside in the church. Jacqueline took these words seriously, and after gathering the rest of the girls, she was at the altar again. The mockery of the principal resulted in a second apparition.

KISSING THE CHILDREN'S HANDS

As soon as the girls knelt before Mary, her face became sad. She slowly spoke these words: "**Tell the little children to pray for France, for her need is great**." Then the visionaries asked her if she was the Heavenly Mother. Mary replied, "**But of course, I am your Heavenly Mother**." When Jacqueline asked about the angel, Mary looked at him, and he said: "I am the angel Gabriel."

Then something completely exceptional in the entire history of apparitions happened. Mary asked the

FRANCE

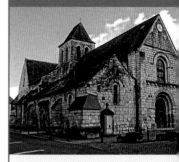

children to let her kiss their hands. She bent down low to kiss Jacqueline's and Nicole's hands. Jeanette's and Laura's were too small, and their outstretched hands did not reach the Heavenly Mother. Jacqueline lifted them up to the Most Pure Lady one by one. Then the children talked about the warmth of Mary's hands and the touch of her lips.

Before Mary disappeared into a silvery cloud, she instructed the children to return at five o'clock that afternoon. As they left the church, the girls saw luminous ovals on their fingers. They managed to show them to a certain woman, but by the time they returned

to school, the heavenly marks had disappeared. They were still not believed, not only at school, but also in their family homes.

Only Jacqueline managed to fulfill the wish of the Holy Mother and got to the church in the evening for the Rosary and the Benediction of the Blessed Sacrament. Mary appeared to the girl, but when she motioned with her hand to come closer, Jacqueline hesitated. She looked at the nun kneeling beside her, confident that she also saw the Mother of God. At that moment the bell rang: the priest gave his blessing with the Blessed Sacrament. The child

⋀ The church where an unusual scene appeared to the children praying the Rosary.

◄ The Holy Mother asked the visionaries to come to the shrine every day at one o'clock in the afternoon until the end of the apparitions was announced.

in the afternoon. The children knelt before the Our Lady's altar and began to recite Hail Marys. After a moment, the Blessed Virgin appeared.

The long hair, which had fascinated the children the day before, was now hidden under a veil, and the angel was kneeling on Mary's other side. There was another inscription on the rock that referred to another apparition. These words were read by the children: "I am the Immaculate Conception." This is the name that Mary called herself in Lourdes.

So we have a reference to past apparitions of the Mother of God: first to Rue du Bac, now to Lourdes. Maybe the sadness shown by Mary during the second apparition was a reference to La Salette? If so, other nineteenth-century apparitions recognized by the Church are being referenced.

The children saw one more inscription, or rather a fragment of it. It was visible on Mary's chest, but it was partially obscured by the Mother of God's hands, which were folded in prayer. The first two visible gold letters were "Ma," the last three were "cat." Later they learned that it said Magnificat, the song that Mary sang during the mystery of the Visitation.

At that moment, the first adult witness of the apparitions appeared. Mrs. Trinson, the owner of a shoe store, entered the shrine. She witnessed a strange scene: she saw Jacqueline and Nicole get up from their knees to kiss something invisible. She saw Jacqueline lift up the younger girls, who also kissed an invisible object. It was an adoration of the cross at the end of the rosary held by the Holy Mother. Their experience was physical; they felt the chill of the metal on their lips, and at the same

looked toward Mary again, but she had disappeared. Never wishing to compete with her Son for attention, she reappeared when the Blessed Sacrament returned to the tabernacle.

"PRAY FOR FRANCE"

The next day, the four visionaries entered the church at one o'clock

time their hearts were penetrated by an inexplicable, deep sorrow. Mary let them feel the pain of her suffering heart.

This wasn't Mary's last reference to the cross. Suddenly, Mrs. Trinson saw the children make the sign of the cross, but they did it so slowly that the gesture seems to last almost forever. The visionaries were imitating the gesture of the Holy Mother, who began to make a slow sign of the cross. Then Mary told them a secret, which they were to reveal after three days, and added emphatically, "**Pray for France, which in these days is in great danger.**" She also asked for the parish priest to come to the shrine at two o'clock, along with the children and a crowd of the faithful. She also asked for a grotto, where her statue and a statue of the angel were to be placed. She promised to bless them, then disappeared.

At the appointed hour, the visionaries, twenty other children, and a few adults came to the church. Father Ségelle refused to come. After a decade of the Rosary was prayed, the Holy Mother appeared with the angel to the chosen four. She asked them to sing hymns and recite prayers. People started singing Marian hymns and reciting the words of prayers that praise Mary. Finally, Mary urged them to return every day at one o'clock, "until everything is over." It was on this day that, to everyone's amazement, the general strike ended.

"I HAVE NOT COME HERE TO PERFORM MIRACLES"
On the third day of the apparitions, one hundred fifty people waited for Mary to appear in the church. The Holy Mother asked for prayer again—this time, she wanted them to sing the Hail Mary.

When the song faded, the amazed crowd saw what Mrs. Trinson watched the day before: Jacqueline lifting the two younger girls with outstretched arms. That day, the ritual of the third kiss took place. This time, the children were to kiss Mary's hand.

The mother of Jacqueline, the oldest visionary, told her daughter to ask Mary for a miracle, but the Holy Mother replied, "**I have not come here to perform miracles, but to tell you to pray for France. However, tomorrow you will see clearly and you won't need to wear glasses anymore**."

Mary also said that she wanted to tell the children another secret, but they had to promise that they would never reveal it. The girls nodded and then heard words unfamiliar to them. The vision lasted fifteen minutes, after which Mary disappeared into a gold sphere. The girls never let themselves be persuaded, whether by pleading or threats, to reveal the secret they received until 1968, when they conveyed it to the archbishop of Tours.

When Jacqueline opened her eyes the next morning, she could see everything clearly, even though she hadn't put on her glasses yet. Her father ran to inform Fr. Ségelle, who only the previous day had mocked the possibility of healing a girl's sick eyes. Now he examined the eyes of his little parishioner and said, "So it's true that she has descended among us!" The parish priest immediately notified the archbishop, who instructed him to be present at the next apparition.

A PROMISE OF FAMILY HAPPINESS
The news of the miracle caused the church to be filled with people at one o'clock that day. When Mary appeared

▲ In the corner of the sanctuary, between the window and an altar, the girls saw the Blessed Virgin Mary and an angel kneeling beside her.

▲ In time, the empty church was filled with crowds of believers who wanted to accompany the visionaries in their meetings with the Virgin Mary.

to the four visionaries, she requested a sung version of the Hail Mary and then asked: "Do you pray for sinners?" The children answered yes.

Then Mary led the decade of the Rosary, but without saying the Our Father. Later, Jacqueline would explain: "One day the Most Holy Virgin Mary asked us to pray one decade of the Rosary and [told us to] start with the Hail Mary, probably because Jeanette and Laura didn't know the Our Father. Mary said only the first part of the prayer—the words spoken by the angel. During the second part she was silent."

Before the Mother of God disappeared, Jacqueline asked her about healing the people who petitioned the visionaries for cures. But Mary promised them something else: "**happiness in families**." The spiritual health of families—the fundamental building block of human life—was more important than the cure of physical diseases. Mary also asked for a grotto, after which she disappeared.

THE SYMBOL OF MARY'S CROWN

On December 12, three hundred people gathered in the church. When the clock struck one, the Holy Mother appeared to the children. The eyes of the visionaries were caught by the crown that Mary had on her head. It was made up of twelve shining rays, each about twelve inches long. Two narrow blue rays were in the center, five wider ones to each side, in order: red, yellow, green, pink, and a dark red.

How should one understand the symbolism of the Marian crown? Blue is the color of the sky, the happiness of eternity, and power. Above all, it is a Marian color. That would explain the double sapphire rays and their central location. Red is the color of life and the spiritual dimension. Perhaps that's why the red in the Marian crown is directly adjacent to the blue color. Yellow is the color of eternal light, glory, dignity, and joy. Green is a symbol of joy, fertility, eternal goodness, and peace. Pink indicates mercy and charity; when combined with dark red, it speaks of great but gentle power.

To the visionaries themselves, the crown resembled a rainbow. It may, then, be a reference to the symbol of reconciliation with God. The rainbow is

▼ *Fr. Ségelle, who initially did not believe the words of the girls and refused to come to the shrine, soon found out that the Mother of God in fact chose his parishioners to witness her message.*

a sign of God's covenant with Noah, in which He promised not to repeat the punishment of the flood. It's a promise of peace—perhaps even a promise not to repeat the Communist "flood" in France. According to Jacqueline, the crown indicated that on that day France had been saved from civil war.

The novelty of this apparition does not end there. Because when Mary lowered her hands, the children saw the entire inscription on her breast: *Magnificat*. The Mother of God once again requested a sung version of the Hail Mary, then led a decade of the Rosary, then she asked the children if they were praying for sinners. When she heard, "Yes, Madame," she said: "**Good, above all pray much for sinners**." Jacqueline asked for a miracle again, and Mary again said that she did not come to perform miracles, but to ask for prayers for France. She disappeared after reciting one more decade of the Rosary.

On December 13 at one o'clock, five hundred people gathered in the church. Mary appeared without the crown and again asked for prayers, hymns, and songs of praise. She announced that the next day she would come for the last time.

SINGING THE MAGNIFICAT

That day, the town was crowded with pilgrims, and the church could not accommodate everyone who wanted to witness the apparitions. Two thousand people fit inside the church, and many more people remained in the church's courtyard. While waiting for Mary to come, they prayed the Rosary, which many had not said in years.

The apparition of the Mother of God and the angel lasted half an hour.

Again, she asked for hymns and prayers. Then Jacqueline read a few questions, including those from a local nun: "Madame, what should we do to console our Lord for the suffering sinners cause Him?" Mary answered this question with the words she had spoken in Fatima: "**Pray and make sacrifices**."

The people sang and prayed. Suddenly, the Holy Mother asked the congregation to sing the *Magnificat*. It's as if she wanted to pour into the hearts of the gathered people what lived in her Immaculate Heart, what the visible inscription on her breast symbolized: humble worship of God and faith in bringing justice to the world—without communism or other false ideologies.

Jacqueline felt the meeting was drawing to a close. She asked for some proof of her presence. The Blessed Mother replied with a smile: "**Before I go, I will send a bright ray of sunlight**." As she said this, she began to bless the assembled. At the same time, a ray of sunshine streamed in through a pane in the southwest

▲ *"France has no idea that she was saved by the prayers of these four children."*

▲ *A stained-glass window adorning the shrine in L'Île-Bouchard.*

A During one of their seven meetings with the Holy Mother, the girls prayed, adoring the cross that was part of the rosary held by Mary.

A RELIGIOUS "ISLAND"

The apparitions ended. But L'Île-Bouchard was just beginning to fulfill its new mission. Jacqueline later recalled that, in the week following the apparitions, a certain police officer came from Paris. He went to Fr. Ségelle and said of the strike, "The government fell into a panic. We were sure it would end badly, but we had no way of preventing it. We couldn't understand why nothing happened." When the parish priest told him about everything that had transpired in L'Île-Bouchard, the officer said: "France has no idea that she was saved by the prayers of these four children."

(Curiously, ten years later, when the Soviet Union released Austria from its sphere of influence, as in France, there was no explanation for the decision of the Soviet authorities. There was, though, a great Rosary crusade, a million people praying for this intention.)

Decades after, a Polish priest working near Paris wrote: "On December 7, 2002, in a small church, in a remote area 300 kilometers (almost 200 miles) from Paris in the village of L'Île-Bouchard, not far from Tours, there was a crowd of people engaged in prayer. If I didn't know I was in France, I would think I was in Poland. The Holy Mass was concelebrated with a bishop and priests with clerical collars, some in cassocks. There were people kneeling during the Transubstantiation and praying the Rosary. It's hard to believe that all this takes place in secular France. ... And yet it is a fact: before Holy Mass and after it, crowds of people waiting in lines for confession, adoration of the Blessed Sacrament, filled the church to the brim."

window, illuminating the apparition site. After a moment, the sunbeam became blindingly bright and began to intensify, forcing those standing closest to the altar to shut their eyes. Those on whom it fell said the beam was very warm. The visionaries knelt with their backs to this extraordinary light, but their faces and the flowers they held in their hands began to shimmer with a multitude of colors, as if the light shining on them was a reflection of something inside the grotto, resembling a diamond.

What is the Church's attitude toward these apparitions? They are not officially recognized, but the local bishop allowed a grotto to be built, as the Virgin requested. He also allowed pilgrimages to L'Île-Bouchard and approved devotion to Our Lady of Prayer. This was reaffirmed in November 1988. And on December 8, 2001, the decree of the archbishop of Tours, André Vingt-Trois, authorized these pilgrimages and the public worship in Saint-Gilles Church in L'Île-Bouchard to invoke Our Lady of Prayer and made the shrine a Marian diocesan sanctuary.

◁ The events in L'Île-Bouchard made the faithful, not only from that region but from all over France, knock on the door of the local church.

▽ Saint-Gilles Church in L'Île-Bouchard.

◁ The interior of the shrine in L'Île-Bouchard.

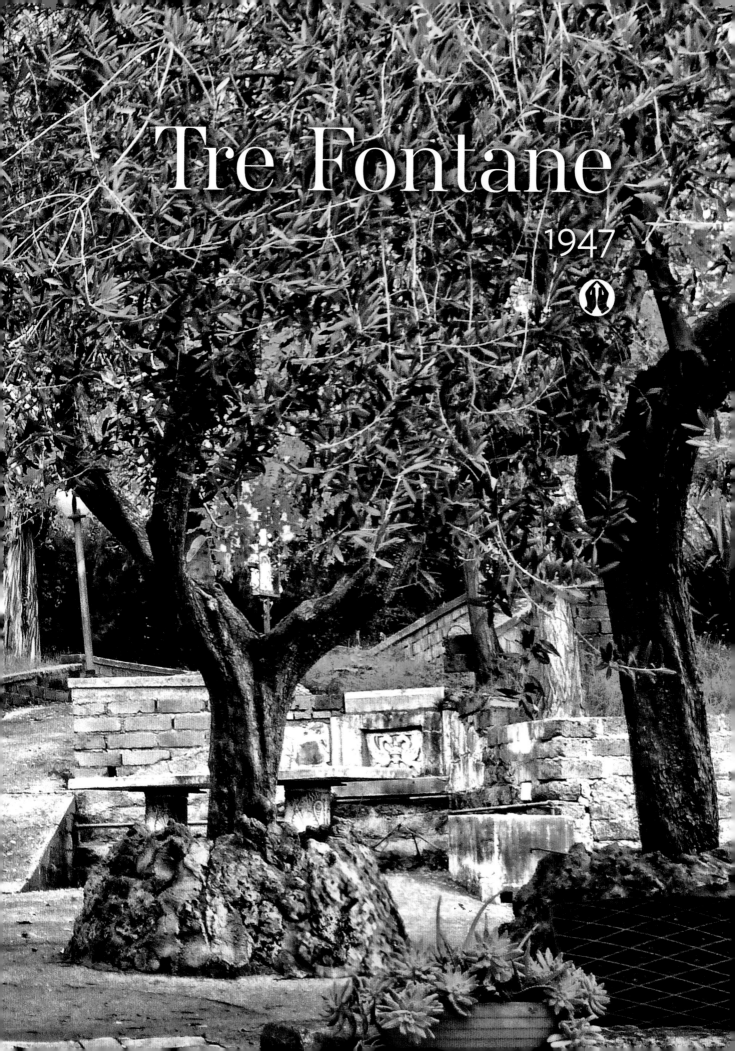

Tre Fontane

1947

> The Holy Mother from Tre Fontane reminds us that God can change evil into good and that no one in His eyes is lost to Heaven.

> ⅄ Peace emanates from the Tre Fontane chapel grounds.

Virgin of
Revelation

The Virgin Mary appeared to a would-be papal assassin—an encounter that changed his life. This unexpected meeting with the Mother of God and the special grace he received freed him from the noose of evil and gave him strength to live according to divine teaching.

In 1937, Luigina Sinapi had an extraordinary vision. The Holy Mother appeared to her, announcing that she would convert the man who planned to assassinate the pope. Luigina was to inform Cardinal Pacelli that he would succeed Pope Pius XI. The visionary met with him and told him about the amazing announcements from the Mother of God, but the cardinal kept their conversation to himself.

Two years later, Pacelli was indeed elected pope. One part of the Marian prophecy had come true. What about

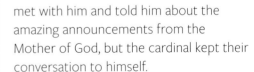

the rest? Ten years later, in 1947, the Virgin appeared in Tre Fontane, Rome, thwarting an attempt on the pope's life.

Bruno Cornacchiola was born in 1913, and from an early age he had a bad reputation. An unappealing character in every way, he held the title of "master of gutter talk." Known for fighting and brawling, he had numerous ties with the criminal world. He fought for the Communists during the Spanish Civil War.

Under the influence of a German Protestant, Cornacchiola became convinced that the papacy was the source of all evil in the world. Inflamed with hatred for the Catholic Church, he vowed to kill the Holy Father. These were not empty words. While still in Spain, he purchased a dagger on which he carved "Death to the Pope." He even determined the day of the attack: September 8, 1947—the Nativity of Mary. He soon became famous for his propaganda attacks on the Church, the pope, and Marian dogmas.

NINE FIRST FRIDAYS

Bruno was married; however, he was far from an exemplary husband. He called his wife, Jolanda, the worst names, cursed her, hit her, cheated, and forbade her from going to church. After returning from the war, he destroyed everything in his home that reminded him of the Catholic faith and ordered his wife to abandon the faith. Eventually, Jolanda agreed to join the Adventists, but on one condition: that Bruno practice nine First Fridays of the month. If afterward he continued to stand by his decision, she would give way.

It's strange, but Cornacchiola agreed and practiced the First Friday devotions,

as revealed to St. Margaret Mary Alacoque. Jolanda believed that God would somehow convert her husband. Unfortunately, nine months passed and Bruno continued to burn with hatred for the Church. With internal reluctance, the wife of Cornacchiola joined the Adventists.

PERSECUTOR OF THE MOTHER OF GOD

On April 12, 1947, God was to show that He is faithful to His promises, although graces are not always granted in the time frame expected.

That year, Cornacchiola was a tram driver in Rome and a staunch Communist. On the first Saturday after Easter, he and his three children went for a picnic in Tre Fontane—specifically, in

the forest in front of the famous basilica that commemorates the site of the martyrdom of St. Paul the Apostle. The name Tre Fontane is tied to a certain legend: when the Apostle to the Nations was decapitated, it was said that his head

Shrine of the Virgin of Revelation in Tre Fontane.

> *Cornacchiola couldn't have guessed that not only would he not realize his murderous plan, but he would desire with all his heart to serve God and the Church, which he was so reluctant to do.*

bounced on the ground three times, and in those places three fountains emerged. Hence, Tre Fontane is also called the Fountains of the Holy Trinity.

Near Tre Fontane was a Trappist monastery, and next to it was a well-known chocolate shop. They waited for it to open, since Bruno and his children had arrived during the afternoon siesta. Cornacchiola sat down in the shade of a eucalyptus tree and prepared a speech ridiculing the dogma of the Immaculate Conception. His hatred for the Mother of God was so great that, earlier the same day, he had defaced a statue of Mary. The statue's pedestal bore the inscription *Vergine Madre*, or Virgin Mother. Cornacchiola wrote: "You are neither a virgin nor a mother."

Meanwhile, the children were playing with a ball. At 3:20, they called him to help them look for the ball. A moment later, the father was no longer looking for a ball, but for his four-year-old son. He found him in a small grotto, kneeling with his hands folded and repeating, "Beautiful lady! Beautiful lady!" The other children came running and knelt beside their brother. They also saw a beautiful figure in the grotto. Bruno tried to lift the children, but they were as heavy as lead. Enraged, he started screaming into the empty grotto. Finally, in his helplessness, he unconsciously recalled the words from his childhood: "Lord, help me!"

PAUL'S CONVERSION

At that same moment, Cornacchiola saw two transparent hands, which touched his face and rubbed his eyes and caused severe pain. After

a moment he saw a small light in the grotto that grew stronger and stronger. It blinded him, though he felt incomprehensible joy in his heart.

When he was able to see again, a beautiful woman stood before him, full of tenderness and sorrow. She was wearing a green mantle and, under it, a white dress with a red belt. In her hands she held a gray book that she pressed to her chest. A broken crucifix lay at her feet.

A year later, Bruno was to place the following inscription at the entrance to the grotto: "Here in this grotto, a hotbed of sin, I, a sinner, on my horse of hatred, immersed in darkness, was ready to fight against the dogma of the Immaculate Conception established by the Church, our Mother. She herself came and threw me down from the horse and won. Taking pity on me in her maternal love, she spoke and told me, 'You persecute me; enough now!' At that same moment, Jesus, who is the Way, the Truth and Life came into me." Clearly, Cornacchiola was aware of the similarities between his own conversion and the conversion of St. Paul.

"OF THE TRINITY"

Mary introduced herself to Cornacchiola as the "**Virgin of Revelation**." Scholars believe this title has at least two meanings. First, it calls on the Church to teach about the Blessed Virgin Mary based on Scripture. Indeed, Mary appeared to Cornacchiola holding a Bible. Second, the title points to Mary as the woman from the Book of Revelation, where she is actively involved in the last chapters of human history.

The Virgin of Revelation spoke to Bruno for nearly an hour and a half, talking to him in a calm, rhythmic voice. Cornacchiola remembered every word exactly as she had said them to him.

Mary announced, "**I am the one who is of the Divine Trinity. … I am Daughter of the Father, Mother of the Son, and the Spouse and Temple of the Holy Spirit**."

Then, she told him, "**I am the Virgin of the Revelation. You persecute me, but enough of this! Come and be part of the holy flock, which is the heavenly kingdom on earth**."

Mary emphasized the importance of traditional forms of Catholic piety: First Friday devotions, the Rosary, and praying the Ave Maria. She said, "**God's promises are and will remain unchanged. The nine First Fridays in honor of the Sacred Heart, which**

∧ "Lord, help me!"—exclaimed Bruno, helpless against what he had witnessed. Heaven immediately responded to his call.

◁ "Here in this grotto, a hotbed of sin, I, a sinner, on my horse of hatred, immersed in darkness … "

◁ According to legend, when St. Paul the Apostle was decapitated, his head bounced three times on the ground, and at each spot it touched, a spring appeared.

▲ *The nook, which had enjoyed the worst reputation, has become a distinct place of devotion thanks to the Mother of God.*

your faithful wife persuaded you to observe before you walked down the road of lies, has saved you. … **The Hail Marys which you pray with faith and love are like golden arrows that directly reach the Heart of Jesus**. … **Pray a great deal, recite the Rosary, and pray for the conversion of sinners, for nonbelievers and for all Christians**."

The Holy Mother also called for unconditional obedience to the Church: **"You must be like the flowers which**

Isola [his ten-year-old daughter] **picked. They make no protest; they are silent and do not rebel**."

MARIAN APPEALS

The Mother of God bound the site of her apparition with a special grace. A notorious area known as a place for illicit trysts, it was to become a tool of grace. **"With this sinful soil**," Mary announced, **"I will perform great miracles for the conversion of nonbelievers and sinners**." Mary called Bruno to "**Live according to divine teachings. Practice the Christian faith. Live it**." Simply professing faith using lips is not yet a journey of faith—to Heaven, to God, to eternal happiness.

The Mother of God also spoke about future problems: "**Science will question the existence of God and refuse to listen to His voice**."

She placed a great deal of importance on her Assumption. For eighty minutes, she taught Cornacchiola about her life. She said, "**My body could not decay and did not decay. I was taken to Heaven by My Son and angels**."

After delivering a secret message to Cornacchiola reserved for the pope only (the visionary conveyed it to the Vatican on May 6, 1947), she advised,

"**You must go to the Holy Father, the pope, the Supreme Pastor and personally tell him my message. Bring it to his attention. I shall tell you how to recognize the one who will accompany you to see the pope**."

The vision came to an end. The Holy Mother smiled at Bruno and the three children, then turned and walked through the walls of the grotto. Cornacchiola was in shock. Together with the children, he went into the Trappist church to thank God for what

Tre Fontane Abbey in Rome's neighborhood.

had just happened to him. Next, he returned to the grotto, where there was a waft of perfume in the air—strange, since the park grounds were littered with filth. Bruno cleaned the grotto and with a key cut in stone this declaration: "April 12, 1947, the Virgin of Revelation appeared in the grotto to a Protestant Bruno Cornacchiola, who converted, and his children."

O ECCELSA MADRE DI DIO
ROMA PARTICOLARMENTE FELICE
DA TE PREDILETTA
VDIVA LA TVA VOCE
IL 12 APRILE 1947
QVANDO DICESTI
IL MIO CORPO NON POTEVA MARCIRE
E NON MARCÌ...
DA MIO FIGLIO E DAGLI ANGELI
SONO STATA PORTATA IN CIELO...

I FEDELI POSERO

IL 1 NOV. ANNO SANTO 1950

GIORNO SOLENNISSIMO IN CUI

PIO XII

PROCLAMÒ IL DOGMA DELL'ASSUNTA

One of the commemorative plaques located near the place of the apparition.

➤ *Today, on the site of the martyrdom of the Apostle to the Nations, stands the Church of St. Paul at the Three Fountains.*

➤ *Votive plaques placed around the grotto.*

⌄ *The main altar in the Chapel of the Apparition at Tre Fontane.*

When Bruno came home, Jolanda smelled a strange scent. When the children went to sleep, the repentant husband told her everything that had happened. He fell at her feet and begged her to forgive her.

MEETING WITH THE POPE

As ordered by Mary, Cornacchiola found the priest who became his spiritual director—and who would eventually help to arrange his meeting with Pope Pius XII. Bruno and Jolanda returned to the Catholic Church. News of the apparition of the Virgin in Tre Fontane spread like wildfire, and numerous pilgrimages set off to the grotto. The police even questioned Bruno and his children. Yet when interrogated separately, they all said exactly the same thing.

A similar examination was carried out by Church authorities, and devotion to the Virgin of Revelation was approved very quickly. On October 5, a month after the planned assassination attempt on his life, Pius XII consecrated a

He asked for forgiveness, which he immediately received. "My dear son," Pius said, "by doing that, you would have added a new martyr to the Church and a new pope!"

AN INCOMPLETE APPARITION?

In 1956, the Conventual Franciscans became the guardians of the grotto. They were the ones who built the chapel on the site of the apparition. The prayer to the Virgin of Revelation received an imprimatur, and the devotion was so widespread that during the Second Vatican Council many bishops came there to pray. In 1987, on the fortieth anniversary of the apparition at Tre Fontane, Cardinal Ugo Poletti, as official representative of the pope, marked the occasion with a special Mass.

As is typical under these circumstances, the Church has not delivered a final judgment on the apparition, mainly because of suspicions that the visionary had lost his credibility. He maintained that he had received twenty-eight other apparitions. The tone of these messages become more and more apocalyptic, and they never came true.

Still, in 1997, Pope St. John Paul II approved the renaming the chapel Holy Mary of the Third Millennium at Tre Fontane.

But no one could deny the depth and sincerity of Bruno Cornacchiola's conversion, which almost seems a miracle in itself.

▼ The façade of St. Vincent and Anastasia Church, the oldest shrine of the abbey.

▼ The fourteenth-century Church of Santa Maria Scala Coeli (*Saint Mary of the Stairway to Heaven*) is located on the grounds of the abbey.

representative figure of Mary from the apparition in the grotto. It was carried from St. Peter's Square to Tre Fontane in a huge procession.

Two years later, on December 9, 1949, Bruno found himself included in the group of people invited to the pope's private chapel to pray the Rosary with Pius XII. After the devotion, the Holy Father asked if anyone would like to talk to him. In a fraction of a second, Cornacchiola was kneeling before him, crying and showing Pius the dagger with which he had intended to kill him.

Montichiari

1947

Mystical Rose

Roses of three colors — white, red, and gold — accompanied the Mother of God during the apparitions in Montichiari. They symbolize purity and faithfulness, a spirit of sacrifice, and conversion, respectively. Be like these flowers: this is the goal that Mary sets before all who want to adore her.

⋏ *Each of these three roses adorning Mary's robe represented a different virtue pleasing to God. The white flower symbolized purity and faithfulness.*

⋏ *The square in front of the cathedral of Montichiari.*

➢ *"Through my coming to Montichiari, I wish to be known as the Rosa Mystica."*

It's 1947. The echoes of the Second World War had not yet faded away, and one could already see with the naked eye the desolation caused by years of war. The oldest generation still remembers those days. It's not only about the enormity of material losses. The *spiritual* devastation is even greater. When the fall of spiritual values began, it turned out to be the beginning of the process that led to today's emergence of — let's use the words of the Pope St. John Paul II — "the civilization of death," "a civilization without God," "life as if God doesn't exist."

People began to act as if they had a right to create a new catalog of values and to choose what is right and what is wrong. What is right became what is easy, what is fun. Wrong became everything that makes demands and limits the individual's freedom. After the war, the process of negating spiritual values became a reality and began to gain momentum. It would be difficult for such a world to love and respect Mary.

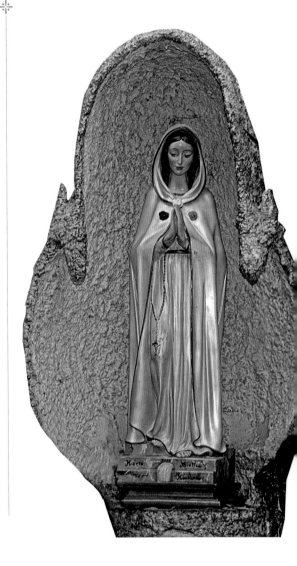

After all, she was humble, and humility became a disadvantage. In her earthly life, she was poor and obscure. On the horizon was a non-Marian epoch, which was unholy, unwise, and bound to fail.

Such an age demands a clergy that itself resists this crisis and bears witness to Christian values. Humanly, this task was extremely difficult. But our priests were not without divine help. Therefore, in 1947, Mary appeared in Montichiari, Italy.

That year was full of Marian apparitions. In addition to the famous Italian Tre Fontane and the French L'Île-Bouchard, the Mother of God also brought her message to the world in Vorstenbosch, Netherlands; in the Italian towns of Varzi, Montepoli, and Grottammare; in Tyromestice, Slovakia; in Tannhausen and Munich, Germany; in Plescop, France; and in Kayl, Luxembourg. She called for conversion and for the strengthening of the Church in the face of a double threat: communism and a false understanding of democracy.

Besides her numerous appearances in many countries in 1947, she left the most enduring message in Montichiari.

ITALIAN LUMINOUS MOUNTAINS

Montichiari is a small town located at the foot of the Italian Alps. The name evokes the most beautiful associations because its translation is "Luminous Mount." From the sanctuary there, the fame of Mary invoked under the title Mystical Rose spread around the world. The name of the town took on a new meaning: it speaks of hope for "luminous days," if man takes the trouble to climb to the peaks of union with God.

Montichiari

ITALY

The very place chosen by the Holy Mother for the apparitions says a lot about the situation of the Church: a hospital. And she chose a lay person as the visionary—Pierina Gilli, a thirty-six-year-old nurse.

In the spring of 1947, Pierina saw an extraordinary visitor from heaven in the hospital room, which was under her supervision. The Holy Mother stood before her, dressed in a purple robe, with tears in her eyes and three swords piercing her heart.

The number three dominated the apparitions in Montichiari. First, we have three swords. The first, as the Holy Mother later explained, is the pain caused by the unworthy celebration of Holy Mass and reception of Holy Communion in a state of sin. The second signifies unfaithfulness to the priestly and religious vocation. The third symbolizes the denial of faith by the clergy.

The visionary reports that Mary is sad, just saying three words: "**Prayer. Penance. Expiation**."

ROSES WITHOUT THORNS AND FATIMA

When, on June 13, Pierina saw the Holy Mother again, the vision was a contradiction of the first. This time, Mary wore a bright robe. She smiled, and there were three roses in the place of the swords. One rose was white, the second red, and the third gold.

Whites symbolizes purity and faithfulness. Red is a sign of giving oneself completely to God, even at the cost of martyrdom. And gold is the color of holiness. When the clergy and religious embody these three virtues, Mary's heart will be filled with joy.

▲ *Votive plaques found in the Apparition Chapel in Fontanelle.*

The message of the Mother of God of Montichiari should be a guide not only for the clergy, but for each of us.

During the second apparition, the Mother of God reportedly said more. She introduced herself: "**I am the Mother of Jesus and the Mother of all of you**." She stated her mission: "**Our Lord sends me to bring a new Marian Devotion to all religious orders and institutes, male and female, and to the priests of this world. I promise to protect those religious orders and institutes who will venerate me in this special way, increase their vocations, and achieve a greater striving for holiness among the servants of God**."

In half a year, the Holy Mother would explain the new devotion and its requirement. But for now, she said only that she desired that the thirteenth of each month become a special Marian day. She assured that on this day she would pour out the grace of holiness on all religious communities who love and honor her.

A TIME OF JUSTICE

On October 22, a new element was added to the message. A warning appeared about the consequences of sin. When Pierina saw the Mother of God again in the chapel of the hospital, Mary warned that God is weary of endless insults and outraged by the contempt that surrounds Him. She said that Our Lord is "tired of the continuous offenses," and that "He already wanted to dispense His justice."

There was one way to salvation. The Blessed Mother described it with a short sentence: "**Live out of love**!"

This is where she said to begin, as if she were recalling the words of Paul the Apostle: "If I speak in the tongues of men and of angels, but have not love, I am a noisy gong or a clanging cymbal. And if I have prophetic powers, and understand all mysteries and all knowledge, and if I have all faith, so as to remove mountains, but have not love, I am nothing. If I give away all I have, and if I deliver my body to be burned, but have not love, I gain nothing" (1 Cor. 13:1–3).

In the next apparition, in November 1947, Mary was said to announce: "**Our Lord can no longer watch the many grievous sins against purity. He wants to send a flood of punishments. I have interceded that He may be merciful once more! Therefore, I ask for prayer and penance to atone for these sins**." The Mother of God gave assurances that, "Whoever will atone for those sins, will receive my blessing and graces." When the visionary asked if people could hope for forgiveness, Mary reportedly replied: "**Yes, as long as these sins are no longer committed**."

Subsequent apparitions followed, and the Holy Mother did not cease to call for abandoning sins of impurity and entering the path of prayer, sacrifice, and penance. She was said to explain that "**penance means to accept, every day, all the little crosses and the duties, too, in the spirit of penance**." This is another element identical to what we find in the message of Fatima: Mary asks us not to look for special austerities and forms of penance because everyday life brings enough opportunities.

She makes another announcement: "**On December 8, at noon, I shall appear again here in the basilica. It will be the hour of grace**." When Pierina asked what this hour of grace

is, she was told: "**This will produce great and numerous conversions. Hardened and cold hearts resembling this marble will be touched by divine grace, and they will become faithful to our Lord in loyal love**."

THE CHILDREN OF FATIMA IN MONTICHIARI

On the eve of the feast day of the Immaculate Conception, the Holy Mother appeared in the basilica in Montichiari. She was wearing a white cloak held by two children: a boy on the right, a girl on the left. As she explained, they are Francisco and Jacinta, blessed visionaries of Fatima. "**They will help you in your trials and suffering. They, too, suffered.**

I wish from you the simplicity and goodness of these two children."

Another guideline: the shepherds of Fatima elevated to the altars in 2000 are to become a model of fulfilling the prayers of the Holy Mother and living her message. This path will not be without hardships and suffering, but apparently it must be so: the Marian paths run in the shadow of the Cross.

Mary announced: "**I shall show my Heart tomorrow, of which the people know so little. In Fatima, I asked that the devotion to my heart be spread**." And she added the words that direct our attention not so much to Fatima as to a little-known place of apparitions, the truth of which she herself confirmed: "**I wanted to bring my heart into Christian families in Bonate**." (Bonate is the small town in Italy, near Bergamo, discussed in chapter 17.) And she immediately explains the meaning of the apparition in Montichiari: "**Here, in Montichiari, I wish to be venerated as the Rosa Mystica, together with the devotion to my heart which must be specially practiced in religious institutes so that they may obtain more graces through my motherly heart**."

APPARITIONS FULL OF MAJESTY

On December 8, the basilica in Montichiari was filled with people, including many priests. The Church was so crowded that Pierina struggled to get inside. She knelt down in the center of the basilica and began praying the Rosary. Suddenly, she stopped with a delighted cry: "Oh, the Holy Mother!" There was a silence. Pierina looked at Mary, who appeared to her on the wide white staircase decorated with

white, red, and gold roses — symbols of purity, fidelity, and holiness. First, she repeated with a smile the words she had said in 1858 in Lourdes: "**I am the Immaculate Conception**," then she began to solemnly descend the stairs, with dignity and majesty. After a few steps, she announced: "**I am Mary, full of grace, Mother of my Divine Son Jesus Christ**." She went down a few more steps and spoke again: "**Through my coming to Montichiari, I wish to be known as the Rosa Mystica. It is my wish that every year, on the eighth of December, at noon, the hour of grace for the world be celebrated. Many divine and bodily graces will be received through this devotion. Our Lord, my Divine Son Jesus, will send His overflowing mercy if good people will pray continuously for their sinful brothers**."

The Holy Mother asked to convey her wish to Pope Pius XII because she wanted the hour of grace for the world to be made known and spread throughout the world. She explained the requirement of the devotion: "**If anyone is unable to visit his church, yet will pray at noon at home, he will also receive graces through me. Whoever prays ... and weeps tears of penance, will find a secure heavenly ladder and receive protection and grace through my motherly heart**."

At that moment, the Holy Mother showed her heart to the visionary, saying: "**Behold the heart that so loves men, while most of them return it with insults. When good and evil are united in prayer, one will obtain mercy and peace from this heart**." Mary explained: "**The Lord is still protecting the good and is**

The yellow rose is a symbol of holiness.

Red means self-sacrifice, martyrdom.

holding back a great punishment because of my intercession." She assured that she has already prepared a sea of graces for her children. It is for those who "**listen to my words and keep them in their hearts**."

These are words we know from the Gospel. They are spoken by Jesus. I wonder if Mary repeats them after her Son, with whom she is perfectly aligned, so that the words of the Savior become her words. Or maybe this sentence (like other passages in the Holy Bible) was taken by the Savior from His beloved Mother, who raised Him for thirty years, taught divine wisdom, and faithfully listened to the word of God and kept it in her Immaculate Heart. One thing is certain: the Holy Mother has the right to the words of Jesus because she is one with Him! It is she who has the fullest right to the words that St. Paul once wrote: "yet I live, no longer I, but Christ lives in me" (*New American Bible*, Gal. 2:20). Perfectly united with the Son, she has in her Immaculate Heart His love and His suffering.

NINETEEN YEARS PASS

The apparitions in Montichiari end. Before departing to heaven, the Holy Mother assures Pierina that she will return and at that time will make public a secret through the authorities of the Church.

Pierina waited nineteen years for Mary. She closed herself in a convent in the nearby town of Fontanelle, where, hidden from the world, she served in the kitchen. On April 17, 1966, which we now celebrate as Divine Mercy Sunday, the Holy Mother showed herself to the visionary once more.

❯ *Stone steps on which the Holy Mother's feet rested during the apparition in Fontanelle.*

LA SCALA SANTA DOVE LA MADONNA "ROSA MISTICA" E' SCESA A PIEDI NUDI IL 17 APRILE 1966. SI FA IN GINOCCHIO PREGANDO IN SEGNO DI PENITENZA E DI AMORE

▲ The interior of St. Pancras Church.

▲ Once again, as in Beauraing, Mary chose the Solemnity of the Immaculate Conception as the day to meet with the visionary.

It was one of the four "new" apparitions near the spring that the Mother of God made "the source of grace," especially for the sick. On May 19, 1970, she would demand that a special medal be struck.

WHAT DOES THE CHURCH SAY?

In 1948, Pierina Gilli appeared before a commission investigating the Marian phenomenon of Montichiari to give them an explanation of the apparitions. Interestingly, the members of the commission were mostly hostile to those events, and during the interrogation, they tried to force the visionary to deny everything. She endured the arrogant and aggressive behavior of the members of the commission. The atmosphere softened somewhat after Pierina swore on the

Gospel. But her patience, peace, and confidence that the Mother of God appeared in Montichiari ultimately did not affect the bias of the commission. Seeing their hostility, the local bishop refrained from releasing judgment. In 1971, the verdict was negative. From a human perspective, it is not surprising, since the apparitions treated the clergy so severely—and it was the priests appointed to the commission who were to decide on their future role. It was easier to question the authenticity of the Holy Mother's words than to acknowledge their truthfulness and accept their sharp criticism of the lifestyle of priests and religious orders. Although many Church authorities took the side of the apparitions granted to Pierina (Bishop Rudolf Graber wrote on July 1, 2013: "We are dealing at the deepest level with Mary's concern for the renewal and sanctification of priests and all persons dedicated to religion"), the official position of the Church remained cautious.

Years passed, and the pilgrimages to the site of the apparitions continued. In 2000, in view of examples of genuine piety and numerous well-documented miracles, the local bishop decided, without invalidating the previous opinion, to accept and welcome public devotion at the site of the apparitions. Those who honor the Mystical Rose received with joy the bishop's 2019 declaration of a diocesan shrine to increase the numerous spiritual fruits at Montichiari.

◀ A cross with a figure of the crucified Christ located on the premises of the sanctuary in Montichiari.

Lipa

1948

> *"Be not afraid, for the love of my Son will soften the hardest of hearts and My motherly love will be your strength, which will crush the enemies of God."*

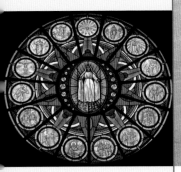

⌃ *Stained-glass image of the Mother of God adorning one of the windows of the monastery.*

Mediatrix of
All Graces

⚜

The apparitions in Lipa are a true kaleidoscope of extraordinary phenomena. There is a blue bird among the vines, a dancing sun, and rose petals falling from the sky.

⌃ *An important characteristic of the Catholic Church in the Philippines is fervent devotion to the Mother of God and deep faith in her intercessory power.*

The Philippines is the largest Catholic country in Asia. More than 80 percent of the population is Catholic. Lipa is a small town located on the southern side of the main island. It is less than an hour's drive to Manila, the capital. In 1948, a young woman named Teresita Castillo lived there.

The year was an important one for her. The girl discovered her calling to contemplation, decided to enter the Carmelites, was accepted to the foundation in Lipa, and began her postulancy, the first stage of her religious formation. By August, she had already experienced nineteen apparitions.

Lipa

PHILIPPINES

MEETING IN THE GARDEN

One day, the postulant strolled around the garden, deep in prayer. She didn't think about what was happening outside the walls of her convent.

When Teresita was passing by a vine, it began to shake. She paused, and after a moment, she was amazed to see the Blessed Virgin Mary standing on the path. Our Lady acted rather like a religious superior. She began giving Teresita various commands, ordering her to kiss the ground, instructing her to have the vine blessed. The Blessed Mother also demanded that a statue of her be placed where she set her feet. She then asked the postulant to come to this place for the next fifteen days.

Teresita obeyed all the Virgin's orders. And because the sisters believed what the young nun saw in the garden, a statue of the Immaculate Mary was placed on the site of the apparition the next day. She was different from the Queen of Heaven young Castillo saw, but neither the Carmel nor anyone in the near and distant surroundings had such an image. Mary had appeared to Teresita on a cloud, clothed all in white. Her dress was tightened with a narrow sash, and her hands were folded in prayer. In her right hand, she held a golden rosary. The Carmelite sisters placed a white statue of the Madonna with her hands extended in a blessing gesture.

APPEALS

During the apparitions in Lipa, the Holy Mother asked that Holy Mass be celebrated at the site of the apparitions each month. It is significant that she chose the twelfth day of every month, the day "before Fatima."

What did the Holy Mother say? First, she gave her identity: **"I am the Mediatrix of all Graces**." Thus, she referred to a truth that divides the contemporary Church. Many Protestants find it off-putting, even offensive. They see it as a return to the era of "Marian exaggeration," which could lead to making Christianity a religion with Mary at the center. Yet the Church has honored Mary with this title for centuries. The only question was whether it would be declared a dogma, an official teaching of the Church.

ROSE PETALS AND OTHER MIRACLES

Many strange phenomena accompanied the Filipino apparitions. We have records of the sun dancing, an intense scent of roses, and, finally, a rain of rose petals, upon which were impressed miraculous images of the Son of God, His Mother, the Last Supper, the Cross, and other scenes from the Savior's life.

This phenomenon was witnessed by other Carmelite nuns from Lipa, then by the entire convent, then by the entire city, and then by the entire archipelago. Hundreds of thousands of people flocked around the monastery, watching the petals with images of Jesus fall like manna from heaven. Witnesses said they saw them appear out of nowhere in the air. These petals also caused numerous healings. One young woman was suddenly cured of a club foot!

We hear testimonials assuring us that when the sick Teresita wasn't able to participate in Holy Mass, she received Holy Communion from the hands of an angel. She was also said to have had revelations of the Sacred Heart of Jesus and supposedly met with angels and saints, including St. Cecilia and St. Thérèse of Lisieux. The visionary was seen falling into a state of unconsciousness, and later she was seen

⋀ *The Holy Mother asked to celebrate Holy Mass at the site of the apparitions on the twelfth day of every month.*

LIPA

> *Teresita's first meeting with the Holy Mother in the convent garden was merely a prelude to what was about to happen a few weeks later.*

▲ *The decision of the Apostolic Penitentiary on the events in Lipa.*

On September 12, 1948 in this Carmel of Lipa, Mary Mediatrix of All Grace appeared on top of a vine. The vine beside Our Lady is the original vine.

▲ *One of the plaques commemorating the events.*

in agony, like Christ on the Cross. Among her witnesses was the local ordinary, Alfredo Verzosa y Florentín, and the superior of the monastery. These two quickly became zealous advocates of the authenticity of the apparitions.

CONFUSION

An uproar broke out over the apparitions. Some of the Lipa townspeople were so disturbed by them that the Vatican decided to remove Bishop Verzosa and his auxiliary, as well as the superior of Teresita's convent—all of whom supported the apparitions. The convent was sealed, and it was forbidden for its residents to speak to anyone from the outside. The sisters were ordered to destroy everything that was in any way related to the apparitions. The obedient nuns burned the priceless diary kept by the visionary. The fire also consumed the records kept by the superior. The statue was removed from the site of the apparitions, but the Carmelite nuns were unable to destroy it. They decided instead to hide it, and the statue survived the next forty years in secret.

Numerous articles appeared mocking the apparitions in Lipa. They contained charges of deception, of pious contrivances, of religious fiction. Teresita found herself in such a torrent of criticism that, a few years after the apparitions, she had to leave the convent. This was the final crowning argument for the falsehood of the alleged apparitions—or so her critics said.

VICTORY, THANKS TO THE POWER OF MARY

The Holy Mother foretold the difficulties ahead, which she referred to as persecution. At the same time, she assured victory. She said to Teresita, "**Be not afraid, for the love of my Son will**

soften the hardest of hearts and My motherly love will be your strength, which will crush the enemies of God." Thus, Mary herself foretold the coming of times when the phenomena would be recognized as a gift from heaven.

Meanwhile, at least five other Filipinos received revelations related to Teresita's: Lola Thelma, a caretaker of a Lourdes grotto in Quezon City; Carmelo Cortes and his older sister, Puring Fruto, from San Francisco del Monte in Quezon City; Lito Valero from Manila; and Alan Robinson, an alleged stigmatic.

And what was the message Our Lady was trying to convey? Why did she draw so much attention to this pious young nun in the Philippines? The appeal from Lipa is simple. Mary says, "**Pray for persecutors! Pray for the end of bloodshed**!"

FORTY-TWO YEARS LATER

In February 1990, a strange phenomenon was reported in the Granja district in Lipa. In the evenings, on the leaves of a coconut tree, outlines of a praying woman were clearly visible. The residents of the city of Lipa began to remember similar wonders seen on rose petals in 1948. Discussion of the apparitions in the Carmelite garden were renewed.

On May 21, one of the Carmelite nuns who witnessed those events died. Sr. Alphonsa pleaded on her deathbed for the statue of the Mediatrix of All Graces to be placed in the convent chapel. Her request was so persistent, so inspired, that the day after Sister Alphonsa's death, the statue originally in the place of the apparitions was restored to a place of honor. The statue stood in the chapel of the Carmelite convent, seeing daylight for the first time after more than forty years in hiding.

Yet this isn't the end of the story.

Once again, rose petals fell around the monastery in Lipa — once again

bearing miraculous images and effecting miraculous healings.

And as the years went on, several bishops who had worked to suppress the apparition admitted on their deathbeds that they had been ordered to do so under threat of excommunication.

As a consequence of "the scandalous suppression of facts, coerced statements from six bishops, the omission of key witnesses and evidence," the Church established a new commission whose task was to examine the credibility of these colorful apparitions. Archbishop Ramón Argüelles of Lipa officially approved the devotion on September 12, 2015.

In 2016 the Vatican intervened, declaring the apparitions "not supernatural." However, in an unprecedented action, it still allows for local devotion.

> ⌄ *In response to the Mother of God's request, the sisters placed a statue of Mary with her hands extended in a gesture of blessing.*

Warsaw

1948

Dispenser of Divine
Omnipotence

On the eve of his death, Primate August Hlond called with great fervor for consecration to Mary. "Work under the protection of the Blessed Virgin Mary," he said. He spoke with great conviction about her impending triumph over Satan. Where did this certainty come from? Probably from the Holy Mother herself.

⌃ *Cardinal August Hlond proclaimed God's victory over evil, which will be the victory of the Virgin Mary.*

Cardinal Stefan Wyszyński, the primate of Poland who "put everything on Mary," considered his predecessor a great Marian visionary. In his final homily—delivered on October 21, 1978, in Rome—he referred to the words of Cardinal August Hlond as an "apocalyptic vision," "a prophetic vision of the Victorious Virgin." Cardinal Hlond's testament says: "Fight under the protection of the Blessed Virgin Mary. The victory, when it comes, will be the victory of the Most Holy Mother."

Do the statements of the primate of the millennium entitle us to talk about the apparition that occurred with the participation of Cardinal Augusta Hlond? Yes, Wyszyński's predecessor was certainly a man whose life had been marked by the touch of the supernatural.

Cardinal August Hlond was born on July 5, 1881, into a family of a railroad lineman who lived near the town of Mysłowice. At the age of fifteen, he joined the Salesians. In 1905, after graduating from the Gregorian

University in Rome, he was ordained a priest. In 1922, Pope Pius XI appointed him as apostolic administrator of Upper Silesia, and three years later, the first bishop ordinary of the newly created Katowice diocese.

Bishop Hlond took the office of the primate of Poland in 1926, and he held it for twenty-two years. It was on his initiative that the weekly news magazine *Gość Niedzielny* (Sunday Guest) was created. He also founded a Polish chapter of Catholic Action. Above all, however, he is the author of pastoral letters filled with divine knowledge, which still make an impression on readers today, as well as several remarkable prophecies related to Mary.

When World War II broke out, the Nazi occupiers would not allow him to return to Poland. Cardinal Hlond spent time in Rome, in Lourdes, and in Hautecombe, France. Then he was arrested and imprisoned in Paris, Bar-le-Duc, and Wiedenbrück, Germany. He was liberated by the Americans on April 1, 1945.

POLAND

Warsaw ✠

◄ The pastoral
ministry of
Primate Hlond was
characterized by a
deep devotion to
Mary.

⬥ In communist
Poland, the
Primate called out
forcefully: "Nihil
desperandum!
Don't lose hope!"

Soon—and despite opposition from the British government—he returned to his homeland, which had been taken over by Communists. When they began to build post-Christian Poland, Hlond began proclaiming God's victory over evil. He assured everyone that it would come—and that it would come through Mary.

His service was interrupted by his unexpected death. The primate died after a successful appendectomy, due to an infection of unknown origin. He died October 22, 1948, on the Feast of Our Lady of a Good Death.

PROPHECY ON THE EVE OF DEATH

The night before he died, Cardinal Hlond spoke an extraordinary prophecy that influenced the lives of successive generations. He addressed the crowd by speaking in Latin, as if in this way he wanted to make his words more solemn and universal. He announced: "*Nil desperandum! Nihil desperandum! Sed victoria, si erit—erit victoria Beatae Mariae Virginis. In hoc certamine, quod certatur inter satanicos conventus*

1948

> "Poland is a nation chosen by the Most Holy Virgin Mary."

▲ Apostolic nuncio Archbishop Philip Cortesi.

et Christum, aliquis eorum, qui se credebant vocatos esse, revocatur in altum et erit sicut Deus ipse disponet."

"Do not despair!" he told the people. "Do not lose hope! However, victory, if it comes, it will be the victory of the Blessed Virgin Mary. In the battle that goes on between a horde of devils and Christ, those who believed themselves to be called, God calls back on high and it will be as God Himself arranges it."

He added, as if in one breath, "Fight with trust. Work under the protection of the Blessed Virgin Mary ... Your victory is certain. The Immaculate One will help you to win."

The victory will come through Mary — the summary of the Primate Hlonda's prophecy became the motto of the ministry of two other "great

helmsmen of the twentieth century":
Cardinal Wyszyński and Karol Wojtyła,
later Pope St. John Paul II.

VISIONS OR PROPHECIES?

The announcement of the victory that
will come through the Holy Mother are
Primate Hlond's most famous words.
But he made several such prophecies,
each of them Marian.

He gave another "testament" from
the same year, equally radical, and
certainly more harsh in its political and
theological content. In a famous speech
during the consecration of the figure
of the Mother of God in Wrocław in
September 1948, Primate Hlond said,
"Because we need this Mother, because
this future is coming, and this future will
be better, because it will be resurrected
by this omnipotence that in our times
God gives in the hands of Our Lady. She
holds this omnipotence in her hands.
She will be the one to give directions to
this world. She will lead the nations with
this Omnipotence of God, the Mediatrix
of Whom she becomes for the nearest
years."

⋀ *Cardinal August
Hlond's prophecy
became the motto
of the ministry
of the pope from
Poland, John Paul II.*

around him? Where did his radicalism and his certainty come from?

And where did his other, equally amazing predictions arise from? Let us quote a few of them:

> "On a new rainbow of glory, the Immaculate One rises above the Church. She will take special care of Christianity during the toughest trials and will give it victory. Let us entrust to Her protection the mission of the Church in Poland and our Polish apostolic struggle."

> "The Blessed Virgin Mary leads the Church through the storms of the ages. The more the dangerous waves tossed Peter's boat, the more the Star of the Sea shines on the horizon. Let us embrace her. May she reinvigorate us with the spirit of the cenacle. May she prepare us for the Vienna of the twentieth century. May she, as the helper of the faithful, lead us to victory over ungodliness and disbelief, armed with the spirit of the knights of Christ. May none of us be missing from her ranks."

He mentions Vienna in reference to the Battle of Vienna in 1683, when Christian forces rebuffed an invading Ottoman army. It was Christendom's greatest victory against Islamic conquerors, second only to the Battle of Lepanto in 1571.

These words indicate something more than just Cardinal Hlond's deep Marian devotion. They suggest some other "knowledge" the primate could not get from readings and conversations. So where is its source? How important is it that Hlond dared to say the words that did not fit into the theological teachings

According to the cardinal-visionary, this "Marian way" to a better future leads along the path of the Immaculate Heart. Cardinal Hlond recalled:

> "Our Mother, indicated by signs in the sky and on earth, is calling us that we may prepare ourselves in

the Holy Spirit for service, which she assigns to us. Poland is to be the General Commander of God's cause, and the truth is to free the souls who got entangled in mistakes, who revolted against the Creator. Where heresy has devastated the honor of the Queen of the Universe, Poland is to restore Her gracious Kingdom of Her Immaculate Heart."

On January 10, 1948, Cardinal Hlond wrote to the Salesian bishop Giuseppe Cognata asking him to pray to the "Immortal King of Ages and His all-powerful Mother, sweet Helper of Christians. We will see events bigger than those that took place in Lepanto and Vienna."

OUR VICTORY — IN OTHER WORDS, OUR COOPERATION WITH MARY

Primate Hlond assured us that those who are hidden in her maternal Heart can be certain that no evil will touch them and that the great prophecy announced on his deathbed will be fulfilled: "The victory, when it comes, will be the victory of the Most Holy Mother."

The primate immediately added, "Work." Because Christianity, as John Paul II used to say, "is a religion of human cooperation with God." The cardinal pleaded, "Work under the

⋎ *A nation that fights in the name of God has the right to God's help.*

1948

> The primate preached that Mary's victory is a victory of the Church. Mary is — and works solely in — the Church.

∀ A memorial plaque in honor of the primate of Poland in the Gniezno cathedral.

protection of the Blessed Virgin Mary." He wanted us to understand that we have a task to do. A difficult task. This work is a battle. After all, in the hour of his death, he said: "Fight with trust." The announced victory—an irrevocable victory—will have two authors.

Primate August Hlond spoke about the victory of the Mother of God and ours. He announced: "Victory, when it comes, will come through Mary." But he immediately added: "Your victory is certain." Whose victory? The victory of the Mother of God—and ours.

THE TRIUMPH OF MARY, THE TRIUMPH OF THE CHURCH

On August 6, 1948, Hlond said:

We witness a fierce struggle between the empire of God and the empire of Satan. Although this battle has been going on relentlessly without cease-fire, today it is more fierce than ever before. On the one hand, we have a triumphant march of the Kingdom of Christ. On the other, the paw of Satan weighs heavily on the world, more greedily and treacherously than ever before. Modern paganism, possessed as if by the cult of a demon, rejected all moral ideals and erased the notion of humanity. It basks in a vision of a society in which the name of God is no longer heard, and in which the concept of religion and Christian morality are destroyed forever. The result of this battle between the empire of God and the empire of Satan is clear. The Church has her victory secured. "The gates of hell shall not prevail against it" (Matt. 16:18). What is at stake, however, is that each

person contribute the merits of his and her moral deeds onto the scales of victory. ... Each of us has a designated role in this battle. If one does not do his best on his designated post, one is a traitor to God's cause and puts others at risk. Whoever removes themselves from this battle out of comfort is a deserter.

Cardinal Hlond announced the victory of Mary will be accomplished in the Church. Without Mary, there is no victory, but also without the Church there is no victory. Whoever wants to share in Mary's victory must be in union with the Church, for Mary works in the Church, not outside of it.

John Paul II carried Hlond's prophecy in his heart. He referred to it in many conversations. He emblazoned this confidence in his motto *Totus Tuus*: "Totally yours"—that is, Mary's. And he gave the prophecy a universal dimension by sharing it with people of all nationalities. For example, an Irishman named Frank Duff came to him asking to found a society called the Legion of Mary. John Paul approved, saying, "Remember, victory will come through Mary." Today, with more than ten million members, the Legion of Mary is the largest lay movement in the world.

A GOLDEN AGE IS COMING "THROUGH MARY"

Mary's victory lies ahead. That is what the entire tradition of the Church wants. When the time of the triumph of the heart comes, the prophecies that St. John Chrysostom had announced in the fifth century, about the coming of the "golden age," will

be fulfilled," It will be the age of the Church, where there will be unity, peace, and joy, and the guide will be the Gospel.

For centuries, dozens of saints took up the same thread. The last one of them, John Paul II, announced the coming of the "spring of Christianity," "new spring of the Church, "civilization of love." The Kingdom was to come through Mary.

Maybe the former Polish cardinal, declared a Servant of God, and perhaps in the future a saint, will be proclaimed the first prophet of the new age, which draws closer to us every day.

But today he can be the patron of all those who forge a better future for the world, remaining under the heavenly banner of Immaculate Mary.

⋁ *Primate Hlond's tomb in St. John's Cathedral in Warsaw.*

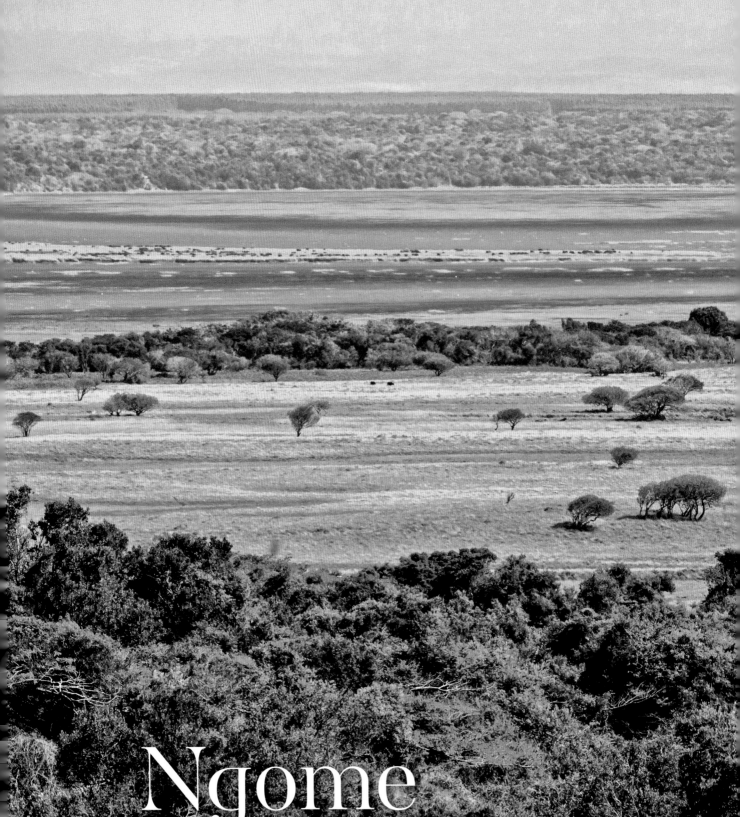

Ngome

1955

Mary, Tabernacle of the Most High

Mary, Tabernacle of the Most High, directs our eyes and hearts to Christ. By demanding honor not for herself but for her Son, she makes Him the center of attention. In Ngome, South Africa, she asked us to follow her example. We are to be living monstrances, bringing Christ to the world by proclaiming His glory.

▲ *The Zulu are an African ethnic group inhabiting the southern part of the continent.*

Not many Marian apparitions have occurred in Africa—only twenty, as of 2000. (For comparison, by the end of the twentieth century, 859 apparitions had taken place in Europe.) Yet, astonishingly, most of the African apparitions occurred in the twentieth century.

The first modern apparition in Africa took place in 1955. That year, on the feast of the Immaculate Heart of Mary, the Holy Mother appeared in Ngome, in the Zulu region of South Africa. There, she revealed a new eucharistic title: Tabernacle of the Most High.

Mary appeared to Reinolda May, a fifty-three-year-old Benedictine nun from Germany. Usually, Mary appears to children. Rarely does she reveal herself to adults, especially those who have passed the half-century mark. Then again, St. Juan Diego was fifty-six when Our Lady of Guadalupe appeared to him.

REINOLDA, A MISSIONARY SISTER

Francisca May was born on a German farm in 1901. She was one of eight children of devout Catholic parents. The local parish priest was also very devout. He awakened a desire for religious life in many young people, including Francisca. She entered the Missionary Benedictine Sisters of Tutzing and took the name Reinolda. Soon, she was sent to South Africa, where the sisters had a mission. They ran a hospital in Nongoma and a farm in the nearby town of Ngome.

At the mission, Sr. Reinolda worked as a seamstress, then as a midwife, and finally as supervisor of the maternity ward at the Benedictine hospital. She was always composed and balanced, calm and patient, kind and smiling. Many of her patients and colleagues remembered her as the best missionary in the country.

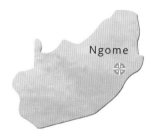

While Reinolda was working at the mission, she experienced ten apparitions. They ended with a command for the Benedictine nuns to convey Mary's eucharistic title to the world.

LIVING TABERNACLES

The first apparition occurred in 1955 on the feast of the Immaculate Heart of Mary, which, at the time, was celebrated on August 22. (In 1969, Pope St. Paul VI moved the feast to the day after the solemnity of the Most Sacred Heart of Jesus.)

Sr. Reinolda later recalled:

Shortly after Holy Communion, Mary stood before me, very close by. Everything was seen in spirit. I was drawn into another plane. Mary showed herself in a wonderful light more beautiful than the sun. She was robed all in white, with flowing veil that ran from top to toe. Upon her breast rested a large host, surrounded by a brilliant corona radiating life. She was a living monstrance. Mary stood upon a globe, hands and feet not visible.

The Mother of God said to the visionary: "**Call me 'Tabernacle of the Most High.'**" After a moment, even more amazing words came from her lips: "**You, too, are such a tabernacle**." Sr. Reinolda took this to mean that, when we receive the Eucharist, our hearts also become vessels for Christ's presence. We ourselves become monstrances.

"**I wish to be called upon by this title for the glory of my Son**," she continued. "**I wish that more such tabernacles be prepared; I mean human hearts**." Then, she explained: "**I wish that the altars be surrounded by praying people more frequently**."

◄ *Our hearts, like the heart of Mary, are to become a dwelling place for the eucharistic Lord.*

▲ *Mary's message at Ngome spoke of the Eucharist and its saving power.*

◄ *Mary appeared to Sr. Reinolda as a living monstrance glowing more beautifully than the sun.*

Our Lady's first conversation with Reinolda ended with a request for the visionary to make Mary's message known.

"**Don't be afraid**," said the Holy Mother. "**Make it known**."

"To whom?" she asked.

"**Don't be afraid**," Mary repeated. "**Tell your priest**."

A TANGIBLE EMBRACE

The Holy Mother appeared to Sr. Reinolda again two months later, in October 1955. After Holy Mass, the missionary saw Mary in the shape of a monstrance. The Mother of God repeated the lesson about becoming living tabernacles for Christ. Then she commanded Reinolda once more to tell others about the apparitions.

"**Make these words known to everybody**," she said, adding: "**Do not be afraid. You are God's tool**."

On March 15, 1956, the Holy Mother appeared to the nun for a fourth time, leaned down, and embraced the visionary to her heart. Unlike the previous three apparitions, this one occurred on the physical plane.

"THE PLACE WHERE SEVEN SPRINGS COME TOGETHER"

Since October, Sr. Reinolda had been praying for a sign that would convince those who didn't believe her testimony.

"**You asked for a sign**?" said Mary. "**I wish that a shrine be erected for me in the place where seven springs come together. There I will let my graces flow in abundance. Many**

▼ *In the land of the Zulu, Mary said that an inexhaustible sea of graces awaits us, as long as we meet certain conditions.*

people shall turn to God." Regarding the conversions and graces that would flow from the shrine, Mary added: "**It is my work**."

Sr. Reinolda believed the seven springs referred to the seven gifts of the Holy Spirit. Our Lady asked for a shrine to be built beside actual springs of water, said the nun, so that pilgrims could see a physical symbol of the heavenly gifts being bestowed upon them.

In 1957, a year after Mary made her request for a shrine to be built, several springs were discovered near the Benedictine school in Ngome.

The next apparition occurred on June 5, 1956, on the solemnity of the Most Sacred Heart of Jesus. During Benediction, Mary came out of the monstrance and approached Sr. Reinolda in the form of "a living monstrance." This vision concluded the first phase of the Ngome apparitions.

"FEARFUL THINGS ARE IN STORE FOR YOU"

In March of the following year, the Virgin appeared again. She told Sr. Reinolda, "**I come to strengthen you. I will make use of your nothingness. Be totally humble**." Then, she said: "**I want to save the world through the Host, my fruit. I am completely one with the Host as I was one with Jesus under the Cross. ... Fearful things are in store for you unless you convert**."

The visionary was confused. Who needed to be converted?

The Holy Mother elaborated that dreadful things would happen "**if the religious do not convert and the world does not convert**."

At the same time, the Mother of God announced that those who believe and convert would receive a sign from her: an

extraordinary outpouring of grace. Her next words to Reinolda were an order: "**Hurry up; the hour is advanced. I must keep back the streams of grace with force because you do not make any effort to help me. I am asking for help from you, my chosen ones**!"

What are the followers of the Holy Mother to do? "**Be hosts**," she said. "**Prepare hosts for me — hosts who put themselves completely at my disposal. Only a flaming sea of hosts can drive back the hate of the godless world and restrain the angry hand of the Father. Do not get tired. I find consolation in revealing myself to you. I shall never abandon you**."

TWELVE YEARS LATER

The last two apparitions in Ngome occurred in March 1970 and May 1971, after a twelve-year hiatus.

By this time, devotion to Mary under her new title had begun to develop, and her message was growing in popularity. An image of Mary, Tabernacle of the Most High, was painted. It hung in the chapel of the Benedictine school. Then, in 1966, the shrine Our Lady requested was built, and the painting was displayed there.

Then, in this time of spiritual peace, the devil appeared to Sr. Reinolda. She wrote: "It was the second night after the devil's terrifying appearance. Something woke me up. There was brightness all around, and Mary, Tabernacle of the Most High, stood by me. She took me in her arms and comforted me. She said: '**I know about your anxiety. I stand by you. I shall not abandon you**.'"

A year later, another apparition occurred, this time in public. Sr. Reinolda recalled that during one of her visits to the shrine, a catechumen

⋏ *"**I am completely one with the Host as I was one with Jesus under the Cross**."*

⋏ *Prayer — this is one of Mary's signposts that will allow us to become living tabernacles for Christ.*

The shrine
dedicated to
Mary, Tabernacle
of the Most High,
was built in the
place where seven
springs meet.

was complaining about the behavior
of her neighbor, who was most
likely ridiculing her for wanting to
be baptized. Sr. Reinolda entered
the chapel and began praying aloud
in front of the painting of Mary,
Tabernacle of the Most High, along
with some other women. They asked
Mary for help for the catechumen and
for the conversion of her neighbor.

"Suddenly," the visionary wrote, "I
noticed that the picture was very much
alive. She stepped forward and her
face was immensely beautiful. In my
excitement I shouted: 'Look at Mary.' I
am convinced that the women too saw
Mary. I personally was so moved that I
walked away silently." She added that the

man who was troubling the catechumen
"asked the priest for forgiveness, and
was at peace thereafter."

Two additional apparitions occurred.
During one of them, Mary promised: "**I
find consolation in revealing myself
to you. I shall never abandon you**."

THE CHURCH ON THE APPARITIONS IN NGOME

In 1989, a group convened to study
the apparitions in Ngome. Its members
included Bishop Mansuet Biyase, the
ordinary of the Diocese of Eshowe,
where Ngome is located; Fr. Michael
Mayer, O.S.B., a parish priest; and Fr.
Paul B. Decock, O.M.I., chairperson of
the Theological Advisory Commission

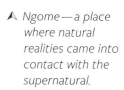

◄ An image inside the shrine depicting Mary, Tabernacle of the Most High.

⋀ Ngome—a place where natural realities came into contact with the supernatural.

of the South African Catholic Bishops' Conference. In their statement, they announced: "There is nothing objectionable" in the promotion of the sanctuary at Ngome and the veneration of Our Lady under the name of Tabernacle of the Most High. "The content of the visions is doctrinally acceptable."

A year later, Fr. Mayer wrote in his newsletter: "The Marian shrine at Ngome is a sign of the presence of Our Lady in the life of the local Church. ... Devotion to Our Lady at Ngome will be an opportunity to work and pray for peace in our country. ... Many believe that the Marian shrine at Ngome is the work of Our Lady."

In 1992, Bishop Biyase blessed the open-air altar at the sanctuary and declared Ngome a place of prayer, inviting the faithful to make pilgrimages to the site of the apparitions. He himself made three pilgrimages there in 1993. The following year, the ordinary invited the bishop of the neighboring diocese to bless the statue of Mary, Tabernacle of the Most High. In 1996, the bishop blessed the pilgrimage center in Ngome.

What about the visionary? Sr. Reinolda retired at seventy-four, which did not prevent her from continuing to work among the sick. She spent the last eight years of her life at the mission station in Inkamana, Zululand, South Africa, where she died on April 1, 1981.

⋀ One of the active springs on the grounds of the sanctuary.

Rome City

1956–1959

Our Lady
of America

▲ Pope St. Pius X.

In this small Midwestern town, Mary was said to ask for the consecration of the United States to her pure heart. She desires people to come to her with trust and simplicity. She encourages them to follow her, opening themselves up to the Holy Trinity and to divine indwelling, which will sanctify them from within.

The story of Our Lady of America begins on May 10, 1846. Twenty-three bishops gathered in Baltimore, in the first Catholic diocese of the United States, and issued an unusual petition to Rome. The American bishops asked for the Blessed Virgin Mary, invoked under the title of the Immaculate Conception, to be proclaimed the Patroness of the United States. Pope Pius IX gave his consent.

The title of the Immaculate Conception is all the more noteworthy because the dogma of the Immaculate Conception would only be proclaimed eight years later. Without a doubt, the American bishops' petition was an important sign for the pope regarding what theology calls "sense of the faith of the Church," which makes God's people intuitively believe the truth revealed from on high. One would expect the gesture earned Heaven's special gratitude for the American Church.

But this is only the first chapter of the story. The next pope named Pius was chosen in 1913. It was his intention to build a national Marian shrine dedicated to the Immaculate Conception in the United States. Pope St. Pius X personally donated four hundred dollars for its construction, an amount worth more than ten thousand dollars today. The sanctuary was built and became the spiritual center of the country, the only such church in the world that bound its history with the Immaculate Conception.

FIRST COMES THE DEVIL

Years passed. Then, as the summer of 1956 was ending, Sr. Mary Ephrem Neuzil was sent to Rome City in northern Indiana. This was the beginning of a new chapter in the history of the American Church.

Sr. Mary Ephrem was born in 1916 to a family of Austrian immigrants and was baptized with the name Mildred Marie. She joined the Sisters of the Precious Blood at the age of fourteen and remained with them until 1979. Then, she was transferred to a contemplative monastery, where she stayed until her death in 2000. The sisters affectionately

▲ *From Baltimore, the first Catholic diocese in the United States, a request pleasing Heaven sailed to Rome.*

called her "Millie." Until the end, the visionary remained unknown; she even managed to prevent the distribution of pictures of herself. Her mysticism remained private until her spiritual diary was found in her cell.

Sr. Mary Ephrem was frequently moved from one mission to another. She had spent a while in Washington, D.C., and in Cincinnati, Ohio, before her superiors decided to move her to Rome City.

Yet she accepted her transfer with some reluctance. She sensed that something evil was in the air. After stepping over the threshold of her cell, she felt that "something jumped out the window." She left the room at night and went to the chapel; however, the strange feeling did not leave her. "I felt like I was in a ring of evil. I couldn't get out of it and, at the same time, something told me I had to get out of it," she wrote. One night, she awoke with the sense that something (or someone) was sitting on the pillow behind her head. Before she could see what it was, it put a paw over her eyes and ran its claws down her face. When

she looked in the mirror afterward, there wasn't a scratch on her face.

For Sr. Mary Ephrem, too much was happening in the new convent!

And so the devil achieved his goal: in the morning, the nun went to her superior and asked for permission to immediately return to her old convent. She received approval, but under one condition: she would have to find someone to take her place. Failing to do so, she stayed in Rome City. And as a result, a meeting with the Blessed Mother awaited her.

MARY AS THE LADY OF LOURDES

Sr. Mary Ephrem saw the Virgin Mary for the first time on September 25, 1956—which, on the Church calendar in the United States, marks the eve of the Feast of the North American Martyrs. Mary came to say she was promising America greater miracles than the ones that occurred in Lourdes and Fatima. They will multiply in this country only if its residents will do what the Mother of God desires.

Rome City, Indiana

UNITED
STATES OF
AMERICA

⋎ *As a result of the initiative from Baltimore, the United States bound their history with the Immaculate Conception before the dogma was officially proclaimed by the Church.*

She also reportedly said,

My children, I am pleased that in America my children love and honor me, especially through my glorious and unique privilege of the Immaculate Conception. I promise to reward their love by working through the power of my Son's Heart and my Immaculate Heart miracles of grace among them. I do not promise miracles of the body, but of the soul.

Why? Again, Mary anticipates our question: "**For it is through these miracles of grace that the Holy Trinity is glorified among men and nations**."

OUR LADY OF AMERICA

The day after Mary was reported to appear in the form of the Immaculate Mother of Lourdes, the Holy Mother was said to appear twice in a different form.

The first time Mary appeared was after morning Holy Mass. The visionary writes in her diary: "I saw her beautiful face and a lily held in her right hand. She was wearing a white veil reaching almost to the waist and a mantle and a dress of pure white. It was tied around the waist with a narrow, white sash made of the same material as the dress. The mantle was fastened at the top with a gold brooch. She wore a tall, gold crown on Her head."

It seemed to the visionary that Mary's eyes, "like her hair, are brown." Millie

◢ *The Basilica of the Assumption of the Blessed Virgin Mary in Baltimore, the oldest Roman Catholic cathedral in the United States.*

◄ *The Chapel of Our Lady of the Rosary in the Basilica of the Immaculate Conception in Washington, D.C.*

also wrote down that Mary's "feet were bare, sometimes covered by the moving clouds," that "the Mother of God did not stop smiling when the Immaculate Heart appeared on her chest encircled by a wreath of red roses, from which fiery flames came out. With her left hand, she slightly raised the mantle so that her Heart could be seen."

The visionary did not understand yet the depth of all the symbols. She just felt that the roses encircling the Heart symbolize the suffering of the Holy Mother. She heard Mary announce: "**I am Our Lady of America. I desire that my children honor me, especially by the purity of their lives**." And then she disappeared.

The visionary felt the presence of the Holy Mother with her all day long. It was something completely new for her. And in the evening, Our Lady of America appeared to her again. Half an hour after Millie began praying the Holy Hour, Mary stood in front of the nun, who understood her to say,

My child, I entrust you with this message that you must pass on to my children in America. I wish it to be the country dedicated to my purity. My children must firmly believe in my love. I desire that they be the children of my Pure Heart. I desire, through my American children, to strengthen faith and purity among peoples and nations. Let them come to me with confidence and simplicity, and I, their Mother, will teach them to become pure — like my Heart and pleasing to the Heart of my Son.

Here is a mighty pillar of good that can restore order in the whole world with its

Y *When Sr. Mary Ephrem saw the Mother of God for the first time, Mary looked just like she did in 1858, during the apparitions in Lourdes.*

▲ On October 13,
1956, Mary appe-
ared to Sr. Mary
Ephrem holding a
replica of the Shri-
ne of the Immacu-
late Conception in
her hand.

strength! There is one condition: a trend of purity must reign in America.

THE NEXT APPARITIONS

"Then," confessed the sister, "I saw the Holy Mother very often." After the initial emphasis on the power of good, further apparitions showed the duality of the American people. The power of evil also exists in the nation.

The next day the nun claimed to see the Mother of God holding a globe in her hands. Mary leaned over her and cried. She reportedly said,

> *These are the tears of your Mother! Will I cry in vain? I come to you as a last resort. I am begging you to listen to my voice. Cleanse your souls in the Precious Blood of My Son. Live in His Heart. Invite me to teach you to live in great purity of heart, which is so pleasing to God. Be my army of chaste soldiers, ready to fight to the death to preserve the purity of your souls. I am the Immaculate One, Patroness of your land. Be my faithful children, and I will be your faithful Mother.*

The visionary also heard Mary say,

> *Cry, my children. Cry with your Mother over people's sins. Intercede with Me before the throne of mercy, for sin is*

The Basilica of the Immaculate Conception is a national shrine, although it does not have the rank of a cathedral; from a historical point of view this title belongs to the Basilica of the Assumption in Baltimore.

USA

overwhelming the world and punishment is not far away. It is the darkest hour, but if men will come to Me, My Immaculate Heart will make it bright again with the mercy which my Son will rain down through my hands. Help me bring once again the sunshine of God's peace upon the world!

NATIONAL SANCTUARY

The Mother of God spoke a great deal about the sanctuary. For example, she said, "**I desire for all of America to be my Shrine, in that every heart will open to the love of My Son**."

But this "all-American sanctuary" was to find its expression in a material sanctuary. On October 13, 1956, Mary appeared to the visionary in the form of Our Lady of America. However, the vision was missing the Immaculate Heart on her chest and lilies in the Mother of God's hand. Instead, Mary was holding a small replica of the completed Sanctuary of the Immaculate Conception in her hand.

Later, Sr. Mary Ephrem noted that she was delighted with the smile that lit up the Mother of God's face. She also wrote down her words: "**This is My shrine. I am very pleased with it. Tell My children I thank them for it. Let**

1956–1959

ROME CITY

THOU ART THE GLORY

⋀ *Our Lady of America desires for faith and purity to grow stronger in the hearts of nations.*

⋁ *Mary asks for a special reform, for a renewal of humanity, which is to bear the fruit of an inner union with the Most Holy Trinity.*

them finish it quickly and make it a place of pilgrimage. It will be a place of miracles. I promise you this."

The Basilica of the National Shrine of the Immaculate Conception in Washington, D.C., was completed on November 20, 1959. Only three years had passed before Our Lady requested yet another sanctuary in the United States.

The Holy Mother also promised that the statue of the Blessed Virgin Mary once placed in the National Shrine of the Immaculate Conception will be "**protection for the whole country**." If we place pictures and statues of her in our homes, those images "**will be protection for the family**." She also promised that her medal "**will be protection against evil for all who wear it with great faith and piety**."

"WITHIN"

One of the most astonishing apparitions took place on the night of November 22, 1957. On the Holy Mother's chest, Millie saw a "triangle and an eye, as if being viewed through a veil." This is a symbol of the Holy Trinity dwelling in the human heart. Mary alone stood on a globe, and a strong light emanating from the Presence of the Divine Trinity illuminated the earth.

The Holy Mother announced that peace must come from "within," that there is no other way. She said our hearts will please her Son more, but we must come to her, His Mother, and learn her spiritual life. She said, "**The Holy Trinity looks down with infinite delight upon such souls and makes them its heaven upon earth**."

She spoke many times about the divine indwelling, sanctification from within. This is how she understood the reform of society and the renewal of humanity.

FROM HEAVEN TO EARTH

In the last years of her life, Sister Mary Ephrem suffered greatly. Her friend Audrey Frank gave a heartbreaking testimony: "If anything related to Our Lady of America occurred, Millie was asked to suffer; she always agreed and there was always something painful coming into her life."

She died believing that America will change, that it will choose God's way. A nun living with her in in the convent recalled, "She said if the world does what God asks, everything will be fine. But if it doesn't, something will happen eventually. God is not going to look calmly at all these abortions. [Millie]

was worried about the whole world and America, which leads it. She was very worried with impurity spreading among young people."

For Mary had announced:

> **Unless my children reform their lives, they will suffer great persecution. If man himself will not take upon himself the penance necessary to atone for his sins and those of others, God in His justice will have to send upon him the punishment necessary to atone for his transgressions.**

On May 7, 2020, Bishop Rhoades of the Diocese of Fort Wayne declared that he could not approve the revelations as objective occurrences of supernatural origin (*non constat de supernaturalitate*) or authorize public devotion; however, private devotion to Our Lady of America is allowable.

⋏ *The Chapel of the Immaculate Heart of Mary in the basilica in Washington, D.C.*

⋏ *A tympanum located above the main entrance to the sanctuary.*

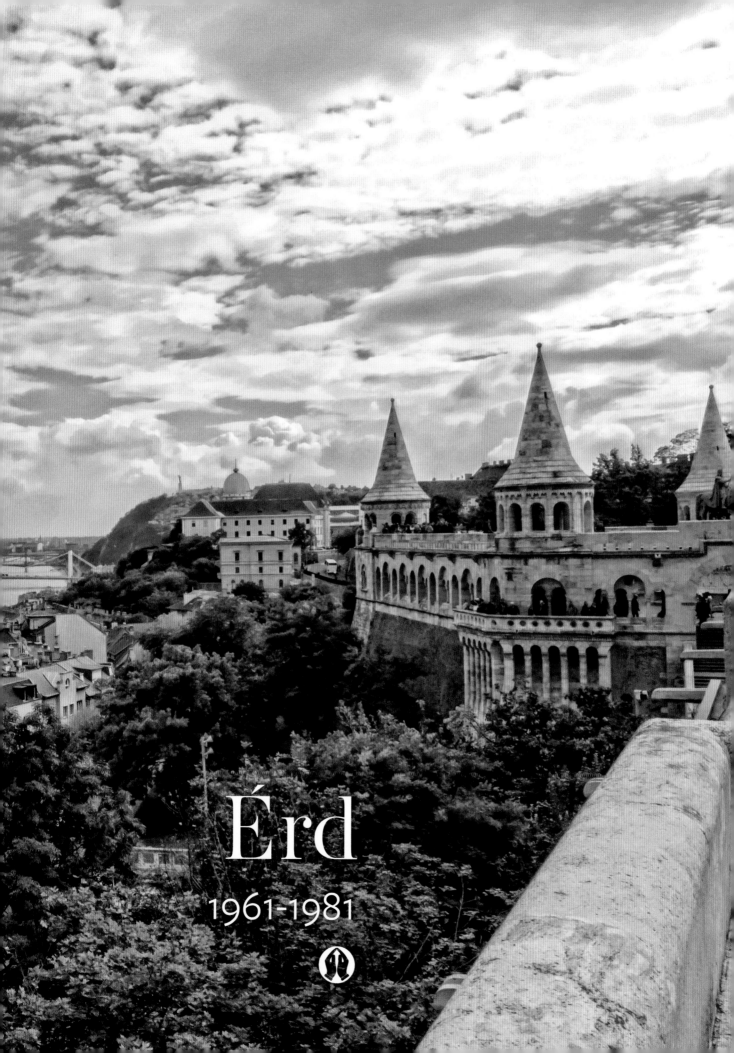

Érd

1961-1981

Flame of the
Immaculate Heart

*Elizabeth always wanted to be as close to God as possible. Not accepted to the convent, she recognized that her vocation was married life. She did not think, however, that she, a simple woman, would be entrusted with such an exceptional mission. She heard Mary say, "**My daughter, I am providing you with a powerful grace: the burning Flame of Love that comes out of my Heart.**"*

A *Elizabeth's vocation was marriage. It was family life, not convent life, God had predestined for her.*

Who was the visionary who heard that through the intercession of Mary the world can receive the greatest graces in the history of the Church? Life did not spoil her. When she was eleven years old, she lost both her parents. At thirty-three, she became a widow. At forty-eight (when the visions began), she was raising six children alone in Communist Hungary. She worked at two full-time jobs from six in the morning until ten in the evening. Into that arduous life came unexpected help from heaven: she was the first chosen one to whom Mary revealed the mystery of her Immaculate Heart.

Elizabeth Szántó was born in 1913. She completed only four grades of primary school. She wanted to enter a convent, but was denied, so she tried again. When her request was rejected a second time, she filed one more application. When it, too, was rejected, the girl realized that

God was calling her to follow a different path.

She discerned a call to the married life, and at the age of seventeen she was married to Karoly Kindelmann, an honest craftsman. Her husband died shortly after the end of World War II, leaving her to care for their six children. To support and educate them, she worked in an iron foundry, among other grueling jobs.

Fifteen years later, the Holy Mother and Jesus began appearing to her, and she began to keep a spiritual journal. By the time she died on April 11, 1985, she had filled 423 pages.

The Holy Mother revealed to Elizabeth that when we accept her light from God into our hearts and pass it on to others, we will blind Satan! This is why the Holy Mother announces: "**I want the Flame of Love of the Immaculate Heart to be known everywhere, just like my name.**"

HUNGARY

◁ *Elizabeth Kindelmann was the first one, because of Mary, who got to know the mystery of light radiating from her Immaculate Heart.*

BLINDING FLAME OF LOVE

The Holy Mother wants the devotion to the Flame of Love of the Immaculate Heart to engulf the whole world. She announced that through this Flame we are invited to be active participants in the task of salvation. We are to blind Satan, which in turns means filling the road to Heaven with crowds of people so far lured by trinkets of the devil.

Mary says: "**This Flame of graces, which flows from My Immaculate Heart, must go from heart to heart. It will be the great miracle whose Light will blind Satan. It is the fire of love and unity. We shall fight fire with fire: the fire of hate with the Fire of Love! I obtained this grace from the Eternal Father—for you, by the merits of the Five glorious Blessed Wounds of My Divine Son.**"

She later tells Elizabeth, "**My daughter, I am providing you with a** powerful grace: the burning Flame of Love that comes out of my Heart. It has never before been offered as it is now. Since the Word became Flesh, I have never taken a greater step as when I offer you the Flame of Love from my Heart that rushes to you.**"

After all, in the Hungarian apparitions, the Holy Mother says, crying, "**My dear soul, wish me many souls! This is My only prayer: souls! Oh, souls! How I languish for them**!" Mary sees how hard Satan works to pull as many people away from God as possible. She is a witness to the sins that spill all over the world, killing so many souls for eternity. She announces: "**Today I am the Mater Dolorosa, for I have to see so many of my children go to Hell. Help me save them! I do not want a single soul to be lost.**"

At last, she adds, "**Until now, nothing could have effectively blinded Satan. But it is up to you not to reject it. This rejection has a simple name: a disaster.**"

"I NEED ALL OF YOU"

Our Holy Mother recommends choosing Thursday and Friday as days of special grace. She wants families to perform an hour of reparation on those days. During it, she suggests reciting the Rosary and leading spiritual readings. She calls for fasting, offering everyday hardship and worries ("**If you are not ready to make sacrifices, you are not capable of serving the outpouring of my graces**"), and participating in Holy Mass as often as possible. Her Hungarian apparitions also bring a new prayer that is to open our hearts to receive the Flame

▼ *The Holy Mother emphasizes that it depends on us whether the Flame of the Immaculate Heart will soon embrace the whole world. So let us not hesitate to take the most important first step.*

of Love, which has engulfed the Immaculate Heart of Mary.

Mary says: "**You must make a great effort to blind Satan! I need you, individually as well as collectively. You must abandon all delay. Satan will be blinded to the extent of your participation**."

We hear further: "**We have a great responsibility. But your effort will not be in vain. If the whole world unites with Me, the soft light of my Flame of Love will then burn and set the globe aflame. Satan will be humiliated and made incapable of using his power any longer, provided this time** of preparation is not indefinitely prolonged! No, do not prolong it! Do not procrastinate in response to my holy requests!" She adds, "**Take the first step today. Will I finally see a sign of your goodwill? Believe me: only the first step is the hardest. You must do it, I am begging you**!"

In Elizabeth's journal we also hear the words of Mary's Son, Jesus. When it comes to participating in the message of the Mother of God, the Savior calls: "**Do more than you can! Go beyond your limits! Think of the three wise men who made a superhuman sacrifice. They certainly exceeded**

their natural limits." If we follow the example of the Magi, "**This Flame will kindle the fire throughout the earth and take over the world**."

WHAT IS THE FLAME OF LOVE?

The Hungarian priest Fr. Gabriel Róna, international coordinator of *La Flamme d'Amour du Coeur Immaculé de Marie* (The Flame of Love of the Immaculate Heart of Mary Movement), compared the Flame of Love to the light beam of a laser. "The Holy Mother says that it is a ray of light," he said. "We know in nature of a highly condensed beam of light that can be used to perform wonderful operations (I am referring to the laser beam). The Flame of Love is a beam of divine, supernatural light which is not of this world. ... With its help, the Mother of God wants to inflame our hearts and urges us to accept it and to pass it to others. And when the Flame of Love engulfs the whole world, it will burst with fire,

which Satan won't be able to bear. The Flame of Love of the Immaculate Heart of Mary will blind Satan. He will be unable to do the damage that leads souls to ruin."

Likewise, we read in Elizabeth's diary that she once asked Jesus and Mary what exactly is the Flame of Love. The Son and Mother gave short answers. Christ said: "The Flame of Love of My Mother is for you what the ark was for Noah." As humanity's refusal to obey God led to disaster, so too would our rejection of Mary's request lead to ruin. We also have to build a "shelter": surround ourselves with the Flame of Love of the Immaculate Heart. If this barrier wall of grace is missing, we will die.

As always, though, Mary is calling us to greater devotion to her Son. As she told Elizabeth, "The Flame of Love of My Immaculate Heart is Jesus Christ Himself!" This, indeed, is the experience of any form of true devotion to the Holy Mother. Whoever honors Mary honors Christ.

⋀ *For families performing the hour of reparation, the Holy Mother desires for it to be a time of offering God everyday hardships and worries.*

∨ *Praying the Rosary and frequent participation in Holy Mass—Mary does not ask for much, while she alone desires to offer us priceless graces.*

Zeitoun

1968

Giotto di Bondone, Flight into Egypt.

Silent Lady

It's hard to believe that in 1968 none of the big television stations mentioned the unusual events in Zeitoun. Yet this did not prevent the Holy Mother from changing the lives of hundreds of thousands of people, witnesses of the apparition, who carried her silent message to their homes and families.

Places where Mary lives radiate with light and attract people.

The Church of Our Lady of Zeitoun was built in 1924. If you believe the stories, it did not arise so much from the needs of the faithful but from the desire of Mary herself. A wealthy Copt (Egyptian Christian) named Khalil Pasha Ibrahim had a vision of the Holy Mother, who instructed him to build a shrine in her honor. Mary was also supposed to have made a promise that she would appear there fifty years later. Her promise has been fulfilled. It happened on April 2, 1968.

There is still another vision of the Mother of God tied to the apparition in Zeitoun, which was received by a woman who lived in Oslo, Norway. Mary purportedly appeared to her and announced that the apparition in the Marian shrine in Zeitoun happened exactly where she rested with Baby Jesus in the hardships of her journey through Egypt.

Yet these private revelations were only the beginning of a series of public apparitions that would leave their mark on the Church forever.

THE FIRST "STROLL"
The date was April 2, 1968—about half an hour after sunset. The streets were crowded with laborers emerging from a bus depot and returning home from work. They were the first witnesses of the apparition of the Mother of God. Several of them, lifting their heads, saw a woman dressed in white walking on the dome of the Church of Our Lady of Zeitoun. These simple people started screaming, "Watch out! You can fall! Don't move! Wait!" The dome was impossibly steep, and no mortal could walk across it without falling to his death. Those laborers didn't know that they were calling to the Queen of Heaven.

As they cried out, a crowd surrounded them, looking up. Some of the passersby

EGYPT

◄ During the apparitions in Zeitoun, Mary was dressed in a luminous dress.

started shouting, "That is the Holy Mother, the Holy Mother!"

Yes, it was her. She was wearing a white dress covering her feet.

Christians, mixed with Muslims, observed the luminous figure in suspense. Suddenly, the Mother of God bent down and knelt before the cross.

Traffic stopped. The crowds looked up. There was no mistake: everyone saw Mary. Later, when questioned by authorities, all the eyewitnesses interviewed described the same phenomenon down to the last detail.

This was the beginning of a heavenly spectacle, which continued for three years. The apparitions lasted from ten minutes to nine hours. The Holy Mother strolled on the domes and between them; she bowed at the gathered crowds, blessing them. Sometimes she folded her hands in prayer and knelt before the cross crowning the middle dome; the cross would emit a bright light.

Sometimes she appeared with an olive branch in her hand. Some nights she was joined by heavenly creatures, like

⋏ Two thousand years ago, the Mother of God stopped in the capital of Egypt, to rest after the hardships of the journey. In the twentieth century, she visited this place again.

doves circling the domes. Sometimes people observed streaks of red smoke rising up out of the Church during the apparition. Once in a while, the apparition was accompanied by flashes of lightning. Sometimes she covered everything with a luminous haze that smelled strongly of incense.

THE MEANING OF THE SIGNS

The apparitions in Zeitoun were full of silence. Not a single word was spoken that could provide us with the meaning of the message. The language of images is all that remains—which, in most apparitions, has a secondary meaning. But in Zeitoun, like in Knock, it has only one meaning. The question remains, *What?*

Mary of Zeitoun did not stand in place, as she did in Knock. She was constantly on the move there. She went on a spiritual pilgrimage, showing us, in short, the "milestones" of our journey to God. It is primarily love for people and blessing them, striving for their eternal well-being. It is prayer and love for the Cross. The Cross is the main signpost in Zeitoun. It calls us to forget about ourselves, to rid ourselves of selfishness, to sacrifice our time, and if necessary, our life, to praise Christ, who, on the Cross, humbling Himself to the point of a death, exalted us and redeemed us.

The road to heaven leads through the Cross and there is no other way, according to the saints. Christianity

The place where Mary revealed herself has belonged to the Coptic Church for centuries.

must be Christocentric, and Christians must imitate Christ's love—a love so great it is ready to die for "your friends," theologians will say. The very strolling of the Mother of God over the domes of the shrine shows us the place where God lives. The Church is a holy place. The supernatural is present there. It can be touched by faith in every shrine, even in the most modest chapel where there is the Blessed Sacrament, where the sacraments are celebrated, where the Savior's Cross hangs as well as the image of His Holy Mother. These places deserve respect and honor. The Church is not a concert hall, a meeting place, or a museum! God lives there.

And the doves? They are larger than earthly ones, flying at night. They proclaim peace that the world will share in if it goes along the paths shown by Mary. The same assurance is given to anyone who wants to enter the paths of Mary. They will experience peace.

This message is strengthened by the sight of the olive branch in Mary's hand—a symbol of blessings and peace.

And what do the stars mean, larger and brighter than those that hang in the sky, that descended upon the Church, sometimes resembling lanterns suspended in the air? If it were one star, we would have called for St. Ignatius of Antioch, that it is the revelation of the mystery of Christ, symbolized by a star brighter "than all the stars. Its light was indescribable, and its novelty caused amazement. The rest of the stars, along with the sun and the moon, formed a ring around it; yet it outshone them all." There are many of these stars in Zeitoun. They symbolize Christians, disciples of Christ, new saints—saints of the end times, about whom St. Louis de Montfort wrote: "Almighty God and His Holy Mother are

to raise up great saints who will surpass in holiness most other saints as much as the cedars of Lebanon tower above little shrubs." He continued, "The formation and the education of the great saints are reserved for her. For it is only that singular and miraculous Virgin who can produce, in union with the Holy Ghost, singular and extraordinary things."

Mary wants to be better known and loved, and through this knowledge and love, she will help to form multitudes of new saints. And, indeed, thousands of those who witnessed the apparitions

A *The apparitions in Zeitoun took place in total silence, and yet Mary's message is clear.*

1968

The Cross is the main signpost in Zeitoun. There is no other way to Heaven than the one leading through the Cross.

at Zeitoun converted to Christianity and became devoted to the Holy Mother.

The silent message from Zeitoun has much to say.

MEDIA OPPOSITION

This apparition probably has the most witnesses in history and can be seen in photos and videos that captured these supernatural events. Hundreds of professional photojournalists and television camera crews broadcast the images of Mary. President Gamal Abdel Nasser himself was a witness of the apparitions. He could not explain the phenomenon he was watching, and so refrained from making any comments.

World television stations followed Nasser's lead. They ignored the facts. They were not interested in the message from Zeitoun. It's puzzling: why didn't the media at least use the apparitions as a way to increase their viewership? It makes for a sensational report.

SEARCH FOR PROJECTOR

Just as with Knock a hundred years prior, it was claimed that the apparitions at Zeitoun were the result of casting beams of light to the top of the church. The police searched the area in a twelve-mile radius. No projector was found that could show images on the domes of the Coptic shrine. Additionally, the city shut off

electric power to that section as a test, but the Mother of God still appeared, bathed in light.

The state police did not believe in miracles, seeing as Nasser was an avowed socialist. Yet their unsuccessful search for a "technically advanced device" is an additional argument for the Christian case. They searched high and low for a natural cause to explain away the appearance of Our Lady—and found none.

Meanwhile, the witnesses believed. Even Muslims looked at the Mother of God in delight. They sang her verses from the Koran: "O Mary! Allah hath chosen thee and purified thee—chosen thee above the women of all nations."

The Coptic patriarch, Kyrillos VI, appointed a special committee, which stated that there is no doubt that on the roof of the Church of the Mother of God in Zeitoun, the Most Holy Virgin Mary appeared. The patriarch himself felt the same way.

ZEITOUN, SECOND EDITION

The apparitions in Cairo have their own sequel. In 1986, Mary, bathed in light, was seen on the roof of St. Demiana Church in Shoubra, a small town near Cairo. Thousands of Egyptians watched her again. These apparitions, lasting up to five hours, were seen for several years.

The commission appointed by the patriarch announced in 1987:

⋏ *Christianity must be Christocentric, and Christians must imitate Christ's love.*

Let us thank the Lord for this blessing on the people of Egypt and for the repetition of this phenomenon. We should also thank the police and the Department of the Interior for their untiring efforts at maintaining safety and good order among the thousands of people who have spent day and night in prayer. We ask all the people to remain calm. In this way, they may prove to be more worthy of receiving blessing from the Most Holy Virgin Mary.

May God bless our nation. We pray that He may guide Egypt and all His children to every success. May this phenomenon be a pledge of well-being for them and for all nations.

Additional proof of the truth of the apparitions in Zeitoun are the miracles and healings taking place to this day. After visiting the church, the place of the apparitions, many sick people experience a miraculous recovery—from blindness, paralysis, cancer, diseases of every sort and severity. A special commission examining individual cases of sudden healings stated that "there is no medical explanation for these cures." Even though Our Lady left no verbal message for the pilgrims, she continues to preach loudly through the wonders that are worked at Zeitoun.

◄ Millions of people of different faiths and nationalities saw the apparitions in Zeitoun. The phenomenon was repeatedly photographed and filmed. Numerous conversions and healings that were received in this place have been validated.

◄ According to tradition, the Church of St. Mark arose in the place of rest by the Holy Family during their flight into Egypt.

▼ St. Joseph was not only Mary's guardian and protector but also her first devotee.

Fatima

1972

> Mary, speaking to Don Gobbi, made him her instrument.

The Apocalyptic
Heart of Mary

⚑ *"Only the powerful force of prayer and reparative penance will be able to save the world from what the justice of God has prepared."*

For twenty-five years, Fr. Stefano Gobbi listened to the Mother of God's message. Her voice inspired him and gave him strength to start an important community. The Marian Movement of Priests gathers clergy and laypeople from all over the world; crowds of people who, like him, love the Immaculate Heart of Mary in a special way.

One simple man could change the face of the Church. How powerful must his testimony have been for one hundred thousand priests, hundreds of cardinals and bishops, and tens of millions of laypeople to follow him to God? These numbers are like the biblical "fruits" by which we recognize if they are from a good or corrupt tree. His supernatural experiences are best described as "interior locutions" rather than apparitions. Though controversial at first, it gained the blessing of Pope St. John Paul II in 1993. By repeatedly "hearing" her heavenly voice, Don Stefano knew that "the future of the world is in the Holy Mother's hands." Once again we have a common thread: Immaculate Mary, Immaculate Heart …

Fr. Gobbi's locutions started in Fatima and later occurred in Akita, Heede, Knock, Guadalupe, and his hometown of Milan. Almost all historically important apparition sites are found on the visionary's list of encounters with the Holy Mother.

Through Fr. Gobbi, Mary also explained why so many contemporary apparitions are occurring. Heaven is trying to intervene as often as possible because the time of the greatest threat to man has come: "the time of Satan's reign."

ORDINARY, ONE OF A THOUSAND

Fr. Gobbi was born in 1930 and obtained his doctorate in theology at the Pontifical Lateran University in Rome. His life was the typical life of a faithful priest, known and valued by the people closest to him, but anonymous in wider circles of the Church and the world.

A MEETING IN FATIMA

On May 8, 1972, Don Stefano Gobbi traveled to Fatima, where he prayed reverently to the Holy Mother, kneeling in the exact same place where, fifty-five years earlier, Mary had appeared to the shepherd children. He said a special prayer for a couple of priests in his acquaintance who had abandoned active ministry and started an organization to lobby against certain Church teachings and disciplines. These wayward clerics were especially committed to the abolition of clerical celibacy.

At just that moment, Fr. Gobbi received an internal locution from the Virgin Mary. She announced: "**You are to follow the path that the bishop shows you**." She spoke of obedience and fidelity to the Church and entrusted him with an important task: to organize his fellow priests in opposition to this new sect of rebellious clerics. These obedient priests were to consecrate themselves to the Immaculate Heart of Mary.

As Mary explained later, the Church is in great danger of a schism—the largest since the Arian crisis, when all but a handful of the faithful persevered while the rest of Christendom abandoned its faith in Christ's divinity.

Don Stefano was not gullible; he had no inner conviction that what he heard was really a voice from Heaven. So he asked for an unequivocal sign.

Fr. Gobbi soon received an indisputable sign that showed him God's will. But the sign alone was not enough. A second level of verification was needed: the approbation of the Church. Don Stefano confessed everything to his spiritual director and, after reflection and prayer, was told to accept Mary's commission. From then on, Fr. Gobbi started working on organizing the Marian Movement of Priests. He chose October 13 as the formal start date of his work, the day of the "Miracle of the Sun."

On this day, the Italian priest became the Mother of God's instrument, and his twenty-five-year period of locutions began, creating a type of guide for the final decades of the twentieth century and the first part of the new millennium.

Don Gobbi began writing down the messages he received. Then he collected them into a book titled *Our Lady Speaks to Her Beloved Priests*. A later version, which also included new messages, was titled *To the Priests, Our Lady's Beloved Sons*.

This remarkable book has been translated into more than twenty languages and was the main tool used to form the Marian Movement of Priests. It has received the *imprimatur* from three cardinals (Bernardino Echeverría Ruiz of Guayaquil, Ecuador; Ignatius Moussa Daoud of Antioch, Turkey; and John Baptist Wu of Hong Kong), as well as numerous bishops and archbishops.

Fatima

PORTUGAL

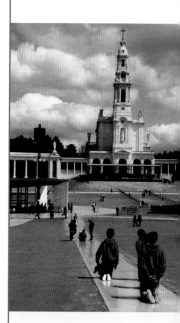

⋀ *"**In my Immaculate Heart you will be consoled**"—these words addressed to Lúcia, Mary repeats to Fr. Gobbi.*

STRENGTHENING THE FATIMA MESSAGE

Our Lady told Fr. Gobbi about her battle against Satan, which would take place during the Apocalypse:

I have come from heaven to reveal to you my plan in this struggle which involves everyone, marshaled together at the orders of two opposing commanders: the Woman clothed in the sun and the Red Dragon. I have shown you the road you must take: that of prayer and penance. I have called you to the interior conversion of your life. I have also prepared a refuge for you that you may be brought together, protected and strengthened during the present tempest which will become even more violent. The refuge is my Immaculate Heart.

On May 13, 1981, Mary said:

The light of my Immaculate Heart now embraces all areas of the world, and my plan for the salvation and the comfort of all stands out with ever increasing clarity. For this I appeared at Fatima to three little children. I have come down from heaven to join you in your journey. Be aware then of the presence of your heavenly Mother at your side. It is a silent and serene presence. She wants to bring strength to your weariness; she sustains you in your work; she defends you from many dangers and leads you each day to carry out well whatever the Father has disposed for you, that the

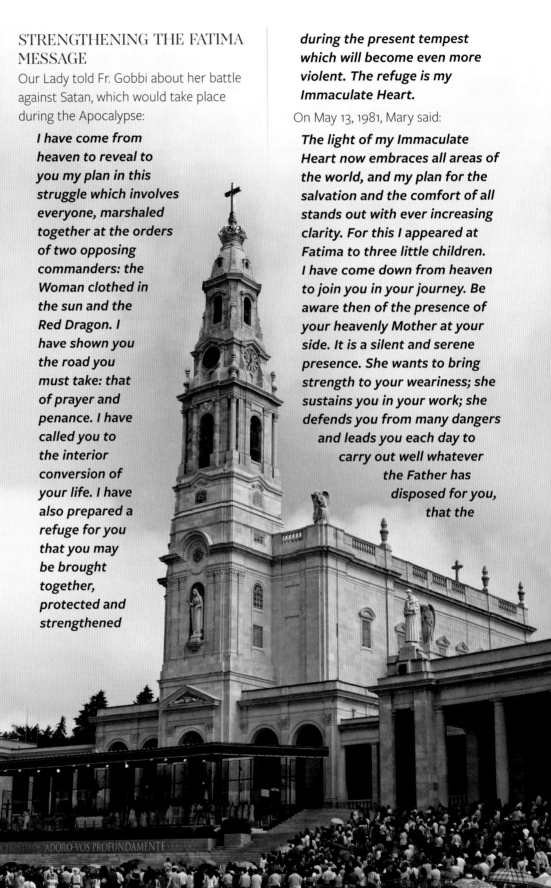

Most Holy Trinity may today be better glorified…. I have come down from Heaven to live once again in you and to love with your heart, to sustain with your labor, to save through your sufferings many of my children who have gone astray and, never before as today, have such need of firm assistance.

ANNOUNCEMENTS OF THE END

It is difficult to summarize the messages delivered by Mary for a quarter of a century. But we know their main motive: it is the "end times," in which a "great schism in the Church" will appear. This time the Holy Mother talks about something more than the punishment of mankind for their sins, even more than about apocalyptic experiences that will consume the whole world. She now says that the "end" is coming.

Over the years, Fr. Gobbi emphasized that "today we are living in the end times shown in the signs." He warned, "Many times in history, this end has been misunderstood by people. But today all the signs of the times are present simultaneously. It is as it was announced in the Holy Bible."

On December 31, 1992, the Holy Mother explained to Fr. Gobbi: "**I have wanted to teach you about these signs, which Jesus has pointed out to you in His Gospel, in order to prepare you for the end of the times, because these are about to take place in your days**." Then she laid out what lies ahead:

I have announced to you many times that the end times and the coming of Jesus in glory is very near. Now, I want to help you understand the signs described in the Holy Scriptures, which indicate that His glorious return is now close.

These signs are clearly indicated in the Gospels, in the letters of St. Peter and St. Paul, and they are becoming a reality during these years.

The first sign is the spread of errors, which lead to the loss of faith and to apostasy.

These errors are being propagated by false teachers, by renowned theologians who are no longer teaching the truths of the Gospel, but pernicious heresies based on errors and on human reasonings. It is because of the teaching of these errors that the true Faith is being lost and that the great apostasy is spreading everywhere.

See that no one deceives you. For many will attempt to deceive many people. False prophets will come and will deceive very many […].

The second sign is the outbreak of wars and fratricidal struggles, which lead to the prevalence of violence and hatred and general slackening off of charity, while natural catastrophes, such as epidemics, famines, floods and earthquakes, become more and more frequent. …

The third sign is the bloody persecution of those who remain faithful to Jesus and to His Gospel and who stand fast in the true Faith. Throughout this all, the Gospel will be preached in every part of the world.

⋀ *Mary announces the battle between herself and the Dragon, described in the Apocalypse.*

Think, beloved children, of the great persecutions to which the Church is being subjected; think of the apostolic zeal of the recent popes, above all of my Pope, John Paul II, as he brings to all the nations of the Earth the announcement of the Gospel. ...

The fourth sign is the horrible sacrilege, perpetrated by him who sets himself against Christ, that is, the Antichrist. He will enter into the holy temple of God and will sit on his throne and have himself adored as God. ...

By accepting the protestant doctrine, people will hold that the Mass is not a sacrifice but only a sacred meal, that is to say, a remembrance of that which Jesus did at His Last Supper. And thus, the celebration of Holy Mass will be suppressed. In this abolition of the daily sacrifice consists the horrible sacrilege accomplished by the Antichrist. ...

The fifth sign consists in extraordinary phenomena, which occur in the skies. ...

The miracle of the sun, which took place at Fatima during my

➤ *The most important response to the prophetic interventions of Mary is entrusting oneself to her Immaculate Heart.*

last apparition, is intended to point out to you that you are now entering into the times when these events will take place—events which will prepare for the return of Jesus in glory. ...

Apostasy is spreading, the wars are multiplying, natural catastrophes are occurring in many places, persecutions are intensifying, the announcement of the Gospel is being brought to all nations, extraordinary phenomena are occurring in the sky, and the moment of the full manifestation of the Antichrist is drawing ever nearer.

Read, with me, the signs of your time, and live in peace of heart and in confidence.

SAFE IN THE IMMACULATE HEART

However, this is not the essence of the locution. The most important response to the prophetic interventions of Mary is to entrust oneself to her Immaculate Heart. "**In these times, you all need to hasten to take shelter in the refuge of my Immaculate Heart, because grave threats of evil are hanging over you. In my Immaculate Heart you will be consoled! For this reason, I say again to each one of you today that which I said at Fatima to my daughter, Sister Lucia: 'My Immaculate Heart will be your refuge and the sure way which will lead you to God.'**"

Mary proposes consecration to her Immaculate Heart. Here is the act of consecration propagated by Fr. Gobbi. It is a summary of the messages he received from Heaven.

> *Virgin of Fatima,*
> *Mother of Mercy,*
> *Queen of Heaven and Earth,*
> *Refuge of Sinners,*
> *we who belong to the*
> *Marian Movement*
> *consecrate ourselves in*
> *a very special way*
> *to your Immaculate Heart.*
>
> *By this act of consecration*
> *we intend to live,*
> *with you and through you,*
> *all the obligations assumed by*
> *our baptismal consecration.*
> *We further pledge to bring*
> *about in ourselves*

⋏ *Mary reminds us of the conditionality of punishment—it can be avoided through prayer, penance, and reparation for sins.*

Mary told Fr. Gobbi that there are many interventions from heaven because "the time of satan's reign" has come.

*that interior conversion
so urgently demanded
by the Gospel,
a conversion that will free us of
every attachment to ourselves
and to easy compromises with
the world so that, like you,
we may be available only to do
always the will of the Father.*

*And as we resolve to
entrust to you,
O Mother most sweet
and merciful,
our life and vocation
as Christians,
that you may dispose
of it according to your
designs of salvation
in this hour of decision that
weighs upon the world,
we pledge to live it according
to your desires,
especially as it pertains
to a renewed spirit
of prayer and penance,
the fervent participation in the
celebration of the Eucharist
and in the works of
the apostolate,
the daily recitation of
the Holy Rosary,
and an austere manner of life
in keeping with the Gospel,
that shall be to all a good
example of the observance
of the law of God
and the practice of the
Christian virtues,
especially that of purity.*

*We further promise you to be
united with the Holy Father,
with the hierarchy and
with our priests,
in order thus to set up a barrier*

*to the growing confrontation
directed against the Magisterium,
that threatens the very
foundation of the Church.*

*Under your protection,
we want moreover to be
apostles of this sorely
needed unity of prayer
and love for the Pope,
on whom we invoke your
special protection.*

*And lastly, insofar as is possible,
we promise to lead those souls
with whom we come in contact
to a renewed devotion to you.
Mindful that atheism has
caused shipwreck in the faith
to a great number of the faithful,*

that desecration has entered into the holy temple of God, and that evil and sin are spreading more and more throughout the world, we make so bold as to lift our eyes trustingly to you, O Mother of Jesus and our merciful and powerful Mother, and we invoke again today and await from you the salvation of all your children, O clement, O loving, O sweet Virgin Mary.

CONDITIONALITY

This is not a depressing message about an impending catastrophe. The Holy Mother reminds us that her Immaculate Heart will ultimately prevail. She also reminds us that everything is conditional, that punishment may be remitted. The key to avoiding punishment is conversion—getting off the road to perdition. God's justice also requires penance and reparation for sins. This is the primary task of the members of the Marian Movement of Priests: "Thanks to your prayers, but most of all to the Holy Mass, you priests can balance the scale of God's justice." But Fr. Gobbi explains that Mary wants something more; the Movement itself is not enough. "**Only the powerful force of prayer and reparative penance will be able to save the world from what the justice of God has prepared**."

ᕀ *Rescue and salvation will come through Mary.*

A The interior of
the Shrine of Our
Lady of Fatima in
Zakopane, Poland.

➤ A Holy Mass
celebrated in the
Fatima sanctuary.

A MISSION FULFILLED

Fr. Gobbi died in Milan June 29,
2011—the Feast of Sts. Peter and Paul.

On January 1 of that year, which
happened to be the first Saturday of
the month, the founder of the Marian
Movement of Priests wrote his spiritual
testament: "I accept death whenever and
wherever the Lord desires, renewing in
the Immaculate Heart of Mary my 'Yes'
to the Divine will. ... As I have consecrated
every moment of my life, in the same
way I consecrate to the Immaculate
Heart of Mary the moment of my passing
from Earth to Heaven and from time to
eternity."

Fr. Gobbi also quoted a fragment from
the homily that he delivered at the end of
October 2010 in Fatima. He wrote: "This
year an extraordinary event occurred. On
May 12, here in this Cova da Iria, before
you, Mary, the Holy Father Benedict XVI
consecrated all of the priests of the world
to your Immaculate Heart. Therefore with
this consecration, it seems as if my task
might be finished and that my journey
would have come to an end."

Akita

1973

Apocalyptic
Madonna

When the supernatural entered Sr. Agnes's life, she had doubts. However, when she saw the eucharistic light a second time, she knew it was not an illusion. Indeed, this was just the beginning of the extraordinary phenomena that were to take place near Akita, Japan, in a small convent chosen by the Mother of God.

▲ *The eucharistic light that Sr. Agnes saw was a sign that Jesus is truly present in the tabernacle.*

➤ *A wooden figure of the Mother of God became a source of numerous supernatural phenomena.*

Katsuko Sasagawa was born in May 1931. Born sickly, her parents and older siblings doted on her. During surgery to remove her appendix, nineteen-year-old "Kako-chan" became paralyzed from poorly administered anesthesia. After spending the next ten years in various hospitals, she recovered, thanks to the care of a religious sister.

Her encounter with this nun inspired her to investigate Christianity. At the age of thirty-three, Katsuko was baptized. Shortly thereafter, she decided to become a nun herself, taking the name Agnes.

On May 12, 1973, Sr. Agnes took up residence in a small convent of the Handmaids of the Eucharist, located on the outskirts of Akita. Five months before she entered the convent, she had noticed that her hearing was growing steadily worse. Then, all at once, she became completely deaf. From that moment on, she lived in a deep silence, learning to read the lips of her fellow sisters.

THE SECOND FIGURE OF AKITA: JESUS AND THE EUCHARISTIC LIGHT

On June 12, 1973, Sr. Agnes entered an empty chapel. Because the convent didn't have a chaplain, the sisters had received permission from the bishop to open the tabernacle for Eucharistic Adoration. When Agnes opened the door, the chapel was flooded with a bright light coming from inside the tabernacle.

Agnes fell facedown on the ground and started praying. Over and over again, she repeated the prayer the sisters said while adoring Jesus in the Blessed Sacrament: "Most Sacred Heart of Jesus, truly present in the Holy Eucharist ..."

After an hour, when she finally got up and left the chapel, she began to doubt the supernatural nature of her experience. But the next day, the same phenomenon occurred again. This time, it gave Sr. Agnes a feeling of deep peace in her heart. The

light was not an illusion. This was a sign that Jesus was truly present in the tabernacle.

The next day brought a similar encounter, except that the extraordinary light was surrounded by a red flame. This inspired in her a great love for the Holy Eucharist. In her simplicity, she suspected that the other sisters had the same visions and just didn't talk about them. But when she tried to learn more from them, she found that no one else had experienced such remarkable things.

Agnes saw the light of the Eucharist once more — on the eve of the feast of the Most Sacred Heart of Jesus. This time, as she put it, she saw "an adoring crowd of spiritual beings" who worshipped the Eucharistic Lord.

A MYSTERIOUS WOUND

On Thursday, June 28, Sr. Agnes felt an excruciating pain in her left hand. Amazed, she saw two red lines intersecting to form a small cross. On Friday, the mysterious pain became unbearable, but on Sunday, it was gone, along with the wound. The following Thursday, the wound reappeared, and Agnes began to notice a certain pattern: the pain increased on Thursday, peaked on Friday, stopped on Sunday, and then disappeared until the following Thursday.

On the night of July 6, the pain was so severe that Agnes couldn't sleep. At three o'clock in the morning, a voice came out of nowhere, saying: "Be not afraid. Pray with fervor not only because of your sins, but in reparation for those of all people. The world today wounds the Most Sacred Heart of our Lord by its ingratitude and injuries. The wounds of Mary are much deeper and more sorrowful than yours. Let us go to pray together in the chapel."

Then, Agnes saw a beautiful figure standing beside her. She thought it was her older sister, Tomi, who had died many years ago. But the figure shook its head. "I am the one who is always with you and protects you." It was her guardian angel.

The angel disappeared in the chapel. Agnes walked over to a wooden statue of the Mother of God, which was the work of a Buddhist sculptor. Suddenly, the figure flared up with the same light that had burst from the tabernacle. The statue of Mary seemed to come to life. The sister fell to the ground and heard these words:

On April 22, 1984, Bishop John Shojiro Ito announced that the apparitions in Akita have a supernatural character.

My daughter, my novice, you have obeyed me well in abandoning all to follow me. Is the infirmity of your ears painful? Your deafness will be healed, be sure. Be patient, this is the last trial. Does the wound on your hand cause you to suffer? Pray in reparation for the sins of humanity. Each person in this community is my irreplaceable daughter. ... Pray very much for the pope, bishops, and priests. Since your baptism you have always prayed faithfully for them. Continue to pray very much, very much. Tell your superior [the bishop] all that passed today and obey him in everything that he will tell you. He has asked that you pray with fervor.

When Sr. Agnes asked the novice master to look at the Mother of God's hands on the statue, it turned out that from Mary's right hand blood flowed from two intersecting lines. Just as in Sr. Agnes's case, the bleeding increased on the days of the Lord's Passion.

Soon, Sr. Agnes told the bishop what "the voice full of indescribable beauty" had conveyed to her. Bishop John Shojiro Ito told her briefly, "Be careful not to think 'This phenomenon is intended especially for me. I am someone exceptional.' Seek humility."

On Thursday, July 26, the pain in Sr. Agnes's hand was unbearable, while the statue was bleeding as well. The bishop recommended consulting a doctor.

It was a sleepless night. Before dawn, Agnes went to the chapel. She heard the angel's voice again:

Your suffering will end today. Carefully engrave in the depths of your heart the thought of the blood of Mary. The blood shed by Mary has a profound meaning. This precious blood was shed to plead for your conversion, to ask for peace, in reparation for the ingratitude and outrages against the Lord. As with the devotion to the Sacred Heart, apply yourself to devotion to the Most Precious Blood. Pray in reparation for all people. Say to your superior that the blood is shed today for the last time. Your pain also ends today. Tell them what happened today. He will understand everything immediately. Follow his directions.

The angel's voice faded, and the suffering stopped. Sr. Agnes moved her hand and didn't feel pain. A quick look convinced her the angel's announcement was fulfilled: the wound had disappeared without a trace. The statue also stopped bleeding, but the wound on Mary's hand remained visible.

⋏ *"**Each day recite the prayers of the Rosary**," Mary requested. "**With the Rosary, pray for the pope, the bishops, and priests**."*

A "Many people in this world afflict the Lord. I desire souls to console Him."

AN APOCALYPSE HALTED

Shortly thereafter, on August 3, the first Friday of the month, the apparitions of the Mother of God began. Agnes was praying the Rosary and saw the angel beside her again. This time it was not he who spoke to her, but the statue of the Mother of God. Mary said: "**My daughter, my novice, do you love the Lord? If you love the Lord, listen to what I have to say to you. Convey this to your superior**."

Mary continued:

Many people in this world afflict the Lord. I desire souls to console Him to soften the anger of the Heavenly Father. I wish, with my Son, for souls who will make reparation for sinners and ingrates. Let them offer their suffering and poverty for these people.

In order that the world might know how terrible the wrath of the Heavenly Father is against the modern world, God is preparing to inflict a great chastisement on all humanity. Together with My Son, I have intervened so many times to appease the wrath of the Father. I have prevented the coming of calamities by offering the Father the sufferings of the Son on the Cross, His Precious Blood, and beloved souls who console Him—countless sacrificial souls filled with love. Prayer, penance, and courageous sacrifices can soften the Father's anger. I desire this also from your community: that it love poverty, that it sanctify itself and pray in reparation for the ingratitude

and outrages perpetrated by so many people against the Lord.

Recite the prayer of the Handmaids of the Eucharist with awareness of its meaning and put it into practice. Offer in reparation for sins whatever God may send. Let each one endeavor according to capacity and position, to offer herself entirely to the Lord.

Even in a secular institute prayer is necessary. Already souls who wish to pray are on the way to unity. Without attaching too much attention to the form, be faithful and fervent in prayer to console the Master.

Is what you think in your heart true? Are you truly decided to become the rejected stone? My novice, you who wish to belong without reserve to the Lord, to become the spouse worthy of the Spouse, make your vows knowing that you must be fastened to the Cross with three nails. These three nails are poverty, chastity, and obedience. Of these three, obedience is the foundation. Show complete obedience to your superior. He will know how to understand you and to direct you.

A NEW WITNESS

September 29, the feast of the Archangels, had come. When the visionary prayed the Rosary with one of the sisters in the chapel and looked at the statue of the Mother of God, it gleamed with the same light that shone from the Eucharist. Agnes tugged at her companion's sleeve; soon, both sisters saw Mary's hands were shining with a particularly intense glow. Then, the wounds on the statue's hand disappeared forever.

In the evening, Agnes once again had the vision of the angel. "Mary is even sadder than when she shed blood. Dry her sweat." Drops as clear as water dripped from the statue that was soaked in light. Not knowing what to do, the sisters grabbed a packet of cotton pads and began to wipe away the sweat that flowed from the statue.

Later, the sisters recalled feeling an overwhelming sadness as they wiped the sweat, which smelled of flowers. This scent stayed with the sisters for seventeen days.

THE ANNOUNCEMENT OF A TERRIBLE PUNISHMENT

October 13 fell on a Saturday. The visionary did not know that it was the fifty-sixth anniversary of the last apparition in Fatima. During morning prayer, she saw a supernatural light gush out of the tabernacle. At the same time, the statue of the Blessed Virgin gave off a sweet fragrance that filled the chapel. When Sr. Agnes began to pray the Rosary, she heard these words:

My beloved daughter, listen well to what I have to say to you. You will inform your superior. As I told you, if people do not repent and better themselves, the Father will inflict a terrible punishment on all humanity. It will be a punishment greater than the deluge, such as one will never have seen before. Fire will fall from the sky and will wipe out a great part of humanity, the good as well as the bad, sparing neither priests nor the faithful. The survivors will find themselves so desolate that they will envy the dead. The only weapon you will have left is the Rosary and the sign left by my Son. Each day recite the prayers of the Rosary. With the Rosary, pray for the pope, the bishops, and priests.

The work of the devil will infiltrate even the Church in such a way that one will see cardinals opposing cardinals, bishops against other bishops.

⅄ *Sr. Agnes's conversations with Mary were invoked by reciting the Rosary.*

The mosiac of the Japanese Madonna in the Church of the Annunciation in Nazareth.

The statue of the Mother of God in the convent in Akita cried 101 times over six years.

The priests who venerate me will be scorned and opposed by their brothers; churches and altars will be plundered; the Church will be full of those who accept compromises, and the demon will press many priests and consecrated souls to leave the service of the Lord.

The demon will be especially implacable against souls consecrated to God. The thought of the loss of so many souls is the cause of my sadness. If sins increase in number and gravity, there will be no longer pardon for them.

With courage, speak to your superior. He will know how to encourage each one of you to pray and to accomplish works of reparation.

Today is the last time I will speak to you in a living voice. From now on you will obey the one sent to you and your superior. Pray very much the prayers of the Rosary. I alone am able still to save you from the impending calamities. Those who place their confidence in me will be saved.

The statue was full of sorrow, but it quickly returned to its inanimate state.

Sr. Agnes told the bishop everything. She asked him what "cardinals" meant because she did not know this word. For Bishop Ito, this was one of the most important indications that the apparitions in Akita were not the sister's invention.

In mid-October, the sisters smelled the scent of flowers in the chapel for the last time. The next day, another

smell appeared: the smell of rotting flesh. Despite the unbearable stench, the sisters started to pray the Rosary. Then, the entire chapel floor was filled with maggots. They disappeared the next day, but the stench remained for the next three days.

On October 13, 1974, the visionary regained her hearing, but—as the angel had foretold—the healing was temporary. On March 6, 1975, silence took hold of Agnes again.

TEARS OF THE MOTHER OF GOD

On January 4, 1975, another inexplicable thing happened: the statue began to weep. The wood of the statue of the Holy Mother was dried out, and in several places woodworm holes were visible. But tears were pooling in the corners of the eyes and running down the cheeks. Witnesses agreed that the statue was weeping like a living person.

On that day, Mary cried twice, and, for the next six and a half years, a total of 101 times. The last time this phenomenon was observed was on the feast of Our Lady of Sorrows, September 15, 1981.

In 1975, at the end of the New Year's retreat, Sr. Agnes saw her guardian angel once more, who came to give her the last words of the message:

Do not be surprised to see the Mother of God weeping. She weeps because she desires the conversion of as many people as possible. She wants souls to consecrate themselves to Jesus and the Father through her intercession. The retreat-giver said in today's sermon: "Your faith fades when you do not see. This

is because your faith is weak." The Blessed Virgin Mary is happy about the consecration of Japan to her Immaculate Heart because she loves Japan. She is sad, however, that this consecration is not treated seriously. Although she chose Akita to deliver her message, the local pastor is not afraid of what might be said about him. Do not be afraid. The Holy Mother is waiting for all of you.

THE ROAD TO RECOGNIZING THE APPARITIONS

In the months that followed, the tears, sweat, and blood that appeared on the statue were examined. To ensure objectivity, a non-Christian specialist was asked for his opinion. His expertise would verify the results of research carried out at a Catholic university. The opinion of Dr. Kaoru Sagisaka, who didn't know where the samples came from, was astonishing: "The material present on the gauze is human blood. The sweat and tears absorbed by the cotton pads are of human origin." The blood was type B; the tears were type AB.

In 1975, Bishop Ito began a formal examination of the apparitions. He appointed a famous Mariologist from Tokyo, Fr. Garcia Evangelista, to chair the commission. In May of the following year, the theologian announced the research results. Unfortunately, they

▼ *By listening to the message of Akita, one can better understand the appeal from Fatima.*

were negative. Because the fluids belonged to different types (B and AB), the Tokyo expert believed that the visions of Sr. Agnes had nothing to do with the supernatural and were the result of a type of "ectoplasmic powers" of the visionary. Through these powers, she was able to transfer her own blood, sweat, and tears onto the statue. Fr. Evangelista concluded that Agnes was "a special psychopathic case" and that her visions were "the fruit of detachment from reality and a dual personality." Fr. Evangelista didn't explain why the statue often bled and wept when Sr. Agnes was far away from Akita.

The bishop instructed the sisters to accept humbly the commission's verdict.

A few months later, while in Rome, he was granted the right to appoint a new commission. It turned out that the local ordinary had the deciding vote in such cases, and Bishop Ito wasn't a member of the first commission.

Another examination of the blood and tears was conducted by Dr. Sagisaka of the Department of Forensic Medicine, School of Medicine at the University of Akita. The results were given on November 30, 1981, and revealed that "the object examined has adhering to it human liquids which belong to the blood group O."

Three days later, the statue cried for the last time.

At the same time, the first miraculous healing took place through the intercession of Our Lady of Akita. A forty-three-year-old woman, Teresa Chun, was cured of brain cancer. Her older sister placed an image of the miraculous statue under the sick woman's pillow and started praying for healing through the intercession of Mary. On August 4, 1981, Teresa Chun woke up healthy. The cancer had disappeared without a trace.

On May 1, 1982, Sister Agnes regained her hearing. Perhaps the most important date was April 22, 1984, when Bishop Ito announced that the Akita apparitions have a supernatural character. In his pastoral letter he stated, among other things, that "this message is identical to what the Mother of God delivered in Fatima."

Betania

1976

Betania was to become the Latin American Lourdes—a place of prayer, reconciliation with God, and healing.

Mother of Peace and Unity

Esperanza was only fourteen years old when the Mother of God told her about a place she chose for her. More than a quarter of a century passed, however, before the visionary and her family managed to find it. A piece of land with an old house, a waterfall, and a grotto—a place where Mary was waiting for her, a place of apparitions, healings, and miracles, a place where the sun danced again.

The beatification process of Maria Esperanza de Bianchini began on January 31, 2010.

Padre Pio said about her, "When I leave, she will be your consolation." These prophetic words spoke of the then twenty-six-year-old Maria Esperanza de Bianchini, a woman Heaven has been preparing for an extraordinary mission since childhood. What kind of mission? God told those who asked this question to wait a long time. The answer came after thirty years.

Maria Esperanza was born in 1928 in Monagas, Venezuela. From early childhood, she exhibited an exceptional spiritual sensitivity. She was able to focus so deeply on prayer that people were overwhelmed by fear. She had her first supernatural vision when she was five years old. As her mother departed by ship on a journey, she cried inconsolably. Esperanza saw a smiling woman with a beautiful rose in her hands next to the ship sailing on the river. The woman, St. Thérèse of Lisieux, threw the flower toward the crying child. At the age of twelve and suffering from severe pneumonia, Esperanza saw the Blessed Mother, who assured her she would not die because God had special intentions for her. Mary indicated what medicine would heal the little girl. It was purchased, and Esperanza indeed recovered.

SEARCHING FOR THE PLACE OF THE APPARITIONS

In her youth, Esperanza had at least a dozen similarly amazing meetings with Mary. Naturally, she considered becoming a nun, but God revealed that she was called to become a wife and mother. So, Esperanza headed to Rome, where she prayed in as many churches as she could. In front of one of them, she met her future husband, Geo Bianchini. The young couple

Betania

VENEZUELA

was married on the Solemnity of the Immaculate Conception in 1955. After returning to Venezuela, they settled in Caracas and had six children.

Years went by, but Esperanza still remembered the unusual vision she had at age fourteen. The Holy Mother had assured her that one day she would own a piece of land with an old house, a waterfall, and a grotto. It was to be the place of future Marian apparitions. Esperanza and Geo spent twenty-seven years looking for this place. It turned out that it was located two hours away from Caracas. The Bianchinis, together with two other couples, purchased this piece of land and soon started visiting on weekends. It irresistibly attracted

them: it was overflowing with peace and an atmosphere of prayer.

FIRST APPARITION

In February 1976, Esperanza felt that the Mother of God was calling her to "Finca Betania" ("property of Betania"). The woman was certain she would see Mary on March 25, on the Feast of the Annunciation, and she was right. "I was at the grotto when I suddenly saw a big, beautiful white cloud," the visionary recalled. "My friend said to me, 'Maria, the farm is on fire! It's burning like a candle!' And I said: 'Yes, I know. I can see the fire. But it comes from Mary.' When the Holy Mother appeared, she rose to the top of the tree. She was beautiful: she had auburn hair, light brown eyes, small lips, a straight nose. Her skin was like silk. She was tan, beautiful, very young. Her hair was about shoulder length.

"Mary was a ray of light that penetrated my soul, shaking every fiber of my heart," Maria recalled. "On the inside I felt so humble, so weak and haggard. I was nothing compared to the beauty that blinded me."

Then Esperanza heard an inner voice:

> *My daughter, tell my children of all races, of all nations, of all religions that I love them. For me, their differences do not matter—all my children are the same. There are no rich and poor, ugly and beautiful, black and white. I come to gather them all, to help them climb the tall Mount Zion, ... that they may achieve salvation.*

Mary also explains that her open arms and the radiance she exudes call all people to conversion.

IN THE SPIRIT OF FATIMA AND LOURDES

The second apparition took place August 22, on the day of the Queenship of Mary. Mary assured the visionary that if people take on their daily crosses, there will be no more suffering, tears, and death. "**Each day, everyone will sing together with my beloved Son a constant Hallelujah! Hallelujah! Hallelujah**!"

On February 11, 1978—in memory of Our Lady of Lourdes—the Holy Mother wanted to gather together with the residents of Betania. They were mainly workers living in poverty, neglected by the government, deprived of the protection of the Church. The Mother of God wanted them to accept the Sacraments of Baptism, Confirmation, Eucharist, and Marriage on that day. This required two things of Maria Esperanza. First, she had to prepare these people for the meeting with God. Second, she had to ask the bishop to come to the farm. Geo, who had been involved with Catholic Action in Italy, proved to be well prepared for the task. He created a small team of catechists and for two weeks traveled through villages and banana plantations to prepare people to receive the Sacraments.

But what to say to the bishop? Esperanza was afraid of calling the chancery. Then, three days before February 11, their phone rang. The astonished visionary heard the voice of Bishop Juan José Bernal: "Our Lady of Lourdes wants me to be in Betania, to help you realize what she asks for. Why haven't you called me? How was I supposed to know about all of this? But as you can see for yourself, the Holy Mother has her own ways."

⋏ *Esperanza and her husband searched for the place of future Marian apparitions for twenty-seven years.*

◁ *Mary appeared for the first time to Esperanza when she was fourteen years old. As an adult, she received the grace of many meetings with the Mother of God.*

⋏ *In Betania, the Mother of God underlines the value of daily hardships, sacrifices, and suffering; thanks to them, the Immaculate Heart of Mary will triumph.*

⋏ *"Tell my children of all races, of all nations, of all religions that I love them. For me, their differences do not matter—all my children are the same."*

On the feast day of Our Lady of Lourdes, Bishop Bernal showed up in Betania with a few priests. Many people were baptized and received their First Communion. Special care was taken for the needy. When the poor locals came to the farm on the day of the Annunciation, Mary spread her hands, from which rays of light poured out.

"They came directly toward us," Esperanza recounts, "bathing us with light, in a way that Nasira Mistaje uttered a cry saying: 'Everything is burning up!' Actually, the whole area appeared to be on fire. It was beautiful. The sun began to gyrate, and everyone was shouting with emotion."

During this apparition, Esperanza heard that she was to bring a message of peace and reconciliation to the world. For this reason she will suffer, but her faithfulness will result in great joy and happiness.

FEEL THE MOTHER'S HUNGER

At that time, a new bishop was appointed to the diocese of Los Teques, in which Maria Esperanza lived. Pio Bello Ricardo had a doctorate in philosophy and studied psychology. The case of Betania was of no interest to him; he acknowledged that they are private revelations—something that concerns only heaven and the visionary. But the apparitions did not stop, and their character went far beyond "individual matters" of the visionary. The Holy Mother proclaimed the need for the reconciliation of the world with God. **"You must feel the hunger for God in your hearts—a hunger for His gifts and a hunger for His Mother, who does not cease to give herself every day, in every part of the world, so that people can be saved."**

APOCALYPTIC WARNINGS

Mary repeats the call for reconciliation: **"I come to reconcile my children, seek them, give them faith**," she declared. **"Lust, thirst for power, and material wealth made them cold, indifferent, selfish."** She warned that **"Hell...must be destroyed by kindness, love and the truth of this Mother's heart. Forgiveness must appear because only love can save. ...That is the only way to avoid destruction."**

The tone of the Holy Mother's statement is urgent. It's the "eleventh hour." The time of reconciliation has already been greatly extended. **"Humanity abuses grace and is going toward perdition. If it does not change and not improve, it will die from fire and war."** But God wants to spare us that fate, which is why He sends His Mother to the world.

On May 12, 1981, Esperanza had an inescapable feeling that the following day there would be an attack on the Holy Father. "I spent the whole night in prayer. I was so distraught that I cried out: "Lord, how is that possible? How can you raise your hand against this life, Lord?" May 13, on the day of Our Lady of Fatima, shots were fired in St. Peter's Square. For the next three months, Esperanza felt intense pain in the abdomen area. She felt she was suffering in union with the pope.

ACKNOWLEDGMENT OF THE APPARITIONS

Bishop Pio Ricardo could not ignore the apparitions in Betania any longer. He appointed a special commission and stood at its head. He asked for written testimonies of all who were on the farm in Betania on March 25,

1984, when "the great apparition" of Our Lady took place to more than one hundred people. They all saw her clearly and sharply, so they gave their oral and written affidavit to the bishop. Then he questioned every one of them. He analyzed the information on the healings and conversions. He discussed this topic twice with Cardinal Ratzinger. He also informed the pope himself.

On November 21, 1987, the bishop published a pastoral letter, in which he confirmed the authenticity of the apparitions in Betania.

The message from Finca Betania is simple. It talks about peace and reconciliation, strengthens faith, awakens a thirst for conversion, urges us to use the sacraments, calls for prayer and penance, and above all, encourages us to participate in Holy Mass and to pray the Rosary. All this to extend the hour of mercy, obtain the grace of conversion, and prevent punishment for the sins of the world. Padre Pio is right: the words conveyed to us by Esperanza are of consolation to us.

⌄ *Finca Betania attracts crowds of pilgrims, thirsty for the presence of God and the protection of Mary.*

Deir el-Ahmar

1976

Our Lady of Lebanon

A certain Maronite monk met a mysterious woman on his way toward Deir el-Ahmar, which had been shelled the previous day. The woman, dressed all in black, was heading in the same direction. When he asked her why she had such dirty hands and sleeves, she replied: **"I toiled all night to deflect the shelling from Deir el-Ahmar."** The woman was the Blessed Virgin Mary.

Our world is full of armed conflicts. We know of one argument for the nonexistence of God: if He existed He would not tolerate the death of children, the nightmares of concentration camps, tortures, rapes, the immeasurable ocean of human suffering. We forget that God has written signs of love into many wars. He warned us (usually through His Mother) before they broke out, indicated the best means to end them, and even directly intervened in order to save human lives.

One example is what occurred during the war that was tearing Lebanon apart in the 1970s. God occasioned a whole series of supernatural incidents during the war, which were to make the warring parties aware of the senselessness of war. Our Lady was personally involved in those incidents, wanting to reconcile the warring Muslims and Christians.

During the war, which lasted five years, there were miraculous incidents throughout the country. Witnesses most often speak of the Marian apparitions, where the Blessed Virgin Mary appeared as a light akin to a rainbow that spread over several villages. That usually occurred when villages were under attack. Our Lady was not just an observer from on high, watching her children fighting one another. She was the third party in the conflict, actively involved in bringing about its end. During the aforementioned apparitions, she deprived the attacking soldiers of their warring spirit, extinguished the hatred that burned in their hearts, and, at times, she even changed the direction of shells that had been fired. Pope St. John Paul II comes to mind; he told his would-be assassin, Mehmet Ali Ağca, that "One hand pulled the trigger, another guided the bullet." The Holy Father thus referred to Our Lady's role in saving his life. It was so in Lebanon. The artillery shells did not reach their targets.

MARONITES

The Maronites are the heroes of the Marian apparitions in Lebanon. The Blessed Virgin Mary appeared in 1975 in order to protect them. Maronites are members of the Eastern Catholic Church, who owe their beginnings to St. Maron, a friend of St. John Chrysostom, who both lived in the fourth century. Though few in number, they did not succumb to the heresy of monothelitism, which holds that Jesus had two natures—divine and human—but only one will. The monothelites dominated the Christian world, but the Maronites were an island of orthodoxy in an ocean of heresy. After the arrival of the Crusaders, their unity with the Catholic Church was affirmed and has never been severed. Since then, the community has been called the Syriac Maronite Church.

A BISHOP'S TESTIMONY

When Maronite settlements were attacked, extraordinary phenomena often appeared in the sky. We know that most frequently they were rainbows, upon which stood the majestic figure of Mary. "I collected dozens of Christian and Muslim testimonies pertaining to the apparitions. All those present saw them, but it was not possible to interview them all," wrote Archbishop Elias Zoghby of Baalbek in his April 20, 1980, letter to a French theologian.

I shall describe another miraculous incident," he continued. "The Muslims, on capturing the military barracks in Baalbek in January 1976, seized, with the help of Palestinian fighters, small arms and heavy weaponry. The next day, they placed heavy artillery on a hill above Deir el-Ahmar, a large Maronite settlement. I was there at the time, and I spent the night there. More than one hundred fifty shells were fired

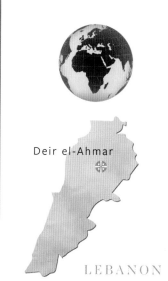

Deir el-Ahmar

LEBANON

⋀ *St. Maron led a pious, prayerful, and contemplative life, preaching the Gospel.*

resumed, but to no avail. The Christians in neighboring villages thought that Deir el-Ahmar would be in ruins, whereas but few walls were damaged. Local Christians prayed.

A Maronite monk, Fr. Boutros Mounsef, known in the area for his saintly life and prophetic spirit, spent that night in a village close to Deir el-Ahmar and observed the shelling. At dawn, he said Mass and then walked to Deir el-Ahmar. He told me what happened to him on the way. As he made his way to the shelled settlement, he came across a woman dressed in black from head to toe. He greeted her and asked her where she was going at such an early hour. "**I am going to Deir el-Ahmar**," she replied. "**And where are you going, Father**?" "I am also going there," he replied.

As he knew all the Maronites who lived in the vicinity, he wondered who the woman could be. 'Who are you?' he asked. "**Do not be so curious. I am the Virgin Mary**." Fr. Boutros bowed and noticed that her hands and sleeves were very dirty. 'Why are your hands and sleeves so black?' he asked. She answered, "**I toiled all night deflecting shells from Deir el-Ahmar. Now I am going to protect the settlement from shells that will be fired this morning. Tell the inhabitants that nothing will happen to them, and that peace will reign there in three days**." After saying that, the Blessed Virgin Mary vanished.

⚊ During the war in Lebanon, Mary helped to reconcile the Muslims and Christians.

at the settlement, each of which weighed nearly forty kilos. ... But of the more than eight thousand inhabitants, not one was even scratched. We spent that terrible night in prayer. The next morning, the shelling was

Her words became true. Indeed, that morning not one person was harmed, and three days later there was a truce in Lebanon. Thanks to the witness of this saintly monk, there were astonishing conversions among young Christians throughout the region.

The apparitions in Lebanon do not fit in with any of the best-known Marian apparitions, like those in Guadalupe or Lourdes. But they have a lot in common with the apparitions pertaining to miraculous Christian victories: at Chocim, Vienna, and Hostýn, for example. In Lebanon, as at the Battle of Lepanto, the Blessed Virgin Mary was personally involved in the armed conflict. *Monstra te esse Matrem*! ("Show yourself a Mother") cry out ancient antiphonies to Heaven. Through her miraculous intervention, she proved herself a mother to the Maronites.

> ⌄ *God occasioned a series of supernatural incidents during the war in Lebanon.*

Cuapa

1980

Mother of Sinners

*Bernardo, although closely connected with the Church since childhood and sincerely devoted to Mary, asked her to choose someone else. He was afraid to take up the task entrusted to him. "**Not everyone can see Me**," replied the Holy Mother and gave him strength. Bernardo was no longer afraid.*

We learn about the apparition in Cuapa, Nicaragua, from the visionary himself. His testimony has been provided to us by Pablo Antonio Vega Mantilla, bishop of the diocese of Juigalpa, who added this short, personal comment: "For our part we are surprised at the emphasis given to the responsibilities that weigh on man and the duty to make peace and to instruct the world. This is a religious emphasis not typical of popular piety, which tends to leave everything up to God." The bishop added: "We hope that the report which we present will serve as an invitation to reflect on the social obligations that very often are largely forgotten by many of our Christians."

Here we have the Church's official interpretation. Cuapa is a call for social involvement, but not *only* that.

Bernardo Martinez took care of the old chapel in Cuapa. It was he who would open and close it. He would ring the bells calling people to prayer. Two women assisted him in this: Auxiliadora

Bernardo and Socorro Barea de Marin. The one day, in March 1980, Bernardo entered the sacristy and saw that a light was burning inside the chapel. He was certain that Auxiliadora hadn't turned it off the day before. A few days later, this time after Socorro's shift, the same thing happened. Bernardo decided to harshly scold both women. The parish had no money, and electricity isn't free.

When he went to their house, he couldn't say a word. He didn't understand how it was happening, but he knew in his spirit that they were innocent. "I saw that I was blaming them without them being to blame. I then thought I would say nothing, and if anything over the minimum was spent, I would pay it myself."

AN ILLUMINATED STATUE

On April 15, at eight in the evening, he knew that inexplicable events were occurring in the chapel. It was dark, and yet he found a statue of the Mother of God bathed in light. At first, he blamed the boys playing nearby, who must have destroyed the roof in this spot — yet there wasn't even the smallest hole in the roof. Then he thought that someone had hung a fluorescent rosary on the statue. "I saw the hands, the feet, the neck ... there was nothing like that." Bernardo recognized that supernatural things were happening. He thought: "The Holy Virgin is quarreling with the people."

Bernardo's first conclusions are puzzling. He said to himself, "I am the one who is to blame." We may wonder why a Madonna illuminated by light would point to the sins of the visionary. The answer came in the following sentences of Bernardo's notes: "As these thoughts were going through my mind, I remembered something that my grandmother used to tell me when I was a child: 'Never be a lamp in the street and a darkness at home.' I understood my sin: I wanted others to make peace, but I was quarreling in my own house." So, "I decided to ask for their forgiveness in front of all the people. I did that. They forgave me."

And so it was indeed. Bernardo helped resolve a dispute among the townspeople of Cuapa over whether to allow their children to be taught by Cuban teachers. The sacristan managed to reconcile the conflicting sides. As a matter of fact, thanks to him, no teacher from Communist Cuba was brought to Cuapa. The problem with these teachers was apparent: in the neighboring town of Comarca del Silentio, a Cuban scolded the villagers who thanked God for the meal they had eaten. "Don't say that," he commanded. "Say as we say, 'Thanks to *Fidel* that I have eaten.'"

Yet, while Bernardo was occupied with solving problems outside the home, he was not involved in family affairs. The encounter with the illuminated statue made him see the error of his ways. He told people about it during his public confession. Then those gathered in the chapel heard from Bernardo the story of the shining statue. From that moment on, the sacristan became the subject of crude jokes throughout the community.

But a woman, Consuela Martin, believed Bernardo's words. She made him promise to let her know as soon as he saw the Holy Mother again.

Cuapa

NICARAGUA

⅄ *The visionary from Cuapa did not want to take on the mission entrusted to him. However, Mary explained to him that it was God Himself who chose him to bring her message to the world.*

A Mary's first great message: *"**Love each other. Comply with your obligations. Make peace. Don't ask Our Lord for peace because if you do not make it there will be no peace**."*

A RELUCTANT VISIONARY

The news of the unusual vision reached the parish priest. He questioned his parishioner in detail and then asked how he was praying. From childhood, Bernardo prayed the Rosary and three Hail Marys every day, and in difficult moments he called out to the Mother of God: "Don't leave me, Mother." This is how his grandmother raised him.

The parish priest told him to pray more, and to ask Mary if there was anything she wanted from the people of Cuapa. But Bernardo asked the Holy Mother for something else: "Blessed Mother, please do not request anything of me. I have many problems in the church. Make your request known to some other person because I want to avoid any more problems. I have a great many now. I don't want any more."

This is how Bernardo prayed. As the days passed, people slowly forgot about the incident.

AN ESCAPE TO THE RIVER

Yet Bernardo's problems only multiplied. In May, financial troubles began. He was at risk of losing his job. All of this resulted in a spiritual crisis. It got to the point that when he woke up in the morning, he asked for death. He thought: "In the chapel I swept ... I removed the dust ... I washed the altar cloths and albs ... and for this very same thing I was scorned, I was called a fool. Even my own family — my blood brothers — would say that I did not prosper financially because of my involvement with things at the sacristy. I have been a sacristan but without earning any money. I began to work in the house of God since I was able to use the dust cloth and broom. ... I was at the time very small. I have done it because, in that way, I serve the Lord."

On the night of May 6–7, Bernardo was unable to sleep, so he decided to go to the river to fish. At last, he "felt happy" and "content" in that "pleasant environment." Noon came, and Bernardo was still sitting by the river, still filled with happiness. An hour later it started to rain, and his carefree time near the water was interrupted. The fisherman took refuge under a tree and prayed his daily Rosary. At three o'clock, he started gathering his things to go home: the animals had to be fed and the church had to be opened.

THE FIRST MEETING WITH MARY

Suddenly, lightning flashed across the sky. Bernardo thought it would rain again but was amazed to see that there was no sign of rain. He had walked a few steps when another flash of light lit up the sky again. He later claimed that this light opened his eyes to an extraordinary vision. The Holy Mother stood before Bernardo.

The written records left by Martinez are torn, and much is sadly illegible. But here is what remains of his testimony about that first meeting: "I saw that she blinked … that she was beautiful … the pile of rocks was … she remained … as if … the cloud … was covered with Jaragua grass." We learn that Mary was standing on a cloud that covered a whole morisco tree. "The cloud … radiated in all directions, rays of light with the sun. On the cloud were the feet of a very beautiful Lady. Her feet were bare. Her dress was long and white. She had a celestial cord around the waist. Long sleeves. Covering her was a veil of a pale cream color with gold embroidery along the edge. Her hands were held together over her breast."

Bernardo went on to say: "She looked like the statue of the Virgin of Fatima." Bernardo raised his hands to his face, as to wake up from a dream. But when he looked again at the Madonna, she looked different. "She had human skin," he said, "and her eyes were moving and blinking." Martin stood there paralyzed. "My mind was the only thing that I could move."

Then Mary extended her arms, "like in the Miraculous Medal, which I never had seen, but which later was shown to me."

Rays shot out from her hands and touched the visionary's heart. Now he could move his tongue. He asked: "What is your name?" He heard the sweetest voice; she said her name was Mary. "I saw the way she moved her lips. I then said, 'She is alive! She spoke! She has answered my question!' I could see that we could enter into a conversation, that I could speak with her."

Indeed, the conversation began. When asked where she was from, Mary replied: "**I come from heaven. I am the Mother of Jesus**." When asked what she wanted, she replied: "**I want the Rosary to be prayed every day**." Bernardo didn't let her finish, assuring Mary that people prayed in Cuapa. But Mary continued: "**I want it to be prayed permanently, within the family … including the children old enough to understand … to be prayed at a set hour when there are no problems with the work in the home**."

She also said that Our Lord does not like mechanically recited prayers. She recommended praying the Rosary using citations from the Holy Bible. She also called to live the Word of God, after which she announced her first great message: "**Love each other. Comply with your obligations. Make peace. Don't ask Our Lord for peace because if you do not make it there will be no peace**."

She added a request about practicing the devotion announced in Pontevedra: "**Renew the five first Saturdays. You received many graces when all of you did this**." It turns out that the First Saturday devotions had been known and practiced in Nicaragua before the recently ended civil war. After God gave the country peace, the First Saturday devotions were forgotten.

We know this kind of thinking: "When in fear, God is near." But once our prayers are answered, we stop praying. When we receive the graces we desire, we give up praying. The Holy Mother reminds us that this kind of behavior is wrong because we always need God's help, because we are always in danger. She says: "**Nicaragua has suffered much since the earthquake. She is threatened with even more suffering. She will continue to suffer if you don't change**."

This threat concerns not only Nicaragua itself because Mary says: "**Pray, pray, my son, the Rosary**

Mary, who appeared to Bernardo, spread out her hands like on the Miraculous Medal, and a light burst from her hand and touched the visionary's heart.

In Cuapa, Mary first and foremost asked people to pray the Rosary every day, in their families, contemplating its mysteries.

for all the world. Tell believers and nonbelievers that the world is threatened by grave dangers."

However, the visionary was reluctant to undertake any kind of mission. "Señora, I don't want problems; I have many in the Church. Tell this to another person." But her answer was short: "**No, because our Lord has selected you to give the message**."

"NOT EVERYONE CAN SEE ME"

As the cloud began to rise, Bernardo remembered Consuela Martin's request. He wanted to stop the Holy Mother, to bring this pious woman. Mary answered: "**No. Not everyone can see me. She will see me when I take her to Heaven, but she should pray the Rosary as I ask**."

Mary raised her hands up, and the cloud carried her up to Heaven. That was the end of the vision.

THE WEIGHT OF THE UNANNOUNCED MESSAGE

For eight days, Bernardo carried a message in his heart. He felt a great burden weighing down on him, and his inner voice repeatedly told him to convey the words of Mary to people. But the visionary did not want to do it. His suffering was increasing, and he was running away from it. He looked for entertainment; he went to bathe in the river. Yet still he lost weight and turned pale. His friends began to ask if he was sick.

Then, on May 16, the Holy Mother appeared to him again, in the same form as before, and again, spreading her hands, she gave him her light. The sacristan felt guilty that he had not fulfilled Mary's requests. He even avoided the place of the first apparition

so as not to risk meeting the Mother of God. He realized that he could not run away from her. "She will be following me wherever I am," he thought. Then he heard a gentle voice: "**Why have you not told what I sent you to tell**?" The visionary explained that he did not want to be mocked. "Señora, it is that I am afraid. I am afraid of being ridiculed by the people, afraid that they will laugh at me. They will say that I am crazy." But Mary assured him: "**Do not be afraid. I am going to help you**."

That day, two ladies heard the story of the apparitions: Lilliam Ruiz de Bernardo and Socorro Barea de Marin. Bernardo trusted them more than anyone, so he confided in them his "problems" with the Mother of God. The women started scolding him that he was not obeying Mary. They made him tell other people. It was the first time Bernardo received correction without answering back.

The next day, Bernardo told his family about the apparitions. Some of them believed, while others laughed at him. The visionary was astonished at his own reaction: the behavior of people didn't matter to him. All that mattered was obedience to Heaven's orders. In the evening, after reciting the Rosary, Bernardo told his story to those gathered in the church. Again, the reactions were all different. Still, it didn't matter to Bernardo. Mary had fulfilled her promise. He felt the touch of grace. He fulfilled the Mother of God's request and was happy.

Two days later, Bernardo told the parish priest everything. He recommended that Bernardo pray the Rosary, and if the apparitions continued, Bernardo was not to speak a word about them.

AN UNUSUAL NIGHTLY VISION

The next apparition took place while he slept. Bernardo dreamed he was at the site of the first apparition and prayed the Rosary, and when he finished, the Holy Mother appeared to him, preceded by two flashes of lighting. Mary showed him four amazing visions. She said, "**Look at the sky**." First, Bernardo, saw a crowd of people dressed in white, marching toward the rising sun. They were bathed in light. They were singing, but the visionary could not understand the words. These people were incredibly happy and joyful. Mary said, "**Look, these are the very first communities when Christianity began. They are the first catechumens; many of them were martyrs**." And she added immediately: "**Do your people want to be martyrs? Would you yourself like to be a martyr**?"

Being a simple man, Bernardo didn't exactly know what martyrs were, but he said he wanted to be one. If we, who know what martyrdom is, were to hear the same question, the answer would not be so easy.

Next, Mary showed Bernardo the second group of people. They were dressed in white and holding rosaries in their hands. Later, from conversations with others, it was clear that they were Dominicans. Bernardo didn't know this order, and he did not know what the Dominican habit looked like. Their rosary beads were the color of snow and emitted a multicolored light. One of the people was holding a book—the Bible—from which he was reading something, while others were quietly contemplating the words. After a moment of silence, they said an "Our Father" and "Hail Mary." Bernardo prayed with them, and when this extraordinary Rosary ended, he heard the Mother of God's words: "**These are the first ones to whom I gave the Rosary. That is the way that I want all of you to pray the Rosary**."

We are reminded of the first apparition of Mary in Cuapa—the Rosary is to be prayed daily in families. Now we also know that it is supposed to be connected with meditation.

Afterward, Mary showed the visionary the third group of people. They were dressed in brown robes and reminded Bernardo of the Franciscans. They also prayed the Rosary. Mary said, "**These received the Rosary from the hands of the first ones**."

Then a great crowd of men and women arrived, dressed like the modern residents of Nicaragua. It was impossible to count the crowd. They walked like an army in battle formation, and their rosaries were their weapons. The visionary looked at them, beaming with happiness. "When one is dressed differently from the other persons, one feels rather strange," he explains. "At seeing the first group I did not feel so attracted to them because of that. I admired them, but I did not feel in their

In Cuapa, Mary renewed her request to practice the First Saturday devotions, announced in Pontevedra.

> ⋎ "**The sufferings of this world cannot be removed. Sufferings are the cross that you must carry. That is the way life is**."

midst as when I saw the last group. I felt at once that I could enter into that scene because they were dressed the same as I was."

But when Bernardo looked down at his hands, they were black, while the others were radiating light. He heard from the Mother of God that he couldn't join them: "**You are still lacking. You have to tell the people what you have seen and heard**." She assured him that everyone can share in God's glory if they obey Christ and His Word and persistently pray the Rosary.

In the morning, Bernardo went to the parish priest, confident that the priest would release him from the order of silence. But he upheld the ban. Again, the visionary carried a weight in his heart, and again he heard the inner voice telling him to speak. Still, he chose to obey the Church. He didn't talk about his vision until June 24, when his pastor lifted the ban.

AN ANSWERED PRAYER

On July 8, Bernardo went to the apparition site, along with forty other devotees. They walked in procession, praying and singing. At night, while he was sleeping, Bernardo had another vision. Once again, he prayed the Rosary, and when he finished, he remembered the request of a woman whose brother was in prison, wrongly accused of causing revolutionary riots. The woman asked for help, as it was forbidden to have contact with the prisoner. When Bernardo prayed for the boy, an angel appeared to him.

The visionary later recalled: "I felt a reverence as I was before him, but my feeling toward him was different from what I felt before the Lady ... as if she were someone greater ... she greater than he ... I don't know how to explain it." Yet, while Bernardo had no trouble talking to the Virgin, in the presence of the angel he had difficulty uttering the simplest words.

The angel had a mission to fulfill. He assured Bernardo that the prayer for the boy had been answered and explained in detail what his sister had to do to free her brother. She was to visit him on Sunday, inform him not to sign anything that they suggested he sign, go to the head of the prison with a request to release her brother, and bring one thousand córdobas with her. Everything came true to the letter—a couple days later, the impossible became reality: the woman was allowed to speak to her brother, and a few days later he was released on bail.

THE PASTOR'S VISION

Before another apparition of the Mother of God occurred, Bernardo understood the attitude of his parish priest. This priest did not believe that the Holy Mother appeared in Cuapa, and he therefore wasn't interested in subsequent events. But one day after celebrating Holy Mass, he asked the visionary to lead him to the place where the Holy Mother had appeared. Bernardo showed him the site of the apparitions, and then an amazing change took place in the priest.

First, he looked around as if he recognized the place. Then, pointing to the exact place of the apparitions, he said, "It is this place that was in my dreams last night." From then on, the parish priest became an advocate of the apparitions in Cuapa.

A MARIAN VERSION OF THE PARABLE OF LAZARUS

On September 8, Mary appeared again to Bernardo. The visionary went on a pilgrimage to the place of the apparitions with a crowd devoted to honoring the Mother of God. After finishing the Rosary, Bernardo saw two lightning bolts announcing the appearance of the heavenly Mother. His heart was filled with joy.

After a moment, Mary appeared on the morisco tree, already stripped of its leaves by pious people. This time she introduced herself in the form of a small child: "I saw her as a child. Beautiful, but little! She was dressed in a pale, cream-colored tunic. She did not have a veil, or a crown, or a mantle. No adornment or embroidery. The dress was long, with long sleeves, and it was girdled with a pink cord. Her hair fell to her shoulders and it was brown in color. Her eyes, also, although much lighter, almost the color of honey. She radiated light. She looked like the Lady, but she was a child. I was looking at her amazed, without saying a word, and then I heard her voice as that of a child ... a child of seven ... eight ... years."

Mary repeated the same message as always. The visionary thought that if she was a child, it might be easier for her to appear to all the gathered people. He exclaimed, "Let yourself be seen so that all the world will believe. These people who are here want to meet you." But Mary replied: "**No. It is enough for you to give them the message because for the one who is going to believe that will be enough. The one who is obstinate in his unbelief, even though he might see me, will not believe**." One is reminded of Jesus' words telling the parable of the rich man and Lazarus: "They will not be persuaded even if someone rises from the dead."

The Holy Mother was right. Some believed, others didn't. There was even a man who believed in the apparitions but was convinced that it was not the Mother of God who appeared to Bernardo. "This is nothing more than beings from other planets," this man declared.

A SPIRITUAL SANCTUARY OF HEARTS

Because they wanted to build a new church for Mary, Bernardo was to ask the Mother of God for a blessing. But he heard that it was more important to rebuild God's sanctuary in people's hearts. The walls of this sanctuary are not made from brick and stone, but with virtues. Mary said, "**Love one another. Forgive each other. Make peace. Don't first ask for it. Make peace**!"

"SERVE YOUR NEIGHBOR"

The Mother of God announced that in October she would not appear on the eighth, but on the thirteenth. She chose the "time of Fatima."

On that day, Bernardo was accompanied by a group of fifty people to the site of the apparitions. Although the visionary felt Mary approaching while praying the Rosary, he chose to pray. His attitude resembles the most outstanding examples of mysticism—saints who believed that obeying the principle was more important than the grace of the apparition.

It was three o'clock. People sang "Shining Morning Star, grant me grace to be able to sing the *Ave Maria*," when suddenly a ring of light appeared on the ground. Everyone saw it without exception. A light fell from the sky, as if it were from a powerful reflector, illuminating the gathered people. After a moment, the same ring appeared in the sky, emitting lights of different colors. It stood exactly where the sun stands at noon.

A little girl tried to break free from her mother's embrace, crying out that Mary was calling her. But her mother didn't let her go. The girl saw the Holy Mother first, then Bernardo saw her. Some, like a woman named Mildred, saw something that looked like a shadow of a statue of the Mother of God. This time Mary introduced herself in the form of Our Lady of Sorrows, "similar to the statue that is carried in procession during Holy Week."

➤ *Mary asks us to actively profess our faith—to seek what pleases God.*

Because Bernardo called on Mary again to make herself known to people, he was convinced that her sorrow was caused by his insistent requests, to which she did not respond. But the Holy Mother said, "**I am not angry, nor will I become angry. It saddens me to see the hardness of these peoples' hearts. But you will have to pray for them so that they will change**." Bernardo could not utter a word. He was crying. And Mary delivered her new message:

Pray the Rosary, meditate on the mysteries. Listen to the Word of God spoken in them. Love one another. Love each other. Forgive each other. Make peace. Don't ask for peace without making peace; because if you don't make it, it does no good to ask for it. Fulfill your obligations. Put into practice the Word of God. Seek ways to please God. Serve your neighbor, as that way you will please Him.

MOTHER OF BELOVED SINNERS

Bernardo said to Mary that he would like to present many requests to her. But Mary replied,

They ask of me things that are unimportant. Ask for faith in order to have the strength so that each can carry his own cross. The sufferings of this world cannot be removed. Sufferings are the cross that you must carry. That is the way life is. There are problems with the husband, with the wife, with the children, with the brothers. Talk, discuss, so that problems will be resolved in peace. Do not turn to violence. Never turn to violence. Pray for faith in order that you may have patience.

At her final appearance with Bernardo, Mary said, "**You will no longer see me in this place**." Bernardo exclaimed, "Don't leave us, my Mother." She told him, "**Do not be grieved. I am with all of you even though you do not see Me. I am the Mother of all of you, sinners**."

She repeated her social message of love, forgiveness, and peace once more, and added: "**A mother never forgets her children. And I have not forgotten what you suffer. I am the Mother of all of you, sinners**."

"Pray, pray, my son, the Rosary for all the world. Tell believers and nonbelievers that the world is threatened by grave dangers."

Medjugorje

1981

1981

Queen
of Peace

"Go and you will believe," say devotees of the Medjugorje apparitions. The unique atmosphere of this place and the special community of prayer make people want to return over and over. However, the many questions and persistent lack of answers keep skeptics from abandoning their doubts. The Church also remains cautious, still holding back final approval of these apparitions.

⌄ Medjugorje attracts and fascinates, sometimes surprises, shocks, and even outrages. Never changing, for nearly thirty-five years it has aroused great emotions among those who believe, doubt, or refuse to believe.

Medjugorje is a beautiful little village in the south of Bosnia-Herzegovina. It's flanked by two hills, the Podbrdo and Križevac. The Adriatic Sea is less than fifty miles away. It is the hometown of six alleged visionaries who claim to have been chosen by the Mother of God herself.

Their names are Vicka Ivanković (born 1964), Mirjana Dragičević (1965), Marija Pavlović (1965), Ivanka Ivanković (1966), Ivan Dragičević (1965), and Jakov Čolo (1971).

In the late afternoon of June 23, 1981, the people of Medjugorje cried, "It is as if the Day of Judgment has come to

Medjugorje

BOSNIA &
HERZEGOVINA

◁ *"I am the Blessed Virgin Mary. I chose this place because there are many deep believers here. Unite with Me in prayer."*

us!" A terrible storm had broken out. Thunder boomed from the sky and echoed between the two hills. Fires broke out and raged. The local post office burned down.

The following day after was the Feast of St. John the Baptist—and it was a hot one. Vicka was napping after her morning math exams. Two friends were headed to see her: Ivanka and Mirjana. Throughout the school year they attended school out of town; during vacation they came to the countryside to visit their grandparents.

Ivanka's mother, Jagoda, had died a month earlier, and her father worked in Germany. She was lonely.

Suddenly, Ivanka cried, "Look, the Holy Mother is there!" She later described a figure dressed in a gray robe moving on Podbrdo Hill. Frightened, they ran to the nearest house: that of Marija and Milka Pavlović.

After some time, Ivanka and Mirjana decided to accompany Milka as she

⋀ *At the end of the twentieth century, this small, picturesque village in Bosnia and Herzegovina became the stage for extraordinary events.*

The Holy Mother, summoning the visionaries to her, seemed to attract them with an inexplicable, supernatural force. Every one of them desired to be at the feet of the Heavenly Lady as quickly as possible.

went to fetch sheep from the pasture. Once they reached a spot from where Podbrdo could be seen, Ivanka looked up at the hill again. "I saw the Madonna with Jesus in her arms. Then Mirjana and Milka also looked in this direction and saw her, too."

Milka quickly left for her herd, while the older girls, terrified, ran to Vicka's house. Because their friend was asleep, they conveyed a request to her mother: "As soon as she wakes up, let her come to Jakov's house." Marija was the cousin of ten-year-old Jakov, and she knew that his house had a perfect view of the hill. If there was something on top of it, it would be clearly seen from there.

When Vicka arrived at Jakov's house, she was scared and did not think to look out the window toward Podbrdo. Instead, she ran away. She only stopped when she bumped into sixteen-year-old Ivan Dragičevic and twenty-two-year-old Ivan Ivankovic.

The boys agreed to come closer to the hill with her. Suddenly, Ivan Dragičević looked at Podbrdo and fled in a panic. Vicka, without looking up, asked the other Ivan if he saw anything. "I see something white turning," he replied. Then the girl looked up at the hill. The Holy Mother, they said, stood two hundred yards away. "I saw her as I see you," Vicka later said. "She wore a gray

dress and a white veil, and a crown of stars on her head. Her eyes were blue, her hair was dark, and her cheeks were pink. In her hands she was holding something, which she covered and uncovered, but I couldn't see what it was. She started calling us to herself, but who would have thought to come closer!"

The experience these children describe is known to theologians as a *mysterium tremendum et fascinans*: they were involved in a mystery that was both fearful and fascinating.

THE FIRST MEETING
The next day, Ivanka, Mirjana, Vicka, and Ivan decided to take a closer look at the

site of the apparition. They hoped to meet the Immaculate. (Not all of them felt the same way. Ivan Ivanković and Milka Pavlović did not go with them. They never saw the Holy Mother again.)

Once again, Ivanka noticed the Holy Mother first, then the three others. Vicka called Jakov and Marija. When the Madonna started summoning the visionaries, they rushed up the hill. "We ran as if we had wings, over sharp stones and brambles," recalled Vicka. Several adults saw them run and couldn't understand what was happening. "To get to the top you need at least twelve minutes," Mirjana's uncle later said. "And they got up there in two minutes. I was scared to death." Vicka said, "We were running toward the Madonna as if something were pulling us. I was afraid. I was barefoot, but the thorns didn't hurt me. When we got close to her, something knocked us to our knees. Jakov was kneeling in the middle of a

⋏ *Crowds of pilgrims visit the place of the apparitions; following in the footsteps of the visionaries, they travel on the steep and rocky path leading to Podbrdo Hill.*

⋖ *"Dear children! I am calling you for years through these messages that I am giving you ... For years I am calling you and exhorting you to a deep spiritual life ... Read the messages I am giving you every day and transform them into life."*

⋀ *A cross placed near the place of the apparitions on Podbrdo Hill.*

⋀ *Along the path leading to the place of the apparitions, cast bronze bas-reliefs were set in 1989, depicting the Joyful and Sorrowful Mysteries of the Rosary.*

thorn bush, and I was sure he would be injured. He didn't have the slightest scratch. We started to pray."

The Holy Mother, they said, was standing right in front of them. "She was beautiful," they later said. "She was surrounded by light." Then, Ivanka asked about her mother. The Mother of God assured her that Jagoda was happy. Since the woman died alone in the hospital, the girl asked if she wanted to pass a message on to her children. "**Only that you are to listen to your grandma**," Mary reportedly said. "**You are to take care of her because she is old and unable to work**."

The vision lasted about a quarter of an hour. Mary did not deliver any other significant messages.

Several men who followed the children up the mountain witnessed the final minutes of the apparition. From that moment, the apparitions in Medjugorje became public.

THE WEEPING MADONNA OF PEACE

The next day, a crowd of several thousand gathered at the site of the apparitions. Mary reportedly introduced herself to the children thus: "**I am the Blessed Virgin Mary. I**

chose this place because there are many deep believers here. Unite with me in prayer."

On April 4, 1985, the children heard her say, "**Today is the day I was going to stop giving you messages because some did not accept me. But the parish has made progress**."

The vision on Podbrdo ended. The visionaries, separated by the crowd, returned to their homes. Marija walked in the company of several women. Suddenly she felt a force telling her to separate herself from the group. After a moment, she saw an unusual vision: a bare cross shining with a rainbow of colors, and in front of it the weeping Holy Mother. "**Peace, peace, you must desire peace**," reportedly cried the Holy Virgin. "**There must be peace on Earth, you must be reconciled with God and with each other. Peace, peace, peace**!"

"It was a moving experience," Marija later said. "I saw the weeping Madonna, and the sight made me devote myself completely to the fulfillment of her requests. She came to encourage all of us to seek peace — peace in our hearts, peace in our families, peace in the world."

In 1981, relations between the world's leading superpowers — the United States and the Soviet Union — were strained. Two years before, the Soviets invaded Afghanistan. Next, they were expected to invade Poland. Many feared that nuclear war was imminent.

AN AVALANCHE OF EVENTS

News of the apparitions drew more and more crowds to Medjugorje. The authorities issued further bans on public gatherings, the police organized blockades, the apparitions moved to other places, and finally, at the request of the visionaries,

A A wooden cross was placed right next to the Church of St. James. Pilgrims gather around it, pray in silence, and light votive candles.

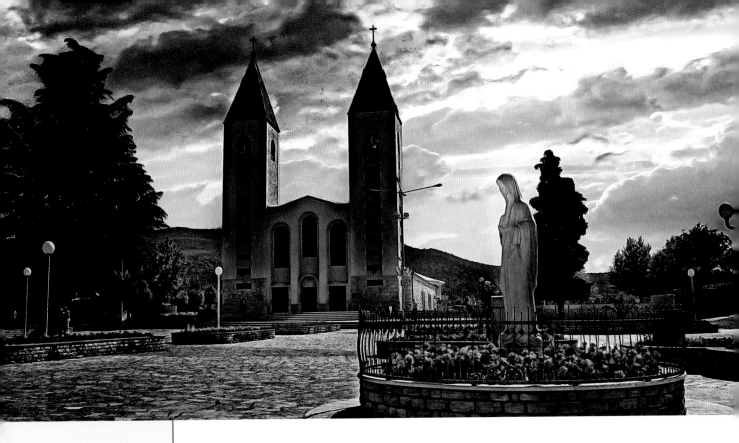

Mary began to appear in the church. The pastor was sentenced to three and a half years in prison for inciting a coup. People saw supernatural signs in the sky: the Fatima miracle of the sun; the inscription MIR ("Peace"); the cross on the nearby hill would disappear and in its place the figure of Christ would appear. Daily apparitions lasted up to forty minutes. They were simple. They were always focused on the need for reconciliation.

Mary announced to the visionaries that she would reveal ten secrets to them. To whomever she passed the last secret, she would stop appearing every day. Mirjana was first given all the secrets, then Ivanka and Jakov. The seventh secret spoke of a punishment that was annulled due to the fulfillment of the Madonna's requests by the faithful.

To this day, Marija, Vicka, and Ivan claim to speak to the Mother of God every day.

The visionaries heard Mary repeat to them: "**Dear children! I am calling you for years through these messages that I am giving you … For years I am calling you and exhorting you to a deep spiritual life … Read the messages I am giving you every day and transform them into life**." There are nearly four hundred such messages. In them, Mary shows the way to peace. It's the way of uniting ourselves with her through zealous prayer, severe fasting, and great sacrifice.

Mirjana also claims to have encountered Satan. "I locked myself in my room and waited for the Madonna. I knelt down … Suddenly, a light flashed and Satan appeared … He looked awful … all black … horrific. I felt weak and fainted.

"When I came to, he was still standing there and laughing. … He said I would be very beautiful and happy, etc., but I don't need the Madonna and my faith. 'She has given you nothing but suffering and difficulties,' he said. But he could give me everything I desire. Then something inside me shouted: No! No! No! … Then Satan disappeared and the Madonna appeared. Immediately my strength returned, as if she had restored it to me ... '**That was a painful trial**," she said, "**but it will not happen to you again**.'"

QUESTIONING THE CREDIBILITY OF THE APPARITIONS

The alleged apparitions at Medjugorje have drawn more than 30 million pilgrims and inspired thousands of conversions.

ordinary, Bishop Pavao Žanić, initially sympathized with the children. But when they told Mary about his conflict with the Franciscans in the diocese, they say that she sided with the friars. "Our Lady said that the bishop is to blame for the disorder in Herzegovina," they told Žanić. He was shocked. "The Virgin Mary would never address a bishop like that!" he exclaimed.

❯ *Crowds of pilgrims continually come, seeking reconciliation with God in Medjugorje, sometimes called the "confessional of the world."*

Medjugorje fascinates, attracts, amazes, shocks, and outrages. One cannot pass through it with indifference. It demands a clear spiritual response. Those who believe in the authenticity of the apparitions usually discuss their personal experience when engaging adversaries. "Go, see and you will believe," they say. They promise an encounter with the "Gospa"—the title they give to Our Lady of Medjugorje.

Others believe the apparitions are a fabrication—or, worse, a ploy of the devil to deceive the Church. For instance, they cite concerns about the Mother of God's involvement in the dispute between the bishop of Mostar and the Franciscans of Medjugorje. The local

Medjugorje's detractors also point to the Virgin's revelation of her "real" birthday. Our Lady of Medjugorje gave the date of August 5, while the Church celebrates her nativity on September 8.

While the Church has not officially approved the Medjugorje apparitions and has continued to study them in depth under Pope Benedict XVI's Ruini commission starting in 2010, Pope Francis lifted the official ban on pilgrimages in 2019. So long as the apparitions continue, the Church will continue standing by as a careful observer. In the meantime, no doubt, thousands will be brought to the Church by the extraordinary power at work in that small village near the Adriatic.

❯ *The Church of St. James is the center of spiritual life not only for parishioners but also for pilgrims visiting the sanctuary from the farthest corners of the world.*

Kibeho

1981

Mother of the Word

Mary's appearances in Kibeho, a small town about twenty miles from Butare in southern Rwanda, were the first apparitions in Africa to receive official recognition from the Church. The message didn't have a local character; it didn't concern only Rwanda. Its content was universal.

Alphonsine, Nathalie, Marie-Claire, Stephanie, Agnes, Emmanuel, and Vestine: these are the names of the seven young people who were witnesses to the apparitions of the Holy Mother in Africa. The Holy Mother said that her African message was directed to the whole world, and yet it was passed on by the visionaries in an unusual way: with the help of singing, gestures, fasting, and even dancing. This is the "language" of the Rwandan people.

There were seven visionaries, but only the apparitions received by three of them have been acknowledged as authentic. Bishop Augustin Misago, who chaired the commission charged with examining the apparitions in Kibeho, said that "when the news of the first apparition in 1981 began to spread all over the country, certain people started going around saying that they, too, had seen the Most Holy Virgin Mary. As a Church, we judged the first apparitions to be sufficient enough for the sake of

⌄ *Mary's message from Africa was directed to the whole world.*

faith. The others were merely imitations of them. They brought nothing new to the original apparitions in Kibeho."

The three approved visions are those experienced by sixteen-year-old Alphonsine Mumureke, her peer Nathalie Mukamazimpaka, and twenty-one-year-old Marie-Claire Mukangango.

"I AM THE MOTHER OF THE WORD"

On November 28, 1981, Alphonsine Mumureke, a student at a school run by the Benebikira Sisters, was on duty in the lunchroom. She was serving her friends when she heard a warm voice calling out: "**My daughter**!" The girl looked around the room but saw that there was no one there who could address her in that way, so she went out into the corridor. There she saw a beautiful woman standing in front of her. Later, the visionary said that the Holy Mother "was not white like the images." She added: "It's difficult for me to determine the color of her skin, but she was unspeakably beautiful."

"Who are you, my lady?" Alphonsine asked.

The woman identified herself as "**Nyina wa Jambo**": Mother of the Word.

Mary asked which truths of the Faith the girl valued the most.

"I love God and His Mother, who gave us her Son, our Savior," she said in reply.

Then Mary said: "**It is true. I have come to assure you of this. I hear your prayers. I would be pleased if your companions had more faith because some of them do not believe enough**."

In Kibeho, Mary said she wanted to help the visionary discover her own vocation. For this reason, she invited her to join the Legion of Mary. Alphonsine expressed her willingness to do so.

"I am the Mother of the Word," Mary announced in Kibeho.

When Mary left, Alphonsine fell into a numbness that lasted close to a quarter of an hour. During subsequent visits, the visionaries would all fall into a similar state.

Alphonsine became an object of mockery and derision. As a joke, some girls began giving her rosaries for the Mother of God to bless. They were amazed when, during the apparitions, the rosaries became so heavy that Alphonsine couldn't pick them up!

The second apparition took place the next day, the first Sunday of Advent. Mary said: "**I love a child who plays with me because this is a beautiful manifestation of trust and love. Feel**

"Never forget the love I have for you when I come to you."

The Sanctuary of Our Lady of Kibeho was established to commemorate the apparitions. Today, it is an important Catholic religious center.

The visionaries from Kibeho.

like a child with me because I, too, love to embrace you. No one should be afraid of their mother. You should not be afraid of me, but you should love me."

NEW WITNESSES

Some people began to pray for the Holy Mother to appear to someone besides Alphonsine to confirm the authenticity of the apparitions. In response to these requests, Mary appeared to Nathalie Mukamazimpaka on January 12, 1982. The message directed to her was more mystical than the one Alphonsine received. It emphasized the necessity of prayer, deep reflection, humility, and sacrifice. The Mother of God repeated one call many times: "**Wake up. Stand up. Purify yourselves and look around carefully. You must dedicate**

yourself to prayer. You must develop in yourself the virtues of love, devotion, and humility." In this message, the Holy Mother reminded us: "**Repent, repent, repent! Convert while there is still time**."

On March 22, the Mother of God appeared to Marie-Claire Mukangango, an impious and sometimes uncouth girl who mocked Alphonsine and always tried to be the center of attention. The Holy Mother urged her to meditate on the Passion of Christ and to recite the Rosary and the Chaplet of the Seven Sorrows.

The Chaplet of the Seven Sorrows (also known as the Servite Rosary) is a way to meditate on the seven dolors of Our Lady: the prophecy of Simeon at the Temple of Jerusalem, the flight into Egypt, the loss of Jesus in the Temple, the meeting with Jesus on the way of the Cross, her presence at the foot of the Cross, the descent of Jesus from the Cross, and the burial of Christ.

When Marie-Claire said she would walk from house to house all over the country and tell people about this chaplet, the Mother of God replied, "**You can spread this devotion all over the world, without even leaving this place. My grace is mighty**."

Then, Mary asked Marie-Claire to sprinkle the crowd that had gathered with the water Mary had blessed. When Marie-Claire attempted to do this, she saw trees and flowers in front of her instead of people.

"There are too many of them," she exclaimed to the Holy Mother. "The field is too big. I cannot do it alone. Please help me." Marie-Claire said that this was Mary's way of showing her how vital it is to accept help from Heaven. Humans cannot do much on their own.

The Holy Mother also told the girl, "**When I reveal myself to someone and speak to them, I am speaking to the whole world. If I am addressing the Kibeho parish now, it does not mean I am addressing Kibeho alone, or the**

▲ The interior of the Chapel of the Apparitions.

diocese of Butare, or Rwanda, or all of Africa. I am concerned with the whole world, and I am addressing it."

Soon there were seven visionaries. Crowds from all over Rwanda came to pray to their "Mariya" and to witness the amazing apparitions. The last one took place on November 28, 1989, the eighth anniversary of the first apparition. Mary appeared to Alphonsine Mumureke and announced that all Christians are called to pray, to repent, to obey and love the Church, to be faithful to the gospel, and to remain in conformity to the hierarchy of the Church.

As she left, Mary said, "**I love you, I love you very much! Never forget the love I have for you when I come to you**." She also assured those present that her message would do much good—not only then but also in the future. Then Alphonsine began singing the Magnificat, and the crowd joined her.

A DARK PROPHECY

During the apparition, all seven of the visionaries saw a terrifying scene of a river of blood and headless bodies without number. This vision lasted

▲ Mary reminds us of our spiritual foundation: God and our faith in Him.

➤ Today, the message from Kibeho is an example of unity and reconciliation for the Rwandan people.

several hours; it is, perhaps, Africa's most well-known prophecy.

In 1994, a civil war broke out. Of Rwanda's seven million residents, one million were killed. Among them were Marie-Claire and her husband. Another two and a half million Rwandans fled their homes.

It is interesting to recall that Alphonsine, Nathalie, and Marie-Claire saw the Mother of God crying on August 15, 1982. On that day, Mary spoke of the special meaning of suffering, saying that it was the path one must follow to reach heavenly glory: "**No one enters Heaven without suffering**." She added that suffering is a means of reparation for the sins of the world. By participating in the sufferings of Jesus and Mary, we can contribute to the salvation of the world.

MESSAGE OF RECONCILIATION

On June 29, 2001, the Vatican released the declaration of Rwandan bishop

➤ In Kibeho, Mary asked for repentance, a change of heart, and unceasing and sincere prayer.

Augustin Misago on the validity of Mary's apparitions to the three young women. Thus, Kibeho became the first Marian apparition in Africa to receive official recognition from the Church.

Today, the Kibeho message for the Rwandan nation is the way of the future, a way of reconciliation.

San Nicolás

1983-1990

Our Lady of the Rosary

The Mother of God in San Nicolás, viewed by a visionary after closing her eyes—which is a novelty in itself—invites her to reflect on passages from the Holy Bible and to interpret them in a special Marian way. However, this is not the end of the novelties. The stigmata that Gladys de Motta received are exceptional because they are different from the wounds of the stigmatists known to us so far.

⋏ *Gladys Herminia Quiroga de Motta received a special honor—the Mother of God herself became her teacher.*

⋏ *"The time has come to pray, beg for forgiveness, and it will be given to you"—this is a fragment of the message from San Nicolás.*

In the bell tower of the cathedral in Rosario, the statue of Our Lady of the Rosary was effectively forgotten. The wooden likeness was more than a hundred years old and extremely valuable. It had been consecrated in Rome by Pope Leo XIII, a great devotee and propagator of the Rosary. The statue was moved from the Eternal City to Argentina in 1884 and was placed in the church in San Nicolás. A Rosary confraternity was immediately established, and a ceremonial procession with the figure was organized yearly. Then one year, during one of the holidays, the statue of the Mother of God fell and its arm broke off. It was assigned for repair, but for unknown reasons it was abandoned in the bell tower and never restored. The Holy Mother asked about her statue in her apparitions in 1983.

When Gladys Herminia Quiroga de Motta saw the hundred-year-old statue, she whispered, "It is the Holy Mother who shows herself to me!" The statue was slightly smaller than the figure of Mary that had appeared to her in San Nicolás, and, of course, not as beautiful. But the rest of the details were the same: a blue mantle thrown over a pink tunic, a white veil, a dark-haired Infant Jesus held in her left hand and, finally, a Rosary held by the Mother and her Son, together.

The visionary did not have to remind herself of these similarities because the Holy Mother unexpectedly stood in front of the statue. "**They have forgotten me, but I am appearing again**," she said. "**Place me on the pedestal again. You can see that this is what I look like**." She also expressed a wish: "**I want to stand on the banks of the Paraná River. Be brave. You will see my light in this place**."

Today, in the place designated by Mary, there stands a Rosary shrine containing the same image of Our Lady found by Gladys de Motta.

ROSARY OF LIGHT

When the apparitions began in 1983, Gladys was forty-six years old. She was a mother of two daughters, the oldest of whom was about to give birth to Gladys's grandchild. The visionary completed only four years of elementary school and could hardly read and write. Her husband was a crane operator in a steel factory. The family lived in a working-class neighborhood of San Nicolás, a city of 150,000 people, a two-hour drive from Buenos Aires.

Her first spiritual vision had occurred in September 1981, when Gladys saw her Rosary glowing with a strange light. In accordance with the Argentinean custom, it had been hung on a nail driven into the wall near the front door. Suddenly it began to shine like molten metal. The woman called her neighbors, who were amazed. From that day on, she began inviting friends and neighbors to pray the Rosary together. How could they refuse, when the Rosary continued to glow with its miraculous light?

THE FIRST MEETING WITH MARY

One day, however, Gladys de Motta felt a calling to pray in solitude. On

San Nicolás

ARGENTINA

◄ *The wooden statue of Our Lady of the Rosary was consecrated by Pope Leo XIII, a zealous devotee and propagator of the Rosary.*

September 25, she took the Rosary off from the nail and knelt down in her room. She began by reciting the Our Father and Hail Mary, concentrating on the prayers and mysteries and closing her eyes to remove any distraction.

Suddenly Gladys saw a strange light behind her eyelids. There stood the Holy Mother. She smiled at the kneeling woman and offered Gladys her rosary. Then, just as quickly as she appeared, she was gone. Gladys de Motta finished her prayers, stood up, and for the first time since leaving school, reached for a pen. She began to write: "*Vi a la virgen por primera vez*" ("I saw the Virgin for the first time"). This was the pattern of the apparitions in San Nicolás. The visionary felt a strange joy

in her heart, and after a moment a light flashed before her closed eyes and Mary appeared. "I felt as if ants were running down my shoulder," she confessed. "I knew then that Mary was coming. I would close my eyes, and she would appear to me."

Three days later, she saw Mary for the second time. When she felt her heart filling up with a strange joy, she closed her eyes and waited. After a moment, the Holy Mother appeared to her drenched in light, once again offering Gladys her great Rosary. Afterwards, Gladys wrote: "*La vi nuevamente*" ("I saw her again").

Gladys de Motta began to prepare for the next meeting. She walked around the house and repeated the short question

The Diocesan Sanctuary of Our Lady of the Rosary in San Nicolás was erected in the place indicated by Mary.

she wanted to ask the Mother of God hundreds of times: "What do you want of me?"

A week later, on October 5, Mary appeared for the third time. In the visionary's notes we read: "I saw her and asked what she expected of me. Then her figure faded away into the air and a chapel appeared. I realized that she wants to be among us." With the help of an image, Mary expressed her desire: she wanted a church to be built for her.

PRIVATE LESSONS FROM THE MOTHER OF GOD

Visions followed, which contained personal messages directed at de Motta. On the anniversary of the Fatima apparitions, Mary said: "**You are**

faithful. Do not be afraid to come see me. You will walk, with your hand in my hand, and you will travel a long road."

Gladys didn't know what Mary meant by the "long road," but the certainty of the Holy Mother being by her side filled her with peace and joy. She felt that Mary was looking after her in a special way. This belief was confirmed by the fact that she was enrolled in the school of Mary. The Mother of God herself became her teacher. She even gave her homework to do. She was to read and meditate on Bible passages. The first [assignment] was from the book of Ezekiel. The visionary found the correct Bible passage with difficulty and read it slowly:

> Hard of face and obstinate of heart are they to whom I am sending you. But you shall say to them: Thus says the Lord God! And whether they heed or resist — for they are a rebellious house — they shall know that a prophet has been among them. But as for you, son of man, fear neither them nor their words when they contradict you and reject you, and when you sit on scorpions. Neither fear their words nor be dismayed at their looks, for they are a rebellious house. (But speak my words to them, whether they heed or resist, for they are rebellious.) As for you, son of man, obey me when I speak to you: be not rebellious like this house of rebellion, but open your mouth and eat what I shall give you. It was then I saw a hand stretched out to me, in which was a written scroll which he unrolled before me. It

⋀ "The guidance given by the Mother of God to the simple housewife, Gladys Quiroga de Motta, is in accordance with the legitimate teachings of the Church."

⋏ Our Lady of the Rosary with Baby Jesus.

Mother pointed to Scripture endowed with a Marian meaning. Sometimes these passages seemed even more difficult to understand. Like the passage from the book of Exodus (Exodus 25:8, NAB): "They shall make a sanctuary for me, that I may dwell in their midst." With this passage, Mary made it clear that she is the Ark of the Covenant of the New Testament. She is the dwelling place of God, and everyone who approaches her receives grace.

FRUITS OF THE INITIATIVES

Gladys read the Bible every day, more than the Holy Mother instructed. She also began making pilgrimages to the cathedral in Rosario. Then, in November 1983, Mary appeared to her again. She said, "**You are my children. You are in need, but I love you. The time has come to pray, beg for forgiveness, and it will be given to you. ... All mankind is tainted. It does not know what it wants and this is an opportunity for Satan, but he will not be the victor. My daughter, Jesus Christ will win a great battle**."

Then, the Virgin assured her, "**I do not take my eyes off my beloved children. Blessed are those who trust in the Mother of Jesus, for their trust will be rewarded. Amen. Amen**."

On March 20, 1984, Mary said, "**You have started to pray, people of God. You are beginning to arise again, as I have risen in presence before you. Live in a way that is pleasing to the Lord**." She also encouraged "her children" to attend Holy Mass and to receive nourishment from the Eucharist. "**When you eat Him, no plague that comes from the outside will touch you. Christ will destroy it**."

was covered with writing front and back, and written on it was: Lamentation and wailing and woe!" *(Ezekiel 2:4–10, NAB)*

Scripture readings were something completely new for Gladys, let alone meditating on them and relating them to herself and her times. But that was just the beginning. Later the Holy

◄ *The Mother of God assured Gladys de Motta, "Blessed are those who trust in the Mother of Jesus, for their trust will be rewarded."*

She also added, "**My children, I am asking you to pray for souls who do not pray and in whom love for God fades away. Let no one believe they live in harmony with God if they are far away from Him. I ask for prayers and for the conversion of hearts. Pray for errant children. Pray for every heart to allow my Son to enter inside, so that rebellion may cease**."

There was a call for de Motta to go to the bishop and convey to him Mary's request to build a shrine. "**Tell him my request**," she said. It was at this time that the visionary came across the abandoned statue in the belfry.

So far, no one knew about Gladys's meetings with the Holy Mother. When the apparitions were made public in late November, the whole neighborhood repeated only one thing: "The Mother of God has appeared." People started showing each other the visionary's

home and they would accost her on the street. It was a trial for this shy, humble woman.

On the evening of November 24, Gladys and a group of people accompanying her went to the place Mary chose for her sanctuary, when suddenly, a powerful lightning bolt pierced the darkness and struck the ground. A nine-year-old girl also saw the lightning strike. Another lightning bolt hit the exact same spot a few weeks later, on January 2.

STRANGE STIGMATA

On Friday, November 16, 1984, Gladys received the stigmata. The wounds appeared on Thursdays and Fridays in Advent that year, then on Thursdays and Fridays in Lent in 1985.

In her last apparition, which took place on February 11, 1990, the Holy Mother promised: "**My children, I invite you to live my instructions step by step:**

▲ *Mary warned: "**Let no one believe they live in harmony with God if they are far away from Him**."*

pray, repent, trust! Blessed are those who seek shelter for their souls in prayer. Blessed are those who make reparation for offending my Son severely. Blessed are those who place their trust in the love of His Mother! Anyone who believes in Jesus and Mary will be saved."

THE COMMISSION AND THE EVALUATION OF THE APPARITIONS

In April 1985, Bishop Domingo Salvador Castagna appointed a commission to investigate the apparitions in San Nicolás. On October 25, the commission announced its results. Although it did not conclude that the apparitions were supernatural in origin, neither did it find any theological errors. The commission also emphasized the inexplicable recovery of a boy suffering from brain cancer; this miracle was closely related to the apparitions. It was not found that Gladys de Motta had any inclination toward hallucinations or mental disorders. So, the ruling was inconclusive. The bishop's actions, however, indicate his personal support for the apparitions. In 1985, he celebrated Holy Mass in the place indicated by Mary for her sanctuary. He said:

> I firmly believe that this is the work of the Mother of God. ... I cannot say more than what the Church says. The Church put all this in parentheses. It neither rejects nor says that it is true, but simply says: "Look: it can be true, therefore

> *"My children, I invite you to live my instructions step by step: pray, repent, trust!"* —asks Mary in San Nicolás.

"Blessed are those who seek shelter for their souls in prayer."

we take it seriously" and there is no element that may say it is not true, on the contrary, the existing elements are positive. ... Therefore, I am allowed to say ... evidently this is an apparition made by God."

Six months later, Bishop Castagna once again celebrated the Eucharist there, and during the homily, he announced that the city had handed over a piece of land for the construction of the shrine and that the cornerstone would soon be laid there. This was done on September 25, 1986, but construction was delayed due to a lack of funds.

Pope St. John Paul II himself, being in Argentina, instructed a helicopter pilot to fly over this new Marian shrine. The helicopter lowered itself over the banks of the Paraná, as if the pope wanted to pay tribute to the Mother of God.

In 2016, Bishop Hector Cardelli of San Nicolás officially recognized the apparitions of Our Lady of the Rosary of San Nicolás. He said, "I recognize the supernatural nature of the happy events with which God through His beloved daughter, Jesus through His Most Holy Mother, the Holy Spirit through His beloved spouse, has desired to lovingly manifest himself in our diocese." With the official approval of the local ordinary, the whole Catholic Church was invited to honor Our Lady of San Nicolás.

Asdee
Ireland
1985

▲ *Almost fifty Marian figures in Ireland became instruments of the apparitions.*

▲ *Out of the few words Mary speaks in Ireland, we find out that she calls for great prayer.*

Madonnas in Motion

In 1985, hundreds of people gathered around Marian statues in many parts of Ireland. They gazed in prayer at the image of the Mother of God, waiting for a miracle to happen. Many of them received the grace of seeing wooden and stone figures come to life, even transforming into the Mother of God herself!

Is what happened in Asdee and in Ballinspittle and so many other places in Ireland a repetition of the events in nineteenth-century Knock? Once again they happened on the same island, the supernatural occurance is Marian, and again they are silent—during these apparitions not a single word fell from Heaven. Even the message contained in the images is raw in its simplicity. But this time it is multiplied many times over—the Blessed Mother delivered her sign in many places. As of September 1985, forty-seven were counted. The sign always remains the same.

On February 14, 1985, many Marian statues scattered across Ireland came alive. Furthermore, testimony exists that these statues were no longer images made out of stone, wood, or plaster, but the Blessed Mother in her glorified body.

THE VILLAGE OF ASDEE

The amazing Irish story of the apparitions of the Blessed Mother began in the village of Asdee in County Kerry, where seven-year-old Elizabeth Flynn saw a moving figure of the Mother of God with the Child Jesus in the parish church. Jesus motioned to Elizabeth with His hand, and the Blessed Mother looked at her with smiling eyes.

As soon as Elizabeth told her brother and sister what she saw, the siblings told the children in the neighborhood, and in a little while thirty pairs of eyes stared at the Madonna in their parish sanctuary. Elizabeth wasn't lying! Shortly thereafter, hundreds, then thousands, of people were witnesses to this phenomenon. There is moving testimony of a child who touched the "Madonna in motion" in Asdee. An eyewitness recalled: "I don't know what it is, but it didn't look like stone.

It didn't look like a figure at all." Could the sculptures of the Mother of God transform into the living Mother of God?

OMNIPRESENT AVALANCHE

A month later, the figure of Our Lady of Lourdes in the grotto moved to the edge of Ballydesmond. Soon an avalanche of these supernatural phenomena flooded all the provinces of Ireland. Through the spring and summer, the figures, located in chapels and grottos, began a strange journey. They moved, raised their hands, sometimes they even spoke, disappeared, smiled, frowned, turned their heads, and, just as in Asdee, changed into the living form of the Blessed Virgin Mary.

Even skeptics confirmed the phenomenon that occurred across Ireland. "The statue's features lost their sharpness," wrote Kevin O'Connor, a reporter for the secular newspaper *Irish Independent*. His editor sent him to the grotto in Ballinspittle to objectively investigate the events. "When I set the focus on the image, Mary's hands were raised toward the face," he reported. Another professional photographer, Jim O'Herlihy, gave a similar testimony. After setting the camera on a tripod, he got ready to take a picture—and then saw the figure move.

The phenomena multiplied. In July, women saw the figure of Mary, placed in a roadside chapel, move forward and backward and raise its hands, and on the Holy Mother's face images of various saints and popes appeared, St. Padre Pio among them. Yet it's hard to find the witnesses, and even harder to find detailed testimonies.

That summer, the narrow streets of rural Ireland were filled with thousands of cars. Mostly on the weekends, but also in the evenings after work, thousands of people, mostly Catholic, set off to see miracles.

Asdee

IRELAND

Y *In 1985, two worlds collided on the "Emerald Isle"—a real and a mystical one.*

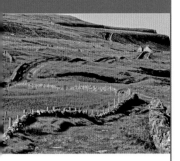

In 1985 Ireland became, to an extent, "the world in a nutshell;" it illustrated the changes that were afflicting traditionally Catholic societies.

The mass media tried using the supernatural element as a weapon to fight the Christian moral tradition in Ireland.

TESTIMONY FROM BALLINSPITTLE

The most well-known place of the Madonnas in motion apparitions is Ballinspittle, located in the southeastern part of the country. Thirty years earlier, on the hundredth anniversary of the proclamation of the dogma of the Immaculate Conception, a stone grotto was built on a slope next to the village, in which a five-foot-tall statue of Our Lady of Lourdes was placed.

On July 22, 1985, Kathy O'Mahony, one of the caretakers of the grotto, went for a walk with her daughter. When they passed by the figure, the women noticed that it was moving.

O'Mahony said, "To me, it was as if she was breathing or lifelike. Maybe breathing or sighing ... chest movements," she said. She and twelve other witnesses said they were suddenly filled with a "sense of peace and protection."

The same experience happened to others. One of them was a local police officer, Sergeant John Murray. When the apparitions began, he went to the grotto out of curiosity, where he found four hundred people in prayer.

"I heard the whole crowd holding their breath," he said, "so I looked at the figure. I saw the statue of the Mother of God floating in midair." He recalled, "The following morning I went up there and checked out that statue. I felt like someone was playing tricks on me, and I was amazed to find no wires or trickery there at all. I was so convinced this was a hoax I had searched behind the statue and also tried to move it," he said. "It wouldn't budge."

Ballinspittle was visited by at least half a million pilgrims from July to October.

"SILLY SEASON"

The reaction of the media was striking. When people started talking about a farmer, Mike O'Donnell, who stepped

back and fell in terror after witnessing an apparition, it was hastily announced that he was intoxicated, that he had a drunken delusion and stumbled and fell as a drunkard might. O'Donnell explained in vain that he wasn't drinking, that he was just trying to get off the path of the figure, which came to life and unexpectedly headed straight at him.

When the media could no longer deny the facts, they resorted to ridicule, mocking not only the witnesses of the supernatural intervention but the apparitions themselves. They gave them the name "Madonna Mania," talked about the events as a "silly season" and tried to capitalize on the apparitions for their secular propaganda.

The media went even further. They cynically suggested that because Ireland struggled with specific difficulties that year, including a rise in unemployment, Madonna Mania had been created both to distract people from real problems and to revive tourism in the country.

Scientific explanations of the phenomenon also appeared. Psychologist Dr. Jurek Kirakowski from University College Cork, explained: "If you stand still, you start wobbling slightly on your feet to hold your balance. Perhaps when you stare too long, your neck begins to tremble. And you see ... that the image is moving. Because you are not aware that you are moving, you interpret this movement as the movement of the motionless figure."

When nearly fifty Marian statues had become instruments of the apparitions, a few of them contained a verbal message. In one of those rare messages, the Holy Mother called for great prayer. Her appeal suggests that Ireland plays a special role to play in calling the world to repentance. What's more, the Holy Mother explained that a new epoch will arrive, which is to be the spring of Christianity—a time of faith, revival, and appreciation for the meaning of the apparitions.

"Consolation and help will come from heaven at that time," wrote one researcher, "when the world wakes up religiously, which will result in a change in attitude toward Marian apparitions. Then Ireland will become a place of particular importance in the eyes of the world because it will be religious and apocalyptic."

The 2018 referendum in Ireland overturning the nation's abortion ban came as a grievous blow to the nation's Catholics. But the moving Madonnas seem to promise that the Emerald Isle may still have a role to play in God's plan for salvation.

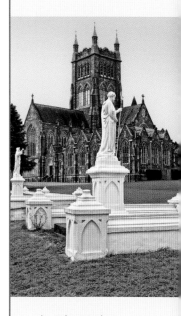

⋀ The apparitions of the Blessed Virgin Mary suggest that Ireland has a special role to play in calling the world to repentance.

⋀ "The Madonnas in motion" prophesied that a dark period is coming for the contemporary world.

Manila

1986

> The Rosary revolution in Manila was directed by the Mother of God.

Λ Epiphany of Saints Avenue (EDSA) — the location of a miracle in the Philippines.

The Lady Who
Commands Soldiers

There were supposed to be bloody clashes, ground and air strikes, tanks, mortars, and rifles. Instead, there was joint prayer and peace. All thanks to the Mother of God, who answered the call of her Filipino children. She listened to their prayers and saved them, changing the hearts of those who were given orders to kill.

From February 22 to 25, 1986, on the Epiphany of Saints Avenue in Manila, a revolution took place. Men and women holding rosaries in their hands marched along the eight-lane road encompassing the capital of the Philippines. It was a powerful force because the Holy Mother stood on the side of the Rosary army. She commanded the people to stop the government's attack. The story of this apparition reads like a thriller novel. As Cardinal Jaime L. Sin said: "The whole scenario of those events was written by God Himself. ... All the action was directed by the Blessed Virgin Mary."

THE STONE THAT FELL TO RAISE THE NATION

In 1972, the Philippines fell under totalitarian control. Just before the next presidential election, the head of state, Ferdinand Marcos, dissolved parliament. According to the constitution, he was no longer eligible to continue as president. His second four-year term was ending. But instead of stepping down, he liquidated the free press and began imprisoning opposition leaders — not to mention about seven thousand dissident soldiers. He also tried to attack the Church, but was met with sharp opposition from Cardinal Sin.

Marcos relented, saying, "I have enough problems. Why would I enter into conflict with the Church?"

The situation in the Philippines became more tense year after year. It was caused by visible government corruption, economic stagnation, a growing gap between the rich and the poor, and bold activities by the Communist partisans in rural areas. The nation's discontent boiled over the day the president's people murdered Benigno Aquino, a member of the Philippine parliament before its dissolution by Marcos.

Before martial law was declared on September 21, 1972, Aquino was an

Manila

PHILIPPINES

uncompromising oppositionist, and he was not afraid to speak out about the scandals of the government. Unsurprisingly, he was one of the first ones to be arrested the day martial law was announced.

He spent seven and a half years in prison, isolated from the world. There

▲ *During the rule of Ferdinand Marcos, the country plunged further into crisis under totalitarian control.*

he fell ill with a serious heart disease that required surgery. Marcos sent him to a hospital in Texas—and refused to allow him to return from exile.

The Aquino family settled in Boston. Benigno devoted three years to studying at Harvard, where he made numerous connections with the resistance in the Philippines. He wanted to return to his homeland no matter the cost. He flew to Manila despite the threats made by Marcos's wife—a former beauty queen—whom he frequently condemned for using public money for private purposes. He was shot on August 21, 1983, when he was departing an aircraft at the Manila airport. He didn't even get to set foot on the Philippine ground.

His death aroused the Filipino people after ten years of apathy. At Cardinal Sin's urging, Aquino's widow, Corazon,

became the head of this dissident movement, despite insisting that she "takes care of housework, not politics."

"GO OUT INTO THE STREET!"

On Saturday, February 22, 1986, Marcos issued an order to arrest the defense minister, Juan Enrile, and several other people. Enrile, General Fidel Ramos, vice chief of staff of the armed forces, and three hundred other military men locked themselves in highway barracks on the Epifanio de los Santos Avenue—Epiphany of Saints Avenue, or EDSA. They announced that they would fight until they fell, but they would not surrender alive to Marcos.

The phone rang on the cardinal's desk. "Your Eminence," said a shaky voice, "you have to help us. If you do not help us, in a few hours we will not be among the living." Everyone knew that a few

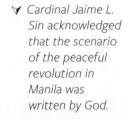

> *Cardinal Jaime L. Sin acknowledged that the scenario of the peaceful revolution in Manila was written by God.*

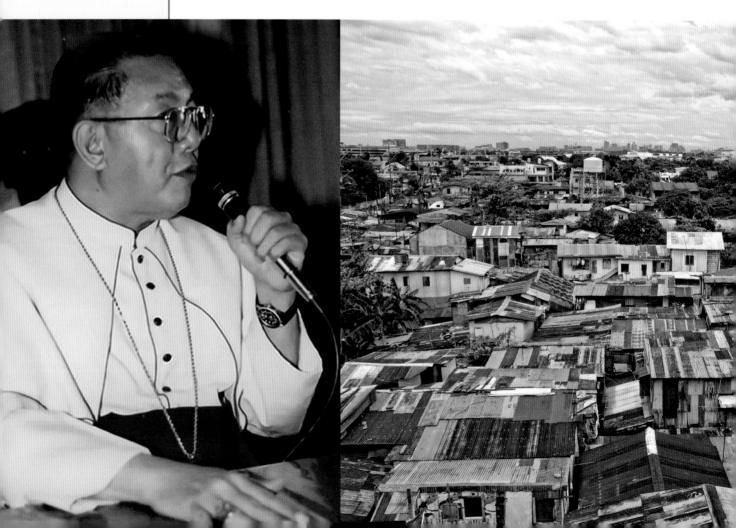

tanks or helicopter squadrons would be enough to eliminate the rebels.

The cardinal prayed in the chapel for half an hour. When he left, he knew what must be done. Through the Catholic radio Veritas, he called on the Catholic people to defend "our friends": "Go out into the street; stand in between the forces of Enrile and Ramos and the oncoming tanks!"

The people heard, and they acted. From all parts of the city, from the slums and more affluent neighborhoods, the crowds flooded in. In a few hours, two million people stood on Epiphany of Saints Avenue. They came with their entire families, including young children. More importantly, they came with rosaries in their hands and prayer on their lips. On the street, huge groups prayed the Rosary over and over. They sang Marian hymns; priests

and bishops celebrated countless Holy Masses on makeshift altars. The people begged the Holy Mother for help. They were very afraid. They knew that Marcos's army was armed to the teeth and could smash them to a bloody pulp. They remained at their posts for four days and nights. At that time, nuns in three contemplative monasteries prayed incessantly for peace. Cardinal Sin told them, "Go to the chapel and pray. Pray with your arms spread out and fast until I say you can stop."

ROSARIES VERSUS TANKS

What was feared soon became reality. The first six tanks appeared on the street. The officers realized they were coming upon a crowd of defenseless civilians. The engines rumbled, and the machines started moving toward the crowd. There were a total of twenty tanks and six thousand soldiers. Two million people, pale and trembling from fear, knelt down facing the oncoming tanks. Nuns were kneeling in the first row. They raised their rosaries and began to pray loudly. Clearly, the people had no intention of stepping back.

Then the tanks withdrew. Not a single shot was fired. The army was defeated by the power of prayer.

In the direction where one of the sisters was leading the Rosary, a tank was approaching with a lone soldier in the turret. The tank stopped before the kneeling crowd. The soldier watched with fascination and then said: "Sister, could you pray louder?" When the nun nodded, the soldier's face beamed a bright smile. After a moment, the tank's crew joined in and prayed.

An old lady in a wheelchair pulled forward. Holding a rosary in her hand, she cried to a different tank

▲ Corazon Aquino, widow of Benigno Aquino, president of the Philippines from 1986 to 1992.

◄ Mary heard the calls of her Filipino children and saved them from inevitable death.

commander: "You can kill me because I'm old anyway! But don't hurt the other people." The tank stopped a few yards in front of the old Filipino woman.

Thirteen-year-old Risa, armed only with fresh daisies, was kneeling and looking at an approaching tank. Under her knees, the asphalt was wet from sweat. "Mister soldier, please don't kill us. We're Filipino, just like you." She handed him her bouquet. The soldier gave her a piercing look for a long time. Finally, he smiled. "Don't be afraid, little one, I won't kill anyone." He jumped off the tank and took the flowers from the child's hands. Risa hugged him. Tears were running down both their faces.

This happened everywhere. "I was speaking with a priest who was there that unforgettable night," Cardinal Sin recalled. "He said you could feel God's presence in the crowd that was absorbed in prayer. He said the soldiers also prayed. He saw their lips moving, uttering the words, 'Hail Mary.' Some of them joined in singing 'Ave, Ave,' under the silent night sky. The crowds chanted the song, which every Filipino had known by heart since early childhood.

The children came with flowers and put them in the barrels of the rifles. Clerics approached the soldiers and hugged them in a brotherly embrace. They were, after all, the same age. Women and girls made sandwiches for those occupying the avenue and offered them to soldiers riding in tanks.

SHIFTING OF THE WIND

Then came the order to use gas to disperse the crowds. But when they began to throw the canisters, the soldiers were the ones who started coughing and running: all of a sudden, the wind changed directions.

Two hours later, the gas attack was repeated and, once again, the wind shifted directions.

"We are still looking for the right purpose for our batteries," the commanding officer explained to Marcos. "We don't want to kill civilians." After another two hours went by, they still sought the right purpose." When

the guns were finally set up, the mortars failed. All the cartridges malfunctioned. Even the helicopters that were sent into action landed among the rebels, and their crews joined them. Why did the squadron commander not attack? "Because he was touched by God's grace," Cardinal Sin later explained.

One of the priests present at the occupation of EDSA "thought of God looking down at His people, blessing and speaking the words once said to Jacob: 'I am the Lord.'"

On the last day of the revolution, Ms. Aquino was chosen as president. Marcos decided to flee the country. He took shelter in Hawaii, where he lived until his death in 1989.

A MARIAN APPARITION?

How was this bloodless revolution possible? This question has been asked many, many times. The cardinal has repeated patiently: "There is no answer. It was a miracle."

Wayne Weible agreed. This Protestant journalist became a zealous Catholic as a result of the Marian apparition he witnessed in Manila. He devoted his entire life to her from the moment of that meeting.

⋏ *During the four-day revolution, Filipinos were aided also by the unceasing prayers of the nuns in the contemplative monasteries.*

⋖ *If people don't pull down miracles from Heaven with their zeal, I cannot expect that I will experience them.*

1986

MANILA

In an interview with Cardinal Sin, Weible revealed that an apparition of the Holy Mother occurred at a crucial moment, seen by hundreds of soldiers of the government's army. He said, "What I am going to tell you, sir, was told to me by many of the same soldiers who were ready to start shooting at people. The tanks tried driving into the crowd. People were praying and raising their rosaries. ... At the same time, a beautiful woman appeared. ... She stood in front of the tanks. She was beautiful; her eyes shining. And this beautiful woman spoke to the soldiers with these words: "**Dear soldiers, stop! Do not proceed! Do not harm my children**." When the soldiers heard this, they left everything and got out of the tanks and joined the people.

That's why when given an honorary degree in Boston, Cardinal Sin could say, "The whole scenario was written by God Himself ... all the action was directed by the Blessed Virgin Mary. We were only actors, but our power came from God.

"I am convinced," he continued, "that all honor, all recognition and all gratitude should be given to the Blessed

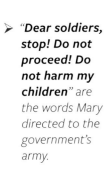

Not a single shot was fired in Manila. The army was defeated by the power of prayer.

*"**Dear soldiers, stop! Do not proceed! Do not harm my children**" are the words Mary directed to the government's army.*

Virgin Mary and through her given to the Son and His Father in Heaven because God truly looked at us with a kind eye, He truly blessed the Philippines and touched us all with His grace."

It's significant that Sister Lúcia, the visionary from Fatima, knew all the details of the revolution in the Philippines. Living in a Carmelite monastery, she had no access to newspapers, radio, or television, but when Cardinal Sin visited her, she told him in great detail about the miracle of the Rosaries said on EDSA.

OUR TASK

Following the events of February 1986, Cardinal Sin warned: "The problem of a dictatorial rule was solved in four days, that's why what happened on Epiphany of Saints Avenue was a miracle. But we have already exhausted the pool of miracles that belonged to us; now we have to solve our problems through smart planning and hard work."

He continued: "During the miracle of the Rosary I saw how all the class differences disappeared. Everyone hurried to help one another, the industrialist stood shoulder to shoulder with the head of the trade union, a businessman shared the same fate as a porter, a college girl as a worker. During the miracle of the Rosary, there was so much care for others. But all of it passed. The class divisions returned, selfishness returned. It's almost as if this miracle never happened."

The EDSA revolt was successful, he said, because during those four days no one thought of worldly matters. Everyone was in danger. Everyone was painfully aware of their need for God's help. Everyone felt Christ's presence among the gathered people. Unfortunately, when everything carries on as usual, the need for God falls to second place in all of us and old habits come back to life.

Today, the Marian apparition in the Philippines has Church approval. Its authenticity was confirmed by Cardinal Jaime L. Sin.

⋏ *Cardinal Sin said that "all honor, all recognition and all gratitude should be given to the Blessed Virgin Mary and through her given to the Son and His Father in Heaven."*

Belpasso

1986

The Immaculate Heart of the Queen of Peace

*The Mother of God unceasingly asks us to pray the Rosary. She repeated that request in Belpasso, but something incredible took place there. During her meetings with the young visionary, Mary herself led the devotion, announcing the mysteries. "**The first joyful mystery: Angel Gabriel announces that I will conceive a Son by the power of the Holy Spirit**."*

⋀ *Today, Belpasso is a well-known place of pilgrimage. A chapel was built on the Rock, which was established as a Marian Sanctuary by the archbishop of the diocese of Catania.*

Rosario Toscano was fifteen years old. He was lying in bed, fighting a stubborn and rare virus. But eventually he was healed, and every first Sunday of the months that followed he would go to the outskirts of the city to have a ten-minute rendezvous with Mary at the site of an unusual rock. The Mother of God also came to southern Italy to announce to the world that mankind needs shelter. In Noah's time, there was an ark that did not sink in the waters of sin. Today that ark is the Immaculate Heart of Mary.

Rosario was born in 1971, the only child of wealthy Catholic parents. Until the spring of 1986, there was no indication that Rosario's life was to be different than what his immediate family planned. But on May 4 of that year, everything started to look different.

The apparitions began that day. At first they took place at the home of the Toscanos, only to move to the outskirts of Belpasso seven days later, in the vicinity of a place called "the Rock." Two meetings occurred in his home, thirty-two at the Rock, and the last one — twelve years later — back in the visionary's home. Altogether, Rosario spoke with the Holy Mother thirty-five times.

IN THE SICK ONE'S HOME

"I was alone, waiting for my parents to return," Rosario recalled. "They went to my school to talk with my teachers about the virus that prevents me from attending classes. Suddenly, lying in bed ... I gasped: I got scared. Something knocked me off the bed. I stood in the middle of the room and felt better. That's when I heard a strange a voice."

"**You've suffered enough**," said someone close by, but although present, still invisible. In a moment, a white light

appeared in the room, and the same female voice instructed him to do three things: to pray for sinners, not to give into despair, and not to spread what he was witnessing. Because, as the Holy Mother said to him later, "**God cooperates with us in silence**."

The woman then began to tell the boy about suffering, of which there is an abundance in this world—not only in Rosario's life, but around the world. And she meant to put an end to it.

Rosario asked to whom he was speaking. The voice from the white light replied, "**I will tell you who I am at the right time**."

Not many days passed before she appeared again and told him, "**I am Mary, the Mother of God, the Immaculate Conception**." And she gave him extraordinary advice: "**If you want to see Me, you must pray the Holy Rosary**." In the Belpasso apparitions, the Rosary is the main theme.

AT THE ROCK

The first proper apparition occurred May 11, 1986. That's when the Holy Mother first appeared on the Rock.

"I saw a beautiful rock in the distance, whose color and shaped looked different from the others," recalled Rosario. "Even its location was different. Certain that this was the place of the apparitions [about which the Mother of God had told him], I started walking down the slope." Then the apparitions began. "The sky was very blue. From it, I saw a white cloud slowly floating toward us. Then the cloud began to expand and open like a flower bud: white light began to burst from it, similar to the light I saw at home.

◁ The Holy Mother introduced herself to the visionary with these words: "**I am Mary, the Mother of God, the Immaculate Conception**."

"Then I saw a beautiful Lady dressed in white. A white mantle with gold trim was thrown over her head. She also had a white sash hemmed with gold. She was holding a rosary in her hands."

When on May 18 Mary opened her arms wide, Rosario saw the last element of the visual message: her Immaculate Heart. The theme of the apparition is suffering and faith. Mary explained, "**The less you believe, the more you**

▲ Mary delivered a message to families: "**Your families must be oases of peace, … small signs of the coming reign of Christ**."

will suffer. Keep the presence of the Lord in your hearts, everyone and at every moment**." For the first time, the Holy Mother referred to something that awaits humanity in the near future. During the next meetings, she would give specifics about "tomorrow."

The Holy Mother gave her blessing to the visionary and the group of people accompanying him, and said, "**I bless you in the name of the Father, and of the Son and of the Holy Spirit**," and she made the sign of the cross over the people.

The apparition ended as it began: "The cloud began to close and go up toward the sky. The Holy Mother disappeared."

THE HEALING

Two weeks later, Rosario was sick again. He had a fever; his temperature was over 100 degrees. He spent all his time in bed. Loved ones no longer believed in the Madonna's assurance that the boy would recover, especially since

the child was very weak and sweating heavily.

Suddenly, his fever began to drop. Before dawn, it had returned to normal. By morning, Rosario had completely recovered. He could now go to the planned meeting with Mary. When he thanked her for healing him, he heard: "**Suffering is thorns, but if they are offered to Jesus, they become roses**."

The Holy Mother soon revealed the main theme of her apparitions in Belpasso: her Immaculate Heart. "**My Heart is very sad. I want to make use of you to make known the Immaculate Heart of the Queen of Peace**," she told him.

She would go on to say a great deal about her Immaculate Heart—about its sorrow, about insults it endures, about the role it has to play in the near future of the world. Subsequent apparitions would show Rosario the sorrowful Holy Mother.

Rosario, commenting on the apparitions in Belpasso, underlined that when it comes to the sorrow of Mary, we cannot focus our attention on temporal problems—for example, the wars that plague many nations. "The Mother of God is worried about something else: for the salvation of each of us. She is worried about us, who are attracted to material things, who have stopped being concerned about the true good: God. Each of us should discover that the desire for holiness lives in our heart. … Only one thing gives us hope: the assurance of help from Mary, Queen of Peace, and the triumph of her Immaculate Heart."

During one apparition, Mary completed her message with a sign. When she prayed the Rosary with

Rosario, she pressed the crucifix adorning it to the Immaculate Heart.

THE CROWDS ASSEMBLE

On the feast of Christ the King, which fell on October 23 that year, pilgrims came to the place of the apparitions for the first time. At the end of Rosario's meeting with Mary, the number of pilgrims exceeded 150,000. Witnesses said that entire villages flocked to Belpasso. Archbishop Luigi Bommarito said that "from Bugio itself, a small village of my former diocese, six coach buses left one Sunday to Borrello." This means, everyone, including the pastor, went to the place of the apparitions.

Previously, the visionary was accompanied by only a few people from his close family. On that day, when several groups of pilgrims witnessed the apparition, Mary revealed her secret to Rosario. The boy was very moved and sad. The secret was directed at families:

Your families must be oases of peace. They must be small signs of the coming reign of Christ. But it will come through my intercession. My heart must triumph, and then the final and great triumph of the heart of Jesus will take place. Therefore, my children, those who truly belong to me should find refuge in my heart.

There was a second part to the secret: the Blessed Mother talked about the flood of evil. "**The world is flooded with injustice, oppression, and sin. The nations of the world rely on the superpowers, but they are wrong**." During the fifteenth apparition, the Holy Mother announced her title,

"Queen of Peace." She then introduced herself in Italian, Latin, Croatian, French, English, and German: "**I am Regina della Pace, Regina Pacis, Kralice Mira, Reine de la Paix, the Queen of Peace, Königin des Frieden: I am Mary, Mother of God, I desire that you enter into my heart with great humility and love**."

"I HAVE COME TO WARN YOU"

Halfway through the apparitions, Mary's tone began to change.

My children, I have come to warn you. My children, my warning is related to your salvation. My children, open your hearts, I want to free you from evil. You often fall into temptations that the evil one puts before your hearts. My children, my Son is calling you, but you remain deaf to His call. My Son is always with you, but you are blind.

She added rhetorically: "**What do you think, what is the reason that I came to you**?" It was to implore them: "**My dear children, do not create divisions among yourself, but be united. You are the chosen people**!"

FIRST SATURDAY DEVOTIONS

On December 1, the Mother of God announced that if God gave His consent, she would also appear on a different day than on the first day of the following month. Indeed, the next meeting with the Messenger of Heaven took place on the feast of the Immaculate Conception, December 8. Rosario Toscano was not at the Rock, but at the church of the Philippine Fathers in Acireale, where he participated in a solemn Holy Mass.

⋀ *"My Heart is very sad. I want to make use of you to make known the Immaculate Heart of the Queen of Peace."*

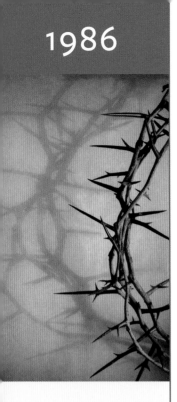

During the last apparition, Rosario saw Jesus Crucified and His Sacred Heart.

The message from Belpasso also speaks of suffering: "Suffering is thorns, but if they are offered to Jesus, they become roses."

There, the Holy Mother gave him another message related to her Immaculate Heart: "**Indeed, I promised assistance at the hour of death with all the graces necessary for salvation to those who every first Saturday, for five consecutive months, would have confessed and received Holy Communion, and above all would have kept me company for a quarter of an hour by reciting the Rosary and meditating on the fifteen mysteries, with the purpose of offering me reparation. I also recommended fasting for world peace.**"

The First Saturday devotion that Mary revealed to Sister Lúcia in Pontevedra in 1925 are clearly mentioned. The message given to the Fatima visionary is identical: we have the same promise, we have a thread of reparation, confession, Holy Communion, and the Rosary, and keeping Mary company for fifteen minutes. When asked why exactly five months, the Mother of God answers the same way as she did to the seer of Fatima:

"**There are five insults directed at my Immaculate Heart: blasphemies against my Immaculate Conception; against my virginity; the refusal to recognize me as the Mother of God and of men; the actions of those who instill indifference and hatred toward me in people's hearts; the actions of those who offend me in my sacred images.**"

Mary added: "**Take action to make reparation for all the attacks and indifferences that hurt my heart. From now on I entrust you with the task of defending the honor of my heart. I promise that if you will accept the task that I have entrusted to you, you will obtain the grace of conversion.**"

THE LAST MEETING

On the day of Mary's last visit to Belpasso, 150,000 pilgrims gathered around the Rock. At the end of the apparition, they heard the boy exclaim: "What? Will you never come again?" People understood that the Holy Mother would not appear again on the Rock in Belpasso. They left the place of the apparitions crying, but not without hope. Mary promised that she would appear once more in the future.

"**I will return one day, which does not mean that I am leaving you now. My Immaculate Heart will always be with you, because peace on Earth has been entrusted to it. When my heart triumphs, you will honor the Queen of Peace.**"

Mary's last message at Belpasso was this:

My children, during these months I have given you many messages to convert you. The Lord has touched many hearts and He has enkindled in them the love for His Heart. He has comforted many inconsolable in pain, He brought peace to many families and to many hearts. He made everyone understand how wonderful and marvelous prayer is, how fruitful is the recitation of the Rosary and my intercession before God, how pleased He is with the sacrifices and penance offered in reparation for sins and for the conversion of sinners. But above all, He made you understand how important the sacraments are for eternal life. He has given you the gift of joy, and He will continue to give it to you during Holy Mass.

Dear children, how many times have I invited you to do what I ask — begging you to accept at least God's commandments. My apparitions have served to revive the spirit of faith, hope, and love in your souls. Spiritual fruits are obtained by perseverance and total trust in God's mercy. I will always protect you, and even if you bend like trees under the blows of the wind, you will remain safe. Trust in me.

At the end, the Holy Mother prophesied about the future:

I have to tell you a very important thing now, and you will pass it on to all people: after the period of peace, which I will give to the world through my heart, many will withdraw from God, many will be ashamed of Him. When the period of peace comes to an end, many unpleasant events will happen in every family, in every city, in every nation and in the entire world: because many will lose their vigilance again, forgetting about God and His laws. The Church will suffer.

Before all this happens, I will warn you so you may tell everyone. This will be the tangible proof of my apparitions, more important than the signs in the sky. Do not be discouraged: always look to the Sacred Hearts of Jesus and Mary. Let the Gospel be in your minds, be your word, but, above all, let it be written in your hearts.

Having said these words, the Mother of God began to slowly rise for the last time toward Heaven. "She's waiting impatiently there for us, like a mother for her children," Rosario declared.

ADDITIONAL APPARITIONS

The apparition announced by Mary at the last meeting did not happen until twelve years later. It was different from the previous ones because it was accompanied by two extraordinary visions. On March 25, 1999 — the Feast of the Annunciation — the Holy Mother directed a request to the world for a special consecration of families, parishes, and dioceses to the Immaculate Heart.

Rosario noted: "On the night of the twenty-fourth to the twenty-fifth of

In Belpasso, the Mother of God once again reminded us about practicing the First Saturday devotion.

1986

➤ *The message from Belpasso reminds us about participating in the holy sacraments:* **"The Lord made you understand how important the sacraments are for eternal life."**

⌃ *Mary tirelessly proclaimed the need to recite the Rosary. In Belpasso she said,* **"Here is the sign of prayer: it is given to all people."**

March 1999, worried about the outbreak of a new war in Europe (in Kosovo), I prayed in my room for peace in the world. I asked our Lord for this through the intercession of the Holy Mother. After a few hours, I got drowsy. I went to bed and fell asleep.

"The first rays of the sun woke me up. I got up, looked around and saw that I was on top of a mountain, from which I could see the whole world.

"I saw the Holy Mother of Belpasso with the Immaculate Heart and a rosary in the right hand. This time she had a small olive branch in her left hand. The Blessed Virgin Mary said:

> *The moment has come to ask the Holy Father to commence, with the help of all bishops, a special consecration of families to my Immaculate Heart, and through it to the Sacred Heart of Jesus. And also parishes and all dioceses, in accordance with the will expressed by our Savior.*
>
> *Many souls follow a path that distances them far from God, but He, in His infinite mercy, wants to save them, entrusting them to the care of my Immaculate Heart. Initially, there will be many difficulties on the road to fulfilling my request, but eventually it will be declared a bastion and many souls will be saved. You must offer a lot of prayers and sacrifices for this intention.*

"The Mother of God pointed to the olive branch in her hand: '**Here is the sign of reconciliation and unity: it is given to all mankind. Humanity, reconciled with the Father for the merits of Jesus Christ, will again find in God the ties to love and peace**.'

"Pointing to the rosary, she added: '**Here is the sign of prayer: it is given to all people. When they open their hearts to God and meditate on His words of eternal life, they will fulfill acts of mercy**.'

"She also pointed to her heart: '**Here is the sign of dedication to God: it is for all who are united in Christ's Eucharistic suffering, who comfort the Sacred Hearts of Jesus and**

Mary, who offer reparation for the conversion of those who are infected with sin.'"

At that moment, the visionary saw Jesus Crucified and His Sacred Heart. On the same height as the Sacred Heart, there was a chalice and a Host, as if they were suspended in the air. Drops of blood and water were falling into the chalice, overflowing it and falling into the world. A loud voice came from heaven: "**Salvation and sanctity**."

WHAT IS THE CHURCH'S STANCE?

The archbishop of Catania, Luigi Bommarito, was in close contact with Rosario Toscano during all the years of the apparitions. In numerous interviews, he spoke positively about the boy. In a May 5, 1989, issue of the magazine *Jesus*, he admitted that he visited the site of the apparitions many times, in both an official and a private capacity. He also described the visionary as a "healthy, level-headed and calm boy, who tries not to draw attention to himself." The bishop recalls, "He told me once: 'I am happy that people have stopped looking for me, but they are going to the Rock and praying there to the Blessed Virgin Mary.' He said it without realizing how important it is. ... He often repeated: 'If Your Excellency wants me to go to the Rock and pray there, I'll go. If you don't want me to go, I won't. If Your Excellency wants to set a day for me to go there, no problem.' In short: he is completely obedient." And obedience to the Church is one of the basic criteria for authenticating the apparitions.

Today, the Rock in Belpasso is a well-known place of pilgrimage, under the protection of the Church. In May 2000, Bishop Bommarito blessed the figure of the Madonna that is placed on the Rock and consecrated the chapel that was built, as requested by Mary, on the site of her apparitions. He awarded her with jubilee indulgences in 2000 and established the Marian Sanctuary of the Diocese of Catania.

▼ *Mary also drew attention to the priceless gift of the Eucharist:* "**The Lord has given you the gift of joy, and He will continue to give it to you through Holy Mass.**"

Yagma and Louda

1986

1986

Lady of Assumption, Mother of Peace

Usually, it is the miracle of the Marian apparitions that ignites a devotion in a given place. The shrines in Yagma and Louda are an exception to this rule. They were created by those who carried love for Mary in their hearts and wished to have a place where they could pilgrimage to honor her. The Holy Mother blessed their efforts by appearing there.

⌃ *The apparitions in Burkina Faso highlight traditional forms of piety, such as the Rosary and pilgrimages.*

⌄ *In Yagma, a Marian sanctuary was created on a beautiful hill overgrown with shrubs.*

The apparitions of Burkina Faso started in 1963 when Fr. Constantin Guirma was installed as a pastor of the second largest parish in the nation's capital, Ouagadougou. The parish of Kologh-naba was dedicated to Our Lady of the Rosary and had a special devotion to Our Lady of Lourdes. Some of the parishioners traveled on a pilgrimage to distant France, to personally stand on the land chosen by the Holy Mother in 1858.

Suddenly, a strange initiative emerged among the lay parishioners. They wanted to establish a great Marian devotion in their country. People started looking

intensely for "land for the Mother of God." Shortly thereafter, Laurent Ghilat and François Dakoure arrived to tell Fr. Guirma that they had found a beautiful hill overgrown with bushes, about ten miles from Yagma. In their opinion, it would be the right place for the Holy Mother's home. The pastor, whose parish encompassed the hill, personally looked at it and encouraged his parishioners to clean it up and erect a grotto, as in Lourdes.

In 1968, three nearby parishes organized the first official pilgrimage to the new shrine. The priests strongly supported this initiative, urging their faithful to participate in it and, as Fr. Guirma recalls, "the pilgrimage was a success." The following year was also successful. Yagma slowly started attracting more and more people as Fr. Guirma and other priests encouraged the faithful to visit it and pray to their beloved Mother. The pastor from Kologh-naba set an example of zeal for others; he was there often to pray and talk to Mary about problems entrusted to him.

THE SECOND INITIATIVE OF THE BISHOP

In June 1969, the zealous priest Fr. Guirma was appointed bishop of the newly formed Kaya Diocese. Because he was connected to the Yagma sanctuary, he decided to create a similar home for the Virgin on his territory. After much searching, he found a beautiful hill near the city and built a place of pilgrimage. The owners of the hill (non-Christian villagers who every year offered sacrifices there for their ancestors) willingly gave the hill to the bishop for religious purposes. Soon a cross was erected, and then an

Yagma and Louda

BURKINA FASO

◄ *"I am the Mother of Peace"* — said Mary to Maria-Rose — *"I come to bring peace and reconciliation to my children in Burkina."*

altar. Construction began on a small sanctuary under the invocation of the Immaculate Heart of Mary.

Yagma and Louda mirrored each other. These closely linked places of Marian devotion become the destination of annual pilgrimages. Beginning in 1970, those pilgrimages were led by now-Archbishop Guirma.

When a bloody Communist revolt broke out in the country in 1983, all the people came to the hill to seek comfort there and entrust their misfortunes to Mary. As in Louda, not only Catholics sought out that place, but also Protestants, Muslims

⋏ *The farmers of Burkina Faso.*

Yagma and Louda point to the role of the Immaculate Heart of Mary as the way to peace.

An almost unknown place on maps was met with extraordinary goodwill from Heaven when the Mother of God came to its zealous followers.

and animists. The sanctuary in Louda was consecrated in 1984, the same year the whole world was consecrated to the Immaculate Heart of Mary.

ANSWER FROM HEAVEN

In 1985, another grassroots initiative appeared: a large prayer movement led by children, who regularly went to Yagma to pray all day long to the Blessed Mother. In the sanctuary, they celebrated traditional devotions, such as the Rosary and the Stations of the Cross. Older youths and adults joined them.

At this time, the Marian apparitions began. The visionary was one of the children from the prayer group. "Young Maria-Rose, a parishioner from my previous parish of Kologh-naba, chose me as her spiritual father and advisor," the archbishop wrote. "Since 1986, the Blessed Virgin Mary and her Son appear to her regularly. Mary appears to her in Yagma, where she often spends time praying with a group, and in Louda, in the diocese of her spiritual father, where she also visits often."

Little is known about the content of these apparitions. We know that Mary appeared in Yagma and Louda, as well as the diocesan oratory in Kaya. Sources

say that Maria-Rose received messages related to both shrines, among others. In June 1988, Mary announced that "**Yagma will be a holy place, an international pilgrimage center, and the pope himself will personally come to bless this place**." Sure enough, in January 1990, Pope St. John Paul II visited Yagma during his visit to Africa.

About Louda, Mary said: "**I am taking possession of Louda. Everyone who comes to that hill in the bishop's footsteps, repenting for sins, will receive absolution, eternal salvation, and many needed graces**." The local bishop explained that the absolution of sins of course required the Sacrament of Reconciliation, unless the conscience of the pilgrim is burdened only with venial sins. In accordance with canon law, one could speak about the promise of an indulgence given by the Holy Mother, which anyone who comes to this place can receive, chosen and built by people, but approved by Heaven. The Mother of God also said that "**Louda's hill is a holy place and God the Father sent His angels to take possession of it and to guard it, as a continuation of**

Yagma. The Eternal One sent graces prepared by Him first to Yagma and then to Louda."

In one of her apparitions, the Blessed Mother also said that she is "**Our Lady of Assumption, Mother of Peace. I come to bring peace and reconciliation to my children in Burkina**."

The initiatives of the laity did not end with the construction of the chapel or grotto. People organized pilgrimages on the Marian hills. They made Yagma and Louda their houses of prayer by coming there often to meet with their Mother. When the apparitions began, they built a sanctuary in Louda and next to it a monument commemorating the visits from the Heavenly Mother. Under the monumental cross stands a life-size figure of Christ and the Blessed Virgin Mary of the Assumption.

The bishop himself wrote, "As a result of the signs we received, after prayers for discernment, after getting opinions of great Mariologists and international experts on supernatural phenomena, by virtue of the apostle's charism given to me and the episcopal power, I confirmed and announced in my diocese that the apparitions of the Virgin Mary to little Maria-Rose in Louda and Kaya, located in my diocese, are real, and thus I confirm the authenticity of all the apparitions of the Virgin Mary and her Son granted to Maria-Rose."

A MESSAGE FOR US

What's extraordinary is that no previous tradition of Marian worship is associated with the sites of these apparitions. On the contrary: Louda was an important ritual site for animists.

And yet the events in Yagma and Louda are of a piece with several modern apparitions that emphasize the Immaculate Heart of Mary. They echo the messages of Rue du Bac, Lourdes, Pellevoisin, Fatima, Pontevedra, Tuy, Akita, and Bethania, among others. Little wonder, too: as Pope Benedict XVI once said, the Immaculate Heart "is stronger than guns and weapons of every kind."

◄ *Pilgrimages began arriving at the hills dedicated to Mary. People made them places of prayer.*

▼ *The Mother of God promises an indulgence to anyone who will come to these places — chosen and built by people, but approved by Heaven.*

Hrushiv

1987

Madonna of Kiev

In 1987, a small wooden Orthodox church, closed for many years by the Communist authorities, suddenly started to emit a brilliant glow. Prayers persisted, Masses were celebrated. The militia and the KGB were helpless. How do you break up crowds of such fervent believers—especially when you yourself are witnessing a miracle?

A *During the reign of the Grand Prince of Kiev, Yaroslav the Wise, the capital of the ancient state of Rus—Kiev—was elevated to the ranks of a metropolis.*

The icon the Madonna of Kiev is one of the most famous Marian icons in the world. Its beauty is often compared to the Mona Lisa. The viewer's attention is drawn to the Madonna's gentle face, her head nuzzling the Christ Child's.

Today, many nations know the image by the name Our Lady of Tenderness. The icon became the ideal of Marian icons, never again achieved by later artists. It was created by a Byzantine monk around 1132 for Prince Mstislav of Kiev. It came to Ukraine around 1134 and was placed in Vyshhorod, where a beautiful shrine was built to house it. This is why Ukrainians honor her as Our Lady of Vyshhorod. In 1155 (some sources say 1164), Prince Andrey Bogolyubsky attacked Ukraine. Before he demolished Kiev, he took the valuable icon from nearby Vyshhorod and moved it to Vladimir, a city in the north.

The icon survived centuries of wars. In 1395, it was transferred to Moscow.

Today it is kept in the secular Tretyakov Gallery. But the Madonna of Kiev showed that neither the frame of the painting nor the gallery walls could limit its power. After all, St. John of Damascus taught that an icon is not only the image itself but the presence of the portrayed saint. This presence made itself known through miracles and answered prayers in another way in the town of Hrushiv.

SILVER AURORA

In 1987, the Holy Mother began appearing above the tower of a small wooden Orthodox church dedicated to the Holy Trinity and belonging to the Greek Catholic community in Hrushiv.

For more than a century it was an important pilgrimage site. But after the Communist takeover of Ukraine, the authorities shut down the shrine.

The years passed. Then suddenly, the seemingly dead church came to life—literally. For three weeks it was inexplicably surrounded by a silver aura.

Hrushiv

UKRAINE

◄ *Our Lady of
Vladimir icon is
one of the most
venerated icons
in the Russian
Orthodox Church.*

The light shone two hundred yards high; in it, the miraculous Madonna from the Kiev icon appeared. The first witness of this unusual phenomenon was twelve-year-old Marina Kizyn. Seeing the Blessed Mother, she immediately called her mother and several people from the neighborhood. They too saw what Marina had seen: an unearthly radiance and, in it, God's Mother.

News of the apparitions spread quickly. Mere days passed before a huge crowd stood around the humble shrine. They came not only from Ukraine but from other republics of the Soviet Union. Every day about seventy thousand people arrived. The militia and the KGB tried, without success, to regain control of this place. It became difficult for the soldiers to remain at

for you, for your children, for your future. There will come a time when your people, so in love with God, will gain independence and become a salvation for those who keep their faith in Jesus Christ." At the same time, the Blessed Mother's words were cautionary: "**Many will come as false messiahs and prophets. Therefore, I warn you, stay awake and be careful. Happy are the lives of those who are without transgressions and keep God's commandments**."

Two days later, Mary declared, "**Lucifer is losing strength. To keep his place on the throne of darkness, he has already begun announcing that he has improved, but this is not true**." Still, she warned: "**Lucifer is intelligent and cunning**."

Referencing the Ukraine's powerful neighbor, Mary said, "**Pray for Russia. Russia will only convert when all Christians will pray for it**." Yet she was not content to criticize only the Communists. She also said, "**Both the East and the West are evil. The**

The council on the Dormition of the Mother of God, where in the fourteenth century the icon of the Madonna of Kiev was placed.

In Hrushiv, Mary said, "Ukraine, my daughter! I pray for you, for your children, for your future."

their posts, given that they themselves were witnessing the supernatural event. Having received the grace of participation in Marian apparitions, they weren't able to ruthlessly disperse the crowds as they were ordered to do or handcuff and punish the more zealous participants to make examples of them.

LUCIFER'S THRONE

For twenty-one days, the church in Hrushiv became a "free zone" within Ukraine. It is unknown from where priests of the underground Church came out of hiding to celebrate Holy Mass for the crowds of people. In time, the crowds began to receive messages from the Virgin Mary.

Here is one of them, from May 14, 1987: "**Ukraine, my daughter! I pray**

difference is that the godlessness of the West has not been officially announced."

VISIONARY FROM THE GULAG

Joseph Terelya, a thirty-four-year-old Carpatho-Russian from a mountain village near Mukachevo, belonged to a family of high-ranking Communist officials. But Terelya was raised by deeply religious grandparents. He was actively involved in the life of the underground Church, often participating in Masses celebrated in the depths of the Carpathian forests.

When he was nineteen, he was drafted into the army, but was soon imprisoned for trying to evangelize his fellow soldiers. The punishments grew stricter, but Joseph didn't stop preaching the faith and made several attempts to escape. He served time in Soviet prisons on and off until 1987, when he regained his freedom through the intervention of President Ronald Reagan.

During his time in a Moscow prison, Terelya experienced the grace of two apparitions. To the prison notorious for mistreating its inmates came the Madonna, the same one he would later

Since 1917, the Madonna of Kiev icon is located in the Tretyakov Gallery; currently in St. Nicholas Museum-Church.

HRUSHIV

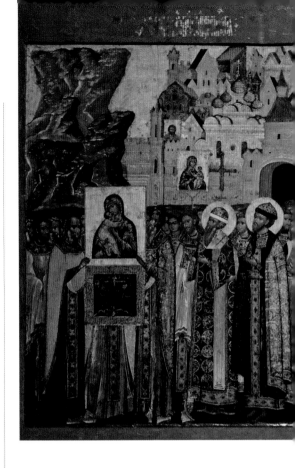

see in Hrushiv. The first apparition occurred on February 12, 1979, while he was alone in his cell, his health quickly deteriorating from the cold, damp jail and his torture at the hands of his captors. During this period, prayer helped him survive. When he woke up one night shivering, he began to pray. Suddenly, he felt his body being filled by an unusual warmth. Then the cell was lit up by a beautiful light—the same one as he would later see in Hrushiv. A moment later, the Mother of God stood in front of him.

Mary said to Terelya, "**You should learn to forgive those who persecute you the most. Difficult years are before you, judgments, degradation. But starting today, you will never be afraid again**."

Terelya later wrote in his book, *Witness*, "It was a brief apparition, lasting a few minutes, but those few moments meant more to me than the whole world. I felt incredibly safe even though I was where I was, despite what awaited me in the near future."

The second meeting with Mary also took place February 12, but two years later, in 1981. From the moment he was convicted for issuing a publication and circulating it underground, Joseph Terelya was transferred to a "freeze cell." An icy wind was blowing inside, and the prisoner was only wearing a thin shirt. He himself described this one night:

> The guard on duty looked through the peephole, saw this, and switched off the light. I sat on my bed and began to freeze. There was an old quilt you could see through and I wrapped myself in it, garnering what little comfort it could afford me. Too weak,

> I finally lay down, praying and awaiting my fate. Within another ten minutes my lips wouldn't move, and my eyelids felt like they too were freezing shut. My head was splitting, my eyes, my temples, my jaws. I could still think but I couldn't move my limbs. I was freezing to death.

> It was then that I became aware of an intense flash in the room, a very powerful light, and heard what sounded like someone walking in my cell.

> My eyes were clamped. I couldn't tell who it was. I can't explain what happened—lying there with my eyes shut, in a state approaching paralysis—but somehow I became aware that the room was illuminated. And the cell was starting to feel warmer. Against my eyelids I felt the palm of a woman's hand and smelled the soft pure fragrance of milk.

➤ *The Madonna, who came twice to the imprisoned Joseph Terelya, was the same apparition he later saw in Hrushiv.*

⌃ *The apparitions in Hrushiv began on April 26, 1987, on the first anniversary of the explosion of the Chernobyl nuclear power plant. Was this Mary's way of warning about the next cataclysm?*

*When the hand lifted I was able to open my eyes. There before me was the young Virgin. '**You called to me**,' she said, '**and I have come**'. The cell grew warmer. My body felt as if it were near an oven."*

During this apparition, the Mother of God delivered many prophecies to Joseph concerning humanity. She also showed him a map. The visionary wrote, "Certain places were on fire. Russia! Neighboring countries were also licked by the flames. Then Mary asked for the sorrow of sins and spiritual purity. At the end, a great flash appeared and the Blessed Virgin disappeared."

The prisoner took off his shirt and began walking around the cell. "It was very hot. The guards couldn't believe I had survived the night. The next day, a commission was convened to find out what happened that night. But they didn't believe that the Mother of God appeared to me."

After Terelya was released, he visited Hrushiv, where he met the Mother of God from his prison years. Together with the long-suffering pilgrims, he heard several messages from Heaven.

During the "thaw" following Stalin's death, Terelya helped work toward the legalization of the Catholic Church in Ukraine. Quite unexpectedly, he received permission to travel to the Netherlands. Alas, once out of the country, he was barred from returning to his homeland.

Now an exile, he decided to settle in Canada and began working to spread the message entrusted to him by Our Lady. Several times in the course of his mission, Terelya met with Pope St. John Paul II—a man who knew a thing or two about Communists.

⚑ *Soviet prison barracks. In Hrushiv, the Mother of God admonished, "**Both the East and the West are evil. The difference is that the godlessness of the West has not been officially announced**."*

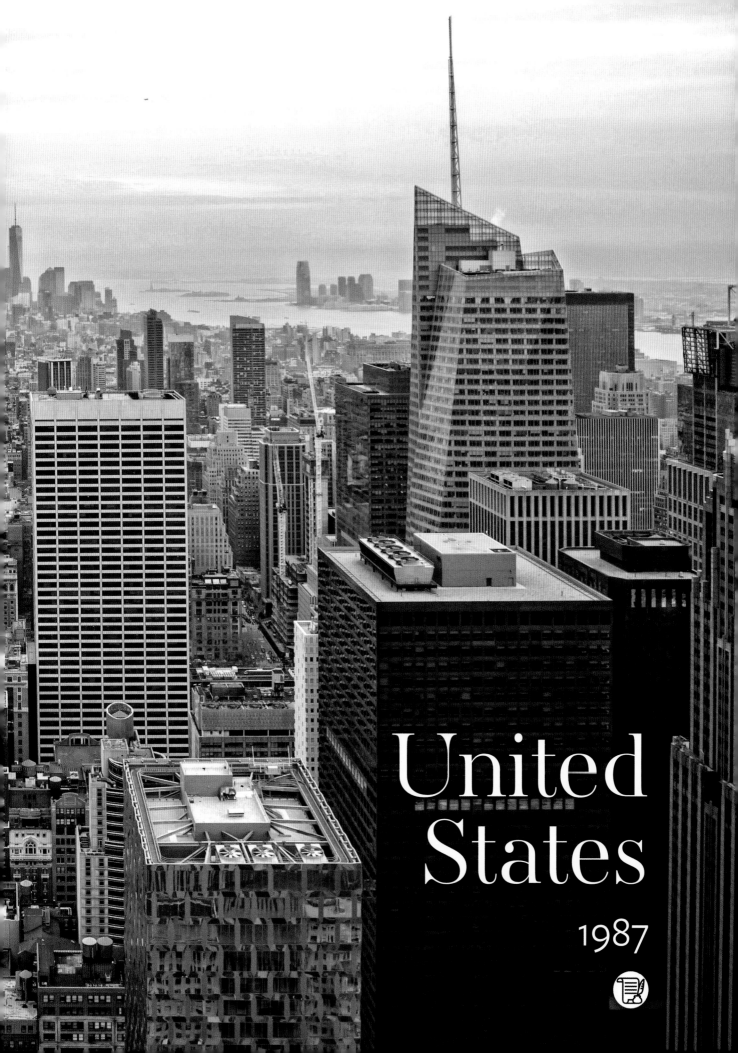

United States

1987

Harbinger of Change

▲ *Pope St. John Paul II was a great advocate of the domestic church.*

"Mariamante" was a mother and a visionary who became the inspiration for those who established the Apostolate of Holy Motherhood; that is all we know about her. She did so much for God, despite the fact that we never came to know her real name. She remained in the shadows, devoted to her family, busy with her daily tasks — just as the Mother of God had promised her.

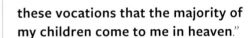

The visionary who inspired the Apostolate of Holy Motherhood remained anonymous to the end. We know only that at the time of the apparitions and locutions in 1987 she was a young mother, and that she lived in the United States.

She went by the pseudonym Mariamante (Latin for "beloved Mary"). The Blessed Virgin Mary promised her: **"I shall always protect you from the public eye."**

MARIAN YEAR

Mariamante's visions occurred during Pope St. John Paul II's Marian Year. The pope identified the modern Church with the family, declaring that "the future ... of the Church passes through the family." So, too, the Blessed Virgin explained to Mariamante: **"As you know, Satan is attacking the family and the priesthood, as they are the holiest of vocations. It is through these vocations that the majority of my children come to me in heaven."**

When asked by the visionary how she was to know whether or not the messages came from her, Mary replied: **"You will know that they come from me by the truth that is contained in them."**

Acting on the Virgin's message, Mariamante initiated the international Apostolate of Holy Motherhood, which pertains directly to families. It brings together mothers who are seeking the path to sanctity in their daily lives. They are directed by, and seek to imitate, Mary — herself a mother and a housewife.

The Apostolate of Holy Motherhood does not have a formal leadership structure. The movement's members want to change the world through everyday holiness. They seek, firstly, to glorify God and fulfill His will. Second, they and their families are consecrated to the Mother of God.

Third, they practice a life of prayer and contemplation, though not neglecting their family and professional duties. They do so with their eyes fixed on the example of Mary of Nazareth.

AROUND THE HEART

Mariamante's visions all occurred during the Marian Year. They can be divided into three stages.

The first stage is comprised of only Our Lady's first apparition, which occurred in January 1987 and was a manifestation of the Immaculate Heart of Mary. It occurred in complete silence, as the Blessed Virgin Mary showed the visionary her Immaculate Heart.

The second stage began on February 8, during which the Blessed Virgin gave Mariamante a detailed, verbal message.

In the third stage, the Sacred Heart of Jesus and the Immaculate Heart of Mary appeared to Mariamante together.

When she spoke, Our Lady primarily focused on practicing the virtue of chastity. "**Pray for chastity and live it. Today's world depends on it**," she said. She also underlined the role of a Christian upbringing, as children were going to live in a different reality from their parents. "**Take care of your children. They are of most importance. They will live during the reign of my Immaculate Heart.**" But only prayer, especially the Rosary ("**which pleases God most**"), and penance will bring about her reign.

The Blessed Mother gave additional guidelines:

Silence and obscurity. This is what I ask of you. May the Lord's light shine through you in your daily duties. Many do not understand this. They think that they must be in the public

UNITED STATES
OF AMERICA

Y *The Apostolate of Holy Motherhood had its beginnings in Mariamante's apparitions.*

*Prayer and humility are of prime importance in the message conveyed to the visionary. "**Pray for chastity and live it. Today's world depends on it**."*

eye in order to do great things for God. It is often quite the contrary. A silent, hidden life counts, like the one I lived in Bethlehem and Nazareth.*

The Blessed Virgin Mary even availed herself of a short, heavenly proverb: "**As love is the queen of virtues, so humility is the king**."

TRIUMPH OF THE IMMACULATE HEART

The messages conveyed through Mariamante referred to Fatima. Our Lady declared, "**The Fatima message contains all that is necessary for you at the moment**."

She said a great deal about the victory of her Immaculate Heart, which was foretold in Fatima:

Good always overcomes evil. Never forget that. ... Satan and his legions cannot prevent my triumph, though they are striving to do so. God has already decided: it is to come about at this time. You are fortunate to be living now, a period of mercy and love. Not everybody had the opportunity to turn away from such a great evil. You will know by a sign in the sky, which will be me, that the time has come for the conversion of many. This will be achieved by a great outpouring of graces upon the earth, graces I received from God. The triumph of my Immaculate Heart will follow, which I foretold in Fatima.

How will this triumph come about? The initiative lies with Mary herself:

Though God gave Me this power, I rarely used it. It was not necessary in the past, as the times were more God-fearing, and the Church was respected. Unfortunately, things have changed. So I have to use other means to communicate with my children.

Our Lady also warned that the road to victory will entail great suffering:

Virtually all those who serve my cause, my triumph, will experience difficulties in proportion to the importance of the mission that I shall entrust to them. Do not be afraid of that. See it as a means to your sanctification.

That suffering is not the work of God, but of the devil. "**Are you prepared to participate in this salvific work through the suffering and crosses that God will send**?" asks the Blessed Virgin Mary. That is why "Mary's children" are to seek help and support in the sacraments: "**You have to constantly partake of the sacraments in order to be strengthened, especially by confession and the Holy Eucharist**."

NEW WORLD

Our Lady also requested: "**Pray for children, all the children in the world. Pray that families might have a great respect for new lives, a great respect for children**."

That is precisely how the members of the Apostolate of Holy Motherhood strive to live. They attempt to reflect Mary in their everyday lives, serving God and their families through long days of prayer, hard work, obscurity, and silence.

"Silence and an inconspicuous life. That is what I ask of you. May the Lord's light shine through you in your daily duties."

Kurešček

1989–1999

Queen
of Peace

Many years passed before France Spelič managed to realize the vocation he carried in his heart. He was ordained a priest when he was over sixty years old. This wasn't the only mission he was destined for, however. Called "Smaverski" by Mary, the visionary saw the Mother of God nearly five hundred times and listened to her words, later to bring her message to the world.

⚐ The Immaculate Conception with Saints *by Piero di Cosimo, c. 1505.*

The apparitions in Kurešček are all tied to politics—specifically, the Slovenian independence movement. Unlike in neighbors Bosnia, Herzegovina, and Serbia, where the terror of civil war prevailed, peace and freedom were achieved in Slovenia after the "Ten-Day War." Mary announced: "The month of May 1991 shall be a month of reconciliation for all. Do everything to make my wish known to all. Do not procrastinate, time is precious." Shortly after, the army of the Yugoslav regime made an incomprehensible maneuver: they retreated.

The connection of this place with Medjugorje has sparked controversy. Mary said, "**The messages from Medjugorje and Kurešček are precious. Do not forget about them or put them on the shelf. Live them**." If one of the apparitions is recognized by the Church, the second will also take on a new value.

France Spelič was born in 1927. At fifteen years old, he fought in the ranks of the Liberation Army. He believed that Communism was the only path to a better world. After the war, the young idealist got married and began his career as an officer under the leadership of the pro-Soviet government. Eventually, he was discharged and began working as a teacher in a small village.

There, in 1954, he came into possession of a Bible. He began reading it and he converted. He left the Communist Party and, as a consequence, was placed under surveillance. Meanwhile, he discovered a new vocation within himself: he desired to become a priest. He knew this dream was unrealistic, however, as long as the Soviets controlled his country. Still, at the age of forty, he began studying theology. During his fifth year of studies, his wife developed multiple sclerosis. For

◄ *The main altar in the Church dedicated to the Queen of Peace on Kurešček Hill.*

▲ *A place of Marian worship—for years destroyed and forgotten—came to life and resounded with prayer.*

the next twenty years, he looked after her with great care and love. In 1993, his dream came true: he was ordained a priest, as announced by Mary. At about the same time, the stigmata appeared on his hands and feet.

VISIONARY'S SECOND LAST NAME AND THE SECOND MEDJUGORJE

The Holy Mother began appearing to France Spelič in 1989. Ten years later, on December 8, 1999, on the feast of the Immaculate Conception, they ended. Mary never called the visionary by name, but from the beginning she referred to him as "Smaverski"—though, to this day, we don't know why.

At the end of 1989—the year of the destruction of the socialist empire—Smaverski visited Medjugorje, where he received a strange message: he was supposed to bring prayer back to life in some forgotten and abandoned place in Slovenia. It later turned out that Mary meant Kurešček, a hill that's 2,733 feet high, located near Ljubljana. There was an old church at the top of it dedicated to the Queen of Peace. For centuries it was a place of fervent Marian devotion, but during the Second World War it was destroyed and desecrated. For half a century it stood half in ruin, forgotten. But three years after the Marian appeal in Medjugorje, the sanctuary in Kurešček was restored and blessed by Bishop Alojzij Šuštar of Ljubljana. "Marije Kraljice Miru na Kureščku" once again began to attract crowds.

The meetings of the Holy Mother with Fr. Spelič became regular. "I was meeting with the Queen of Peace every Saturday," the visionary wrote. Overall, he experienced about five hundred visions.

In Krešček, Mary says: "**Call on Me, trust in Me, and I will help you.**"

Running to Mary, finding refuge in her Immaculate Heart means invoking the Divine Mercy.

GREAT SIGNS OF THE TIMES

Mary placed great emphasis on current events. "**Ignorance toward the signs of the times is like a blind man walking in an unknown place,**" she told him. And yet, "**Many do not recognize the signs. This is why the dragon has begun to spit the fire of evil.**" The Holy Mother warns those who cannot or will not recognize the signs from Heaven: "**Only those who are spiritually nearsighted and blind do not recognize how God is working through me.**"

Likewise, Mary told Fr. Spelič:

Do not try to prove the authenticity of my apparitions and messages. Do not argue with those who do not believe, that I am your Mother and Queen of Peace and that I am coming to the Church also through visionaries. I will provide the proof. The visionaries should try to go unnoticed and should not allow the faithful to put them as the center of attention. They should hide, they should be faithful and offer themselves as examples to others. Those visionaries who are overtaken by greed for admiration eliminate themselves from the circle of my chosen ones. I will prove everything myself. You are to be quiet so I may be heard.

Mary assured the priest, "**I will speak to open hearts myself. I will appear to people even more often than to you …I will speak in Krešček through the help of events. You will recognize me in my works and signs.**" If that should prove difficult, "**Call on me, trust in me, and I will help you.**"

MARY'S APPEAL

Fr. Spelič recounts Mary weeping and speaking in a voice full of pain:

If humanity—all Christians, especially Croats—saw what they lose by not obeying me. … I have been inviting them for ten years, warning and asking for prayers for peace and starting a life devoted to God. But most of them have not accepted me. They rejected the warnings of God's messenger and my invitation to sacrifice. The consequences of this will be serious. Oh, if they would at least recognize me now, the Queen of Peace, and accept me as the Mother through whom God speaks.

Mary described herself as "God's Messenger." She announced, "**I am**

God's Messenger, and the Church is the guardian of my apparitions and messages. And only the Church can verify their authenticity."

And Mary warned not of war, but of a spiritual darkness that will take over Slovenia and will "**penetrate into Christian life and work**." She added, "**One way of defense remains: conversion, life in union with God, bringing peace, living according to the Gospel and the divine messages that you receive from God through my intercession**." The Holy Mother also paid a lot of attention to prayer, above all, the Rosary: "**Pray the Rosary often. Recite it with love and discover the mysteries of this prayer. Each mystery is a source of living water. Pray with your lips, heart, and soul**."

She also appeals to priests.

My heart embraces all priests: strong and weak, the faithful and the fallen. I gladly accept all those who know how to thank me and those who seek refuge in me. I will intercede and bless all who are in distress, trial, and danger, so that the satanic forces may not lead them to compromise the priesthood. Priests, return to the original sources of Christianity! Follow the example of the first Christians, the Apostles, and the holy men and women who lived after them!

TWO HEARTS

As with so many modern apparitions, Mary stressed the need for devotion to the Sacred Hearts. "**Seek refuge in my heart and in my Son's Heart**." Then,

there is only one thing left to do: **"You can only rest in my heart and in the heart of my Son. There is no more time for spiritual laziness**."

The Virgin tells Fr. Spelič that the road to Christ's Heart runs through her own heart. The Holy Mother underlines that the relationship of these two hearts is clearly defined: "**Protect yourselves through my heart in the heart of my Son**." So, she urged: "**Cooperate with my heart! I am your Mother. ... Open your hearts, so that I may enter them**." There is no discussion here of a mystical exchange of hearts, but we hear about the heart being "seized" by the Mother of God and shaped in the image of the Immaculate Heart.

In order to draw nearer to her Son through her, she gives these instructions: "**Pray, fast, offer your sufferings and yourselves to God on the altar. Make offerings and offer them for my intentions**." What are these intentions? "**So that my heart and the heart of my Son may begin to reign in the world**." She also referred to another modern apparition: "**Renew the covenant with the Divine Mercy**."

Mary cautioned against a new foe: "**I know about the opposition who rises against me**." Fr. Spelič recalls her saying at another time, "**Beware! Satanism is at work! Be on guard against the roaring lion, that he not use you to sow discord in the Church, in the family, and in the community**."

Therefore, the Holy Mother announces in Kurešček: "**Be vigilant! Remain faithful, for you live in difficult times. But even more difficult times are ahead of you**."

Mary also said,

⋏ *Smaverski hears the message: "**Seek refuge in my heart and in my Son's heart**."*

⋏ *In Slovenia, the Mother of God said, "**Pray with your lips, heart and soul**."*

My heart and the heart of my Son are terribly offended. Therefore, I am asking you to make reparation through prayer, fasting and offering your sufferings for the grave offenses committed against my heart and against the heart of my Son.

AGAINST SCIENTIFIC THEOLOGIANS

Not a single message of the Mother of God of Kurešček was made public until a local bishop got acquainted with them and concluded that there was nothing in them that was incompatible with the Church's teaching. These make her remarks about modern theology all the more curious.

➤ Mary said, *"My heart embraces all priests: strong and weak, the faithful and the fallen. I gladly accept all those who know how to thank me and those who seek refuge in me. I will intercede and bless all who are in distress, trial, and danger, so that the satanic forces may not lead them to compromise the priesthood."*

The Holy Mother first said, **"Theological science destroyed the faith of many."**

Why? **"Because of their lack of faith, they spread a merely ordinary human theology. Many therefore fall into a crisis of faith."**

She warned,

Some theologians in the Church develop a false philosophy. They want to interpret everything rationally. They claim that no miraculous interventions of God exist, that no angels exist, and that there is no father of evil nor evil spirits. This is a terrible error that kills true spirituality and gives Satan much room for action.

The Holy Mother also warned us against such teaching:

Pray, my children, not to be poisoned by the erroneous theology that some consider to be a scientific theology. Pray for theology professors, especially for the educators of future priests ... and for the superiors of the Church so that they develop a true theological teaching that strengthens faith and does not spiritually destroy others.

PROMISES AT THE FINAL APPARITION

Fr. Spelič recalls that during the last apparition Mary made several promises: "She said that she will always be with me until the moment we meet. She told me to wait for her every Saturday at 6:45 p.m., wherever I am, until the end of my life. She assured

me that in those moments she will be with me, even if I can't see or hear her. She said, '**You and other people will often feel my presence. Others will feel it even more than you. I will prove through interventions and miracles that I am not far from you and others**.'"

ON THE WAY TO RECOGNITION BY THE CHURCH

Archbishop Alojzij Šuštar was asked to investigate the apparitions at Kurešček. He was to answer two questions: Do their messages conform to the teachings of the Church? May the recommendations from the Mother of God of Kurešček be considered a stimulus for personal spiritual development?

The answers were given by Fr. Marijan Sef, chairman of the committee examining the apparitions. After consulting the archbishop, he stated that he answered the first question in the affirmative. As to the value of the recommendations from the Mother of God, he asked for a little patience. "The opinion will be issued at the next session of the committee," he promised.

A year later, the answer was: "It is possible."

The commission's official position is that individual believers must be guided by their own conscience. But if the Vatican approves the apparitions in Medjugorje, no doubt more attention will be drawn to that hill in neighboring Slovenia.

⋀ "*It will be a beautiful place, a place where I will heal wounds and diseases of the soul. Whoever takes refuge with faith in my heart and in the heart of my Son will be healed and filled with peace only Heaven can give*," said Mary on the ruins of the old church in February 1990.

Litmanova

1990-1995

The Immaculate Purity

*In Litmanova, the Holy Mother asked the visionaries to look at the crowds surrounding them. When they did this, they saw that the faces of people are dirty, spoiled by sin. The only way to wash them is the sacrament of penance. Let us not postpone confession. "**If you sin today—wash it away today**," the Mother of God seemed to say.*

Every first Sunday of the month for five years, the Holy Mother would appear to two Slovakian children. She came to Litmanova, a small town located near the border with Poland. Ivetka and Katka, like most residents of this settlement, were followers of the Ruthenian Greek Catholic Church.

⋎ *In Litmanova, the symbol of Mary's mantle protecting her children returns in a special way.*

The first apparition occurred in a small hut built on top of Mount Zvir, which lies next to the town. On August 5, 1990, three children—Katarina Češelková, Ivetka Korčáková and Mikulas Ceselka—played the entire day on this hill. When the church bells chimed five o'clock, the children decided to extend their playtime and not come home. At six o'clock, the apparitions began.

Litmanova

SLOVAKIA

Ivetka, Katka and Mitko were frightened. They began bargaining with God, promising they would go to confession and attend daily Mass for a week if He would spare them.

The boy shouted to start praying as the catechist priest taught. The children began to say the Hail Mary and Our Father, then an inner impulse told Ivetka to pray with the words "Mary, our Mother, hide us under your mantle." Suddenly, in the middle of the room, a magnificent brightness appeared and the children saw the Mother of God. The reaction of the children was quite unusual: they ran away. Mary followed after them in silence, and along the way, she knelt at a cross and began to pray. Then her figure gradually faded into nothing.

Nobody believed that the children saw a heavenly vision. When the three friends returned to the hut on the hill at the end of August, they were accompanied by their parents. The adults stayed outside while the children went inside. After several prayers, including the one about Mary's mantle of protection, a mist began to appear. Within it was an outline of the Madonna.

◄ The image of the Mother of God in Litmanova.

▼ Mary introduced herself in Litmanova with the words: "**I am the Immaculate Purity**."

THE FIGURE FROM HEAVEN

First, the children heard a strange sound. It came from the forest, from the place where the three friends recently lit a bonfire. When it became louder, the children hid in a nearby hut. Once inside, it seemed as though someone were walking around the house. The terrified children latched the door shut. The noise was getting stronger; it sounded like noise coming out of a shaken can. Next it sounded as if someone were dropping an enormous amount of chopped trees down the hillside.

The Blessed Mother once again said nothing. The vision ended as quickly as it began.

Mary gave her first message on September 30. Ivetka was alone on the hill: Mikulas did not see the Virgin during the second apparition and Katka was probably afraid to come to the site of Mary's meeting. Only Ivetka had kept the promises they made to God, and even though she had been to confession two days earlier, she exclaimed, "Blessed Mother, forgive all my sins!"

Mary didn't acknowledge her request, instead asking, "**What can I do for you**?" Ivatka asked for grace—not for herself, but for her mother, who was badly ill. Mary assured her, "**Do not be afraid. Your mother will recover soon because of your tears**." Later, Ivatka recalled, "I cried because the Holy Mother was also crying. I also cried because Katka didn't come."

▼ The message of Our Lady of Litmanova carries many warnings and requests: "My dear children! ... I would be thankful if you had ... strong faith, a pure heart and love me and my Son, because my Son is the true way."

FOG OF SIN

On October 1, when the Ruthenian Church celebrated the feast of the Holy Protection of the Mother of God, Our Lady appeared to both Ivetka and Katka. The former saw her clearly, while the latter saw her only in a fog. "**Because she had sins on her soul**," Mary explained. Mary urged Katka to go to confession, "**today**." She also said, "**I am very sad because Katka did not dedicate the entire month of October to me. She did not pray the Rosary every evening in order to repent for her sins**."

Afterward, Ivetka pleaded for her sick friend, Sonka. "**Every illness is a result of sin**," Mary told her. She warned that Sonka's parents are focused on material matters and they do not live as Christians should live. "**Only fervent prayers to the Blessed Mother will help cure this child**."

During this apparition, the Holy Mother said that in October—the month of the Rosary—the children wouldn't see her. There are busy weeks ahead of Mary. "**I will pray for sinners**." Her absence did not mean that Mary would distance herself from the children. "**I will always be with you**," she promised, and at the end of the apparition she left them a token of her presence.

When the girls were on their way home after the apparition, they were afraid to go through the forested slope. Suddenly Ivetka saw the figure of the Blessed Mother on the edge of the forest. The children began to repeat the prayer that awoke in Ivetka's heart before the first meeting with Mary: "Mary, our Mother, hide us under your mantle." Then the Mother of God came up to them and covered them with her mantle. Ivetka recalled, "The Mother of God guarded us

all the way home. We sang while walking and prayed the Our Father."

Scholars would later identify this phenomenon with an ancient Christian theme that can be dated back to at least the third century, when the faithful composed the well-known antiphon honoring Mary: "Under the mantle of your mercy, we take refuge, Holy Mother of God!"

"I ONLY HELP"

On November 1, the Holy Mother asked the visionaries to visit the place of the apparitions often. Ivetka said that she's afraid to come during the winter, when the snowfall is heavy. Mary told her, "**Do not be afraid. I never inflict pain. I only help**."

After the apparition of November 4, Ivetka recalled, "The Blessed Mother told us that we see her faintly because our hearts were stained with sin. She told us to pray the Rosary three times. Then she told us that she had blessed

Mary emphasized in Slovakia that she is a loving Mother, that she even loves sinners and those who hate her, and that she intercedes with her Son for her children.

Mary calls us to prayer, which she fills with joy, because only people of prayer carry peace.

↗ *Under Mary's mantle, we are able to survive every suffering. We are safe with her.*

the water from the spring. She wanted all people to take the water from the spring. The Blessed Mother is all pure. She was shining brightly and she told us to turn our faces toward the people. When we did, we saw that all the people have dirty faces and then the Blessed Mother disappeared."

Later that month, she told them, "**I am the Immaculate Purity. Help me keep the purity of your heart**!"

The apparitions at Litmanova focus especially on the stain of worldly desires. "**Why don't men make sacrifices as Jesus did so many years ago**?" she asked the children.

People have many material possessions. They have everything they desire. They're even willing to kill each other for it. They only want more possessions. Jesus Himself taught us that we should love one another, that we should forgive one another. Here, however, it's not brought into daily life.

Likewise, she told the children, "**I cannot look at the sins of Slovakia. Many of my children have everything they could possibly want, and yet do not honor me and my Son**." She warned that Jesus will send down a disaster unless the faithful repent and fervently pray.

THE STATUS OF THE APPARITIONS

The apparitions haven't been officially recognized, but the local bishop seems to be cautiously accepting of them. The bishop of that time, Ján Hirka, not only allowed pilgrimages to the place of the apparition, but also wrote a special letter. "Recently we have received many petitions asking our opinion about the events in Litmanova, where it is said that the Blessed Mother appears. Jesus Christ and the Blessed Mother sometimes use individuals to communicate with the world in extraordinary form—appearing to people—to call attention to some sacred truth or duties that have been neglected, or in order to avert punishments. This is in our great God's plan, which we should receive with gratitude and readiness."

He added, however, that danger of misunderstanding the origin of the apparitions exists, and therefore he must take a reserved approach toward them. "I want to stress that at first we must exert a critical attitude, then—if this is a genuine supernatural apparition—it will reveal itself more clearly. St. Augustine, speaking about Doubting Thomas, said that he was greater proof of the truthfulness of the faith than any of the other Apostles." So, "if the apparitions are real, the Savior Himself and the Most Holy Virgin will take care of their proper recognition."

His successor, Bishop Ján Babjak issued a decree in 2004 that recognized Mount Zvir as a place of prayer. He dedicated the chapel that was built on the site of the apparition to the Immaculate Conception of the Virgin Mary.

⌄ As more and more pilgrims came, a chapel was built in Litmanova with an image of the Mother of God.

Aokpe

1992

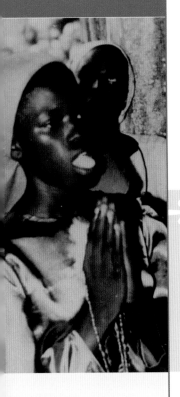

Mediatrix of
All Graces

*Mary in Aokpe asks that the faithful pray the Rosary more fervently than ever before. The appeal is earnest and urgent. The Mother of God also teaches: "**After praying the Rosary, sit and meditate for a while**." Remaining in meditation is the essence of the devotion, she says. It is a time when silence and the fruits of grace fill the hearts of those who pray.*

⋏ *The visionary from Aokpe joined the order of Carmelite nuns in 1996, taking the name Christiana Maria Bambina.*

⋏ *A building on the premises of the Sanctuary.*

Christiana Agbo was twelve years old. She was a shy, simple girl from an underdeveloped Nigerian village. She didn't even speak English, the official language of the country. But suddenly, overnight, she began using the language of former colonizers flawlessly, fluently, with a rich vocabulary. The Holy Spirit gave her the gift of tongues—in this case, the English tongue.

The first news that came to the West was sensational: the Blessed Mother herself asked for the public apparition to be recorded on videotape. Today, the movie *The Mother of God Visits Nigeria* receives flattering reviews from film critics.

What's more extraordinary is that the apparitions have been recognized by the local Church. In January 1996, Metropolitan Archbishop John Onaiyekan officially confirmed the credibility of the apparition of Our Lady of Aokpe. He was the biggest advocate of the apparitions. The reason was rather prosaic: he was granted an apparition of the Holy Mother and she convinced him of the heavenly visits in his diocese. A book about the appearance of the Mother of God in Aokpe received his *imprimatur* and quickly became a bestseller in Nigeria: in one day, in a single parish, as many as a thousand copies were sold. The book's title was taken from the apparition: *Am I Going to Heaven or Not?* One of the Church's eminent Mariologists, Fr. Michael O'Carroll, read it with delight. Many African bishops visited the site of the apparitions; all confirmed their supernatural aspect.

The village of Aokpe is located in the Middle Belt region of Nigeria. It is a small settlement located about four miles from Ugbokolo, the second largest

NIGERIA

◀ *During the first meeting with Christiana, Mary said about herself:* **"I am the refuge of sinners."**

⋏ *Pope St. Paul VI said that the Rosary without meditation is like having a body without a soul*

city in this area. This in turn is located twenty-five miles southwest of Otukpo, the capital of the Idoma region. Fifty miles away lies Makurdi, which, at the time of the apparitions, was the center of the diocese and the capital of the state of Benue. During the apparition, the Blessed Mother herself announced that this forgotten corner of Africa would become known through the world.

It was there on March 29, 1980, that Christiana Inehu Agbo was born to a woman named Regina, longtime

The interior of the chapel in Aokpe.

Mary comes to Aokpe to lead people to the only Savior: Jesus Christ.

they sang. I got scared and ran away. My brother went and called my mom, however, she said she can't see anything. The angels stayed in my room for several minutes, and finally one of them announced: 'I am the Angel of Peace.' Then both of them disappeared."

On December 1, 1992, Christiana was praying in the local church. She finished her Rosary and immediately got up to leave the sanctuary. But Mary herself blocked the door and told her, "**After praying the Rosary, sit and meditate for a while**."

The apparition echoes a renewed emphasis in the Church on the Rosary as a contemplative prayer. Pope St. Paul VI famously declared, "The Rosary without meditation is like having a body without a soul." Likewise, Pope St. John Paul II said, "The Rosary is a prayer of contemplation, in which the most important is meditation, like Mary, on the saving mysteries."

The following year, on October 1, Christiana saw a spherical object on the floor, similar to a globe, and around it, flowers. Suddenly, the Holy Mother appeared and stood on the globe. The girl wanted to ask the lady her name, but before she could finish her question, Mary told her: "**Truly I am the Holy Mother and I will introduce myself on another occasion**." Christiana persisted: "I don't know your name." She heard a response: "**The time to reveal my name has not yet come. The name I bring will be powerful. In the Church of St. Patrick, I will perform many miracles**."

When Mary did reveal her name, she used a controversial title: Mediatrix of All Graces. St. Maximilian Kolbe was an enthusiastic proponent of this title, while Pope John Paul II declined to give

chairwoman of the Catholic Women Association, among other efforts. Regina ensured that her daughter received the best religious education available to their family.

REFUGE OF SINNERS

On September 13, 1992—one of the "Fatima days"—Mary, Mother of Jesus, visited Christiana. The visionary recalls, "I was in my room praying. Suddenly the Holy Mother appeared. When she stood in front of me, she said,

I am the refuge of sinners. I come from Heaven to gain souls to Christ and to shelter my children in my Immaculate Heart. What I want from you is to pray for the souls of Purgatory, for the world, and to console Jesus.

Christiana related, "Later that month when I was in my room, I saw two singing angels. I do not know what

◄ *The authenticity of the Marian apparitions in Aokpe was confirmed in January 1996.*

∨ *During the next apparition, Mary proclaimed herself as the Mediatrix of All Graces.*

it dogmatic status. If the apparitions of Aokpe were ever confirmed by the Church, it would most likely end the debate over this title once and for all.

The apparitions also contain a call for conversion and a warning of the punishment that may fall on humanity submerged in sin. The familiar (if cryptic) anticipation of "three days of darkness" appears in Aokpe, as it does in many other Marian apparitions.

LOCAL FOUNDATION

On December 8, 1995, the Holy Mother asked for a sanctuary to be built in her honor on the site of the apparitions.

She appointed this task to the parish priest in Aokpe, Fr. John Beirne.

Shortly after the final apparition, Fr. Beirne established the Aokpe Shrine Project. The foundation has two goals. First, it aims to spread the message of Our Lady of Aokpe all over the world. Second, it raises funds for the construction of the sanctuary requested by Our Lady.

The parish is poor, and pilgrims visiting the site of the apparitions come on foot—a journey that takes several hours. All income from the book *Am I Going to Heaven or Not?* and the film *The Mother of God Visits Nigeria* goes toward building the sanctuary.

Ireland

2003

A Beacon for Our Times

Through "Anne," Our Lady urges us to "rescue as many souls as possible" by accepting our suffering and uniting it with Christ's Passion. Our hardships may yield fruit in transforming the lives of those who have distanced themselves from God. Someone may well have offered up his suffering for your sake.

▲ *Anne, a lay apostle, is one of us, an ordinary person immersed in an ordinary life.*

▲ *There is anguish over the sin of abortion in these apparitions. Mary declared,* **"I am unable to describe the sorrow that wells up within Me at the very thought of this terrible crime***."*

In 2003, the Virgin Mary and her Son appeared to a certain laywoman, a busy mother of six children. At first glance, the family seemed to have a somewhat dubious past. Our Lady gave her a pseudonym, Anne, that she might anonymously propagate her messages. She asked Anne to be her apostle, assuring her that the task would not bring any suffering or hardship to her family. She also told her that this highly important task would not clash with her family obligations. Raising her children, and the daily toil of home life, would always be of prime importance.

Anne left her first husband when she was barely twenty years of age, taking her daughter with her. She began to receive Holy Communion every day. Anne would later recall: "I then started on the path towards a profound union with Jesus."

She soon began to have extraordinary spiritual experiences, which accompanied her prayers. They started with a dream, during which Our Lady asked her if she was prepared to work for Christ. Anne said yes, and discussions with Jesus soon began. Within six months, Anne began to hear Jesus at various times of the day. "I did not tell anyone about the experiences," she recalled.

"At the same time I also began to experience the grace of being led by the Blessed Virgin Mary. The voices of Jesus and Mary were not difficult to recognize. I did not hear them as external sounds, but in my soul or mind. I began to understand that something special was happening, and that Jesus had a special task for me, more important than my vocation of wife and mother. The Lord Jesus asked me to write down what He said, and assured me that it would be published and distributed." So far, ten volumes of *Direction for Our Times* have been published, and a special foundation has been established to spread the messages propagated by Anne.

IRELAND

and restore light in every corner. However, this is a process akin to attaining sanctity, and, as in your attainment of sanctity, it will entail difficulties and sacrifices. That has to come about in order that light might return to your world."

Our Lady explained what the path to sanctity entailed. "**Being a saint is not an end product, my little ones, but a process ... which sees heaven supplant the world. You are a part of this process, and we are helping you. The more you pray, the more we can push you forward.**"

TO BE A GREAT SAINT

St. Louis-Marie Grignion de Montfort prophesied that in the last days Jesus would ask Mary to form great saints. Have the last days come? The Savior told Anne, "**Your Mother wants to lead you, to form you. Listen to her in purity of spirit.**" He added, "**In these times, My chosen souls must rely heavily on Mary, My Mother. She has made herself available to you in an exceptional way, for she wants to help her children. Be humble, and ask your Mother for help. You will not be disappointed. My Blessed Mother wants to lead her children, for which she has received the heavenly Father's full permission.**" The Savior urged all those who listen to His words to "build a nest" in His Mother's Immaculate Heart, where we shall be safe and filled with grace. He assured Anne that "**abundant graces await all those souls who desire them. My Blessed Mother lovingly offers them to her children in the hope that they will accept them.**"

◄ Anne's daily fatigue, suffering, and cares did not obscure God: [He shone through her as through a window.] He was of prime importance.

▲ "Turn your faces away from this world"—through Anne, this is what Mary wants of us.

TIME IS SHORT

Those messages are full of hope. They say that humanity has reached a turning point in history. Having turned its back on God and living in the darkness of sin, the world will be flooded with light from Heaven. We are approaching the fullness of time, said Anne. Virtue will cease to be an object of ridicule. Evil will no longer reign, and goodness will not be seen as a sign of weakness. And these changes will be made by God Himself—not as a form of punishment, but as a gesture of fervent love.

How soon would this transformation come? Jesus told Anne, "**Your children will live in another world, for which you can sing songs of praise to your Creator, and give Him thanks.**"

Mary likewise said, "**Jesus wants a worldwide renewal. ... Your God wants to purify this world**

> The messages conveyed to Anne are in the form of locutions and visions. The visionary not only converses with Mary, but also with Christ. "**You begged us for a week to convert a soul. But when it cost you a minute, you gave up.**"

⋏ God rejected Saul because he did not observe His precepts and Commandments: "Because you have rejected the word of the Lord, He has also rejected you from being king" (1 Sam. 15:23).

One can only be a "great saint" by committing oneself to fulfilling our Blessed Mother's will. She wants us to help her rescue souls.

> *Look at how many, many souls follow the ways of this world. Perdition awaits them if God's chosen children do not react. Let your hearts soften at the thought of this, my little ones. Help your Mother to lead them all safely back to Jesus. My heart suffers because of my little ones. They are at a loss; in despair. I am close to them, waiting for them to but glance at me so that I might make haste to console them, and show them the way. Unfortunately, they look everywhere but to heaven. Hitherto, the world has not*

seen such times. People are ashamed to ask God for help, as they think it is a sign of weakness. They are afraid to trust. They think that they thus become like children. And it is indeed so. They must become like children to enter the kingdom of heaven, which will be their eternal home. We must help souls to understand that the time has come to return to Jesus. Time is short. It cannot be seen otherwise. I want all souls to be converted to Jesus in the silence of their hearts, and I shall lead them by the hand.

Anne writes that our sanctity translates directly into more of God's presence in the world. She recalls Our Lady saying, "**Turn your faces away from this world. Many of our great chosen ones are living in the world, but not according to the world. You have been placed where you are to be Jesus' ears, eyes, hands, and heart—precisely where you are. If more people were to do that, the world would be a place of great light and consolation.**"

On the other hand, the Blessed Virgin Mary wants us to offer up prayers and sacrifices for sinners, especially our suffering, which God permits in our daily lives.

COOPERATION THROUGH SACRIFICE

Our Lady explained, "**We must rescue as many souls as possible. Think of your suffering as if it were nothing. Remember that some soul most probably suffered for your conversion.**"

Let us avail ourselves of an illustration from the first volume of *Direction*. Anne wrote: "I recall praying fervently for a certain soul. That person wronged me in many ways. I complained when I was wronged by her again." Jesus then admonished the visionary: "**What do you want? The salvation of this soul? You must be prepared for a little sacrifice**."

"What do I want to say?" Anne continued. "Well, I was given to understand that a price tag is attached to the work of salvation. There is no sense in begging heaven for something, to then flee from the suffering it entailed, which would have been used to save people. I recall something that Jesus said, which went something like this: '**You begged us for a week to convert a soul. But when it cost you a minute, you gave up**.'"

Where does one find the grace to change one's life? "From our suffering, united with Christ's Passion," replies Anne. She explains, "Think about Saul, pulled off his horse. Think about your own conversion. Have you ever sinned? Was there a time when you lived in a state of mortal sin? I did. Someone suffered for me, and the Blessed Virgin Mary came and looked after me."

The visionary gives us a simple example. One day she met a friend who was clearly depressed but wouldn't speak about it. "Our Lady asked me if I wanted Jesus to heal her. I said, 'Yes.' She asked if I was prepared to suffer for her. I, of course, said 'Yes.' I understood that I was to suffer for the grace of healing. Well, suffering came the next day."

A NEW WAY
Our Lady described the form that humanity's cooperation in renewing the face of the earth would take:

"Look at how many, many souls follow the ways of this world. Help your Mother to lead them all safely back to Jesus. My heart suffers. They are at a loss; in despair. I am close to them, waiting for them to but glance at me to console them, and show them the way. Unfortunately, they look everywhere but to heaven."

I would like you all to be always immersed in prayer, no matter what you are doing. If you are driving, offer that up to Jesus. If you are working, offer it up to Jesus. If you are doing some menial manual work, I can give it a heavenly value. You can offer up whatever you are doing to my Son for the coming of His kingdom. His kingdom is coming, and I need your help. There are stubborn souls who are doing their utmost to defy God's will and negate His plans. We cannot permit this. We must respond with fervent love and goodness. Your Mother can thus reach out to the world and save many of her children from misfortune.

"Hitherto, the world has never seen such times. People are ashamed to ask God for help, as they think it is a sign of weakness. They are afraid to trust."

▲ Anne heard what the path to sanctity entailed: "The more you pray, the more we can push you forward."

➢ *"The world is turning back to God. Racked with pain, and in utter despair, it is seeking relief. And God responds in His compassionate love and mercy."*

I want you to spend a little time reflecting on God's will for you on a given day. You must do that in silence. You may have many questions, but we shall answer them all in the silence of your hearts. Otherwise you will not hear us above the sounds of the world.

The world wants you to think that you lose a great deal through sanctity. Children, you must ridicule such claims, for you have a great deal to gain. It is the world that forces you to make sacrifices. You will gain nothing through your worldliness, but heartache, loneliness, and coldness in relationships with other people. Today, so many suffer from the coldness of those who are close.

Do not turn your backs on those you are to love. If you turn to Jesus, He will pour so much love into your hearts that it will overflow onto all those you come into contact with. You will never lack love, and it will bring you joy, not burdens nor hardships.

When you serve Jesus, the smallest, the humblest thing you do will become an opportunity to love and save souls. It matters not what you were called to do. In this respect, a street sweeper is elevated to the same dignity as a construction site manager. And to us, your heavenly friends, a street sweeper may have more opportunities to achieve great sanctity.

THE SIN OF ABORTION

In Anne's visions and locutions we come across things that make us stop and think. The Blessed Virgin Mary declared that her Immaculate Heart was torn apart. On the one hand, she was doing everything to stay her Son's punishing hand, as she loves her children. On the other, she calls for God's intervention to save the victims of those sinners—most of all, children who are killed in their mothers' wombs. Our Lady declared that the burden of the crime against innocent babies has become too great. Hence, "**I am one of the voices begging God to intervene in order to save my unborn children. I am unable to describe the sorrow that wells up within me at the very thought of this terrible crime**."

However, she adds elsewhere that thanks to the "knights of the army of light" the process of world transformation may somehow miraculously escape the purification phase:

Be strong, my little ones. You must represent Jesus in this world. This sin appeared because so few represented my Son. Were there to have been enough people following my Son, the crime of abortion would not have come about. There are not enough representatives of Christ in the world to effectively end these outrages. But, as I said, that is changing. The world is turning back to God. Racked with pain, and in utter despair, it is seeking relief. And God responds in His compassionate love and mercy. God will not allow His children to be victims of crime any longer.

AND THE CHURCH?

Anne was obedient to her bishop, Leo O'Reilly. Whatever she writes is not published without his consent. He submitted the following testimony about her: "I have known 'Anne' ... for several years. She is a Catholic in good standing in the diocese, a wife and mother of small children, and a woman of deep spirituality. From the beginning, she has always been anxious that everything connected with the movement be subject to the authority of the Church. She has submitted all her writings to me and will not publish anything without my permission. She has submitted her writings to the Congregation for the Doctrine of the Faith and I have done so, as well. In so far as I am able to judge, she is orthodox in her writings and teaching. Her spirituality and the spiritual path that she proposes to those who wish to accept it are in conformity with the teachings of the Church and of the great spiritual writers of the past and present."

Anne's apparitions have not yet been recognized by the Church, but

Direction for Our Times, an organization dedicated to promoting her writings, has been granted the status of a Private Association of the Faithful with Juridical Personality. The diocese of Kilmore also provides their apostolate with a full-time chaplain. Anne's books have been translated into nearly twenty languages, and Direction for Our Times prayer groups have been established around the world, from the United States and Brazil to India and Australia.

⬆ *Prof. Mark Miravalle, a theologian and Mariologist, wrote, "After examining the messages written down by the visionary, and after conducting a personal interview with her, I personally believe that the messages received by Anne are of a supernatural origin."*

Mexico City

2007

A Strange Light

The events of April 24, 2007, remind us of Mary's constant presence and involvement in our lives, beginning at the moment of conception. On that day, after the Legislative Assembly of Mexico City voted to legalize first-trimester abortion, the image of Our Lady of Guadalupe began to shine with unusual splendor, and in her womb, the unborn Christ appeared.

> ➤ *The miracle in the Basilica of Our Lady of Guadalupe was a clear response to the decision to legalize abortion on demand.*

Defenders of the unborn say that the Virgin of Guadalupe uses extraordinary miracles to reveal her solicitude for all life. The most recent well-known miracle occurred on April 24, 2007. On that day, the Mexico City legislature voted to legalize abortion on demand. After the vote, a Mass for the protection of the unborn was celebrated in the Basilica of Our Lady of Guadalupe. When the liturgy came to an end, a strange phenomenon occurred: the center of the Guadalupe image began to glow with a bright light.

The thousands of people who had gathered to pray began taking photographs. All of the images registered the same phenomenon. Subsequent analysis of the photographs and the light present in the sanctuary revealed that the image was not caused by outside reflecting lights or

Mexico City

MEXICO

other artificial means. Engineer Luis Girault, who studied the photographs, confirmed their authenticity and recognized that the image "had been neither modified nor altered—by superimposition of another image, for example." Girault was quoted as saying that the light "literally comes from inside the image of Mary" and "is very white, pure, and intense, different from the light typically created by flashes."

Perhaps most astonishing was what Girault discovered inside the light: "This light is surrounded by a halo and seems to float within the abdomen of the Virgin.... Indeed, if one examines the image even more precisely ... one can see within the halo certain shaded areas that have the characteristics of a human embryo within its mother's womb." But the people gathered did not need a scientific analysis to know that on April 27 the unborn Christ appeared to them in the womb of His Mother.

A light from within Mary's womb lit up the image of Our Lady of Guadalupe. Within the light was a human embryo—the unborn Jesus.

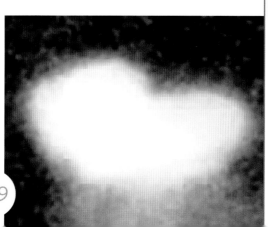

Warraq

2009

Royal Virgin of Giza

Christians and Muslims stand side by side, staring at the dome of the church in Warraq, and honor Mary together. The power of this phenomenon to unite Egyptians of different religions gives hope for alleviating tensions and conflicts dividing Egypt itself.

⚜ *The apparition in Warraq coincided with the beginning of the Coptic month of Kiahk, called "the month of Mary."*

⚜ *Just as in Zeitoun, in Warraq, the figure of Mary appearing on the church's roof gleamed. A bright light also surrounded the domes and the church tower.*

On December 11, 2009 — the first day of the Coptic month of the Nativity — in Warraq, one of the crowded slums of Cairo, something so amazing happened that, despite it being late at night, it attracted crowds of people. It is said that hundreds of Egyptian Muslims and Christians spent that Friday night on the streets, gathering around the Virgin Mary and Archangel Michael Church.

And the phenomenon wasn't limited to Warraq. That year the local press reported that the Holy Mother appeared above various churches in the greater Cairo area: Al-Masarah, Ayn Shams, Ezbet El-Nakhl, Mahmashah, Al Marj, Al Fajjalah, Al-'Umraniyah, and Imbabah, to name just a few. Mary appeared in a long, luminous mantle, a white dress tied with a blue sash. On her head she wore a crown topped with a cross — the same one as on the domes of the church. When she appeared, the crosses on the churches shone brightly. Mary moved between the domes of the church and above the entry gate between the two towers.

MARY'S LOVE FOR EGYPT

The land of Egypt was visited by Mary many times. After Zeitoun (1968), the Mother of God came to the Church of St. Demiana in Shoubra (March

25, 1986). The narrow streets that encompassed the parish were filled with Christians and Muslims. Between August and November 1992, Mary appeared above her church in the city of Edfu. Then between August and September 1997, she appeared in Shentena Al-Hagar. The next Marian apparition took place in the small Egyptian city of Assiut, in Upper Egypt, where she appeared between August 2000 and January 2001. Around the church people sang, "Come, Mary, Come" and "Your Light Is on the Cross."

Thousands of people gathered under the mentioned churches. Hymns and prayers were chanted to the Holy Mother, Mother of the Real Light.

Of all these supernatural occurrences, however, the best known is still the apparition in Warraq. The Virgin's appearance coincided with the beginning of the Coptic month of Kiahk, called "the month of Mary." It lasted from 1:00 a.m. until 4:00 a.m.

The first unusual phenomenon above the Coptic Church was observed by a Muslim named Hassan who around 8:30 p.m. saw a strong light radiating from the church. Pedestrians also noticed a strange light spilling out of the building, as well as doves circling the church. Then at one in the morning, the whole figure of the Mother of God appeared and moved on the church's roof. Luminous doves were also seen flying at night without moving their wings. Larger than normal stars appeared in the sky, which moved toward the church, and then disappeared. A bright aura, with colors from orange to blue, surrounded the church. The crosses on the church were shining a phosphorescent light. Above the Holy Mother's head appeared a snow-white cross. A pleasant smell of

Warraq

EGYPT

▾ *Panorama of Giza.*

incense, floating in the form of white smoke, spread around the church.

It led to miraculous healings. Thirty-nine-year-old Kawkab Munir Shehata could not see in her left eye due to retinal degeneration caused by diabetes; suddenly, her vision was restored. She is convinced that the Holy Mother restored her eyesight. "It was about 3:40 a.m.," she recalled. "I felt severe pain, which lasted about a quarter of an hour. And then I was happy to find out I could see clearly. Now my left eye is even better than the right."

The official announcement made by the bishop of Giza shows just how seriously the local church treated the apparitions. It reads:

> The Bishopric of Giza informs that the Virgin Mary has appeared at the church dedicated to her in Warraq Al-Hadar, on Friday, December 11, 2009, at 1:00 a.m.

The Holy Virgin appeared in her full form, in luminous robes, above the middle dome of the church, in a brilliantly white dress with a royal blue sash. She wore a crown on her head. On top, a cross of the main dome was visible. The crosses on top of the church's domes and towers also glowed brightly with light. The Holy Virgin moved between the domes and on to the top of the church gate between its two twin towers. Local residents saw her. The apparition lasted from 1:00 a.m. until 4:00 a.m. on Friday, and it was photographed and captured by cameras and cell phones. Some three thousand people from the neighborhood, surrounding areas, and bystanders gathered in the street in front of the church to see the apparition. Since Friday, a

⋀ *Muslims, unlike Protestants, honor the Blessed Virgin — Miriam, mother of Jesus.*

◄ *Old Portuguese sources say the name "Fatima" originates from the name of the Muslim princess who fell in love and accepted the Christian faith.*

⌃ Coptic Cathedral, located in the Abbassia District in Cairo.

⌃ The Virgin Mary appeared at the church dedicated to her in Warraq Al-Hadar. "It's a great blessing for the Church and the people of Egypt."

large crowd was gathered in the vicinity of the church, and could observe the emanating light, doves soaring above the church at various times of the day and night, as well as stars, which emerged seemingly out of nowhere, in the sky, traveling a distance of two hundred meters across, then disappearing. The huge crowds gathered around the church were incessantly singing songs and hymns in honor of the Holy Virgin. This is a great blessing for the Church and the people of Egypt. May her blessing and intercession benefit us all."

Signed
Theodosius
Bishop of Giza

"MAYBE THEY WILL LEAD TO FORGIVENESS"

Many believe that the latest apparitions of the Mother of God should be connected to similar apparitions in 1967 to 1971, which took place during difficult times: the military defeat of 1967; ethnic disputes; the death of Kyrillos, the head of the Coptic Church. Several decades later, the persecution of Christians by Muslim authorities and residents is still talked about. Copts make up 10 percent of the population and are marginalized and often become the objects of persecution.

The parish priest in Warraq, Fr. Fishay, took a wider view: "Maybe her apparitions are intended to bring people together. Maybe they will end the tensions between Muslims and

Christians and end extremism. Maybe they will lead to forgiveness, which Egyptians once prized so highly."

The Church confirmed the veracity of the apparitions in a few places: Warraq, Shoubra, and Zeitoun. In his speech, the Coptic pope, Shenouda III, stated that the "Beloved Blessed Virgin Mary loves Egypt" and therefore "appears in Egypt" many times. He noted that the apparitions were also confirmed by Muslims, adding that "unlike Protestants, Muslims honor the Blessed Virgin." He

▼ *Elements of Islam appear quite unexpectedly in the content of contemporary apparitions.*

told skeptics that those who desire to see the Holy Mother can receive this grace because she lets them see her. But she doesn't grant this to "complicated people" who reject the possibility of the appearance of Mary.

WILL ISLAM CONQUER THE WEST?

For centuries, Europe regarded Islam as the embodiment of satanic evil. As 666 years from the birth of Islam approached (the anniversary was in 1264), Pope Innocent IV was convinced that the three 6s imposed on Satan's influence in Islam was a sign of the intensification of evil that must lead to the apocalypse and end of the world.

The prophecy did not come true, but the specter of Islamicization hung over Europe. The destruction of North Africa was a warning for Europe. A once flourishing Christian civilization until the seventh century was totally swept from the face of the earth by the followers of Mohammed. Muslim armies had been driven back several times: at Poitiers in 732, at Lepanto in 1571, at Khotyn in 1621, and at Vienna in 1683. Yet, in the seventeenth century, as part of the alleged apparitions of St. Margaret Mary Alacoque, Christ warned that Europe would be punished with five hundred years of Islamic rule.

In October 1999, during a synod of bishops in Rome, Archbishop Giuseppe Bernardini, who had been living in the Islamic world for decades, spoke of prophecies regarding future invasions by Muslims. In his opinion, several countries will find themselves in serious trouble because of their shaken internal integrity, putting them in immediate threat of a civil war.

Trevignano
Romano

2014

Apocalyptic Protector

There are apparitions occurring everywhere. The loudest one of them sounds rather apocalyptic. It's as if we're so far in the denial of God's laws that the catastrophe had to come. It's as if the first of many walls has collapsed. According to Mary's words, it's not the last one.

"It all started when Gianni and I made the decision to go to Medjugorje to thank the Mother of God for allowing us to meet and for leading us to the sacrament of marriage," recalled Gisella, the visionary from Trevignano Romano. On the morning of August 22, 2014, she started her journey with her husband.

In nearby Tihaljina, where the miraculous statue of the Queen of Peace is located, the first supernatural event occurred. "That day," wrote Gisella, "a Mass was celebrated for a group of Poles in the local church. Gianni and I decided to attend. At the sign of peace, we noticed a very beautiful woman. She had blond hair and marvelous blue eyes that seemed to radiate light. She turned toward us, and, giving us the sign of the peace, she smiled. At the end of the Mass, the priest who accompanied the group of Poles asked us where we were from and suggested that we take a few photos with them. We agreed willingly."

The beautiful woman waited for Gisella after the conclusion of the Mass. "She looked me in the eye and said that at that moment Mary embraced me, and that she would grant me many graces, and above all, that she would give me many gifts." The woman introduced herself as Elizabeth.

Trevignano Romano

ITALY

In the afternoon, the married couple arrived in Medjugorje, where they met the same group of Poles. Gianni and Gisella asked the Poles, "Do you know Elizabeth?" The newlyweds were amazed to hear that no one knew her. Then Gianni decided to show them the photos taken in the morning, only to find that Elizabeth wasn't in any of them. The spot where they saw her was completely empty.

Slowly, the couple realized that they had been speaking to the Virgin herself.

EFFECTIVE PRAYER

A strange sequence of events began. "We started taking phone calls from friends who informed us about their health problems or the health problems of someone in their family. Gianni took down the names of the sick on a piece of paper, and we started praying intensely for their intentions. Over the next few months, the same people informed us of an improvement in health."

⋏ Trevignano Romano is a charming resort near Rome, located on Lake Bracciano. For several years it draws more and more pilgrims. They listen to the words of Mary, who recommends incessantly praying the Rosary, the Chaplet of Divine Mercy, reading the Holy Bible, if possible, participating in the Eucharist every day.

2014

> *The visionary with the notebook in which she writes Marian messages. The Mother of God asks to pray the Rosary. Anyone who teaches others this prayer **"will receive a crown made with pearls of mercy and glory as a reward for helping other people achieve salvation."***

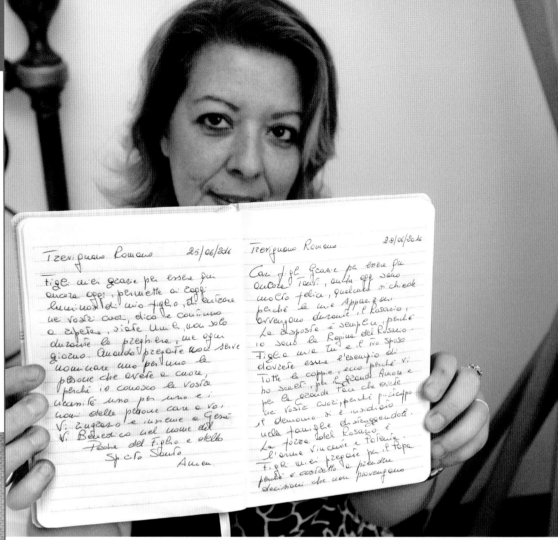

> ⌃ *Not only did the statuette of Mary begin to weep tears of blood; on February 15, 2020, Gisella had an apparition of Christ, who said He is greatly suffering. His heart bleeds because of the people who have rejected Him. He asked for prayers for holy priests, so they may support people in moments of suffering.*

Gisella recalled another apparition: "The Mother of God said that we should open the doors of our home because she would send people to us who were in need of conversion." Gisella's intuition told her to devote herself to the Rosary: "I invited one lady I met by chance at the supermarket for joint prayer of the Rosary in our home, and she willingly agreed. After a very short time, there were almost one hundred people who came to pray with us."

In fact, the apparitions always occurred during the start of praying of the Rosary. Mary explained to her. "**You wonder why I appear during the Rosary. The answer is simple: because I am the Queen of the Rosary. Its strength is great, it is a victorious and mighty weapon.**"

Mary added, "**I feel in my heart—and it fills me with great sorrow—with what falsity and hypocrisy the holy Rosary is recited. Prayer cannot be a careless tune. It has to be sweet music flowing from the heart.**"

THE HEART OF THE APPARITIONS

Many other signs attended these apparitions. The statue of the Queen of Peace, purchased in Medjugorje, bleeds. So does the Divine Mercy image they bought in Poland. The visionary also claims to have received the stigmata and that holy images appear on her body.

As for her messages, the Virgin forewarns of apocalyptic times:

awakening of volcanoes, earthquakes, asteroid impacts, three days of darkness, the advent of the Antichrist, and the cessation of sacramental life.

Gisella has also reported prophecies that are fulfilled in a matter of days or weeks. The most well known comes from September 2019: "**Pray for China, because new diseases will come from there, all ready to infect the air by unknown bacteria**." When the announced epidemic appeared, Mary continued: "**It is not the last virus that will come from earth, but expect other things: earthquakes and plagues. The world is full of them, and many, despite all of this,** **have already given their souls to the devil. Children, this is the time of conversion.**"

IS IT TRUE?

There are reasons to be skeptical of the revelations from Trevignano Romano, however. Supposedly, the Virgin told her visionary that Christ the Judge will return soon, that Antichrist will take over the power of the Church, and that the Church will run out of Eucharists. The Italian bishops view the apparitions with favor.

We can be sure of one thing: the call to conversion, to the Rosary, and to strengthen families comes from God.

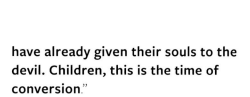

⋏ On September 28, 2019, the Mother of God said, "**Pray for China, because new diseases will come from there.**"

IMAGES IN *THE WORLD OF MARIAN APPARITIONS* COURTESY:

About
Sophia Institute

Sophia Institute is a nonprofit institution that seeks to nurture the spiritual, moral, and cultural life of souls and to spread the gospel of Christ in conformity with the authentic teachings of the Roman Catholic Church.

Sophia Institute Press fulfills this mission by offering translations, reprints, and new publications that afford readers a rich source of the enduring wisdom of mankind.

Sophia Institute also operates the popular online resource CatholicExchange.com. Catholic Exchange provides world news from a Catholic perspective as well as daily devotionals and articles that will help readers to grow in holiness and live a life consistent with the teachings of the Church.

In 2013, Sophia Institute launched Sophia Institute for Teachers to renew and rebuild Catholic culture through service to Catholic education. With the goal of nurturing the spiritual, moral, and cultural life of souls, and an abiding respect for the role and work of teachers, we strive to provide materials and programs that are at once enlightening to the mind and ennobling to the heart; faithful and complete, as well as useful and practical.

Sophia Institute gratefully recognizes the Solidarity Association for preserving and encouraging the growth of our apostolate over the course of many years. Without their generous and timely support, this book would not be in your hands.

www.SophiaInstitute.com
www.CatholicExchange.com
www.SophiaInstituteforTeachers.org

Sophia Institute Press® is a registered trademark of Sophia Institute.
Sophia Institute is a tax-exempt institution as defined by the
Internal Revenue Code, Section 501(c)(3). Tax ID 22-2548708.